THE DOG LOVER'S companion

Dog Heaven Is So Easy To Find

One evening in Berkeley, a man watched an elderly golden retriever press his nose into an invisible spot on the sidewalk, inhaling with deep satisfaction. Long seconds passed. The dog, enraptured, never looked up.

"He's got access to information we can't even imagine," the man said.

It's true. Why, when your dog can get so much pleasure, education and self-fulfillment in just plain dogness from the sidewalk, would you ever leave home without him?

ISBN 0-935701-33-8

THE DOG LOVER'S companion

The Inside Scoop on Where to Take Your Dog in the Bay Area & Beyond

by
Lyle York &
Maria Goodavage

THE DOG LOVER'S COMPANION

Foghorn Press
PO Box 77845
San Francisco, CA 94107
415-241-9550

Managing Editor...................Ann-Marie Brown
Copy Editor ....Nina Schuyler
Cover & Inside Illustrations ....Phil Frank
Cover Layout ....Anon Lee
Book Design ....William T. Power
Maps ....Luke Thrasher

ACKNOWLEDGMENTS

For their great help in researching this book, I would like to thank Bob Flasher of the East Bay Municipal Utility District; John Steiner of the San Francisco Bay National Wildlife Refuge; Ned MacKay of the East Bay Regional Park District; Dan Cather, Superintendent of Open Space, city of Walnut Creek; Ann Nelson of the Point Reyes National Seashore; Casey May of the Marin Municipal Water District; John Pelonio of Mount Tamalpais State Park; Chris Christensen of Sonoma County Regional Parks; Gina Farnquist of the San Jose Department of Recreation, Parks and Community Services; Jill Keimach of the San Francisco Bay Trail Project; Dr. Richard Benjamin, D.V.M.; O'Brien and Burr Heneman; Caroline Grannan and Steve Rubenstein; and most of all, Matt Wilson, without whose navigating skills I would have gotten lost a thousand times. *—Lyle York*

Thanks to Evvy (Golda Lox), the original Joe and Mark, for their support through the journey. To the countless park officials who put up with endless questions. To Drs. Rob Erteman, Cara Paasch and Karl Peter for their sage veterinary advice. And to sweet Pat, whose life was too short, but whose inspiration is everlasting. *—Maria Goodavage*

CONTENTS

FOREWORD

A book needs an introduction, but a dog doesn't. When a dog introduces himself to another dog, he gives a quick sniff and a wag. Right away both parties know where they stand. When a dog book introduces itself, the writer goes on and on about how wonderful dogs are. What a waste of time. Readers of dog books already know how wonderful dogs are. Clearly, dogs are better than people at introductions. Dogs are better than people at nearly everything.

Dogs love people more than people love dogs. Some people don't even like dogs. A lot of these folks own businesses or make rules, just so they can erect signs that say "No Dogs Allowed," three of the most horrible words in the language. This book does not seek to stick its wet nose into other people's business, but to point out businesses where wet noses are sought. It tells where dogs are not only allowed but welcomed, embraced, celebrated for the good company they are.

Unfortunately, more and more places in Northern California are kicking out more and more dogs. Some of these places may be less messy than the ones described on the following pages, but they are also less joyous. For this book is a guide not to geography but to joy—the joy to be had in the company of someone who will never break your heart, although she may break your upholstery.

In this book are beaches where dogs are allowed, restaurants where dogs are allowed, motels where dogs are allowed and even a miniature railroad where dogs are allowed. You can take a dog on a ferry. You can take a dog on a ski lift. You can take a dog to a self-serve dog wash (bring extra towels). This book tells how, where, when, how much. The why is understood.

This book also tells where the policy of "No Dogs Allowed" is replaced by another three-word policy, "Under Voice Control." Translated into English, that means take off the leash. You and your pal may run around with the wind in your hair and fur, not a bad policy. At such places only the dog need be under voice control, not the owner.

The joy is here, on every page. In discovering places that are good for dogs, the reader will find himself discovering places that are good for people, too. It's hard to have a bad time with a dog, but it's even harder to have a bad time when a dog is having a good time.

—Steve Rubenstein, March 1992

·Introduction·

PREFACE

In dog heaven, all doors can be shoved open with a nose. Scratching is permitted and barking encouraged. Digging is OK, too. Cats, chickens, prize-sized rats, children and strange people are available for the chase. Sofas are never covered with plastic.

On Sunday afternoons, dogs gather around meadows and lakes to socialize. The paunchy middle-aged ones tell dirty jokes. Puppies brag about the fine leather shoes they've consumed. And older dogs exchange tales of the 1950s—the good ol' days when Lassie and Rin Tin Tin were stars, and humans were smart enough to follow them.

But no matter what the age, breed or social class of these Elysian dogs, the conversation always comes back to how grateful they are that they no longer have to hear those three words that haunted them during their lives on Earth. They were cruel words—abominable, loathsome, stinging syllables uttered by their idols day after day: "You can't go."

On Earth, dogs have many ways of coping with this news. Joe, who lives with Maria, runs to the front window and stares until everyone is well out of sight and feeling plenty of guilt. Then, according to neighbors, he trots to the back porch and drools over the cats next door until someone comes home—when he mysteriously appears at the front window again as if he hadn't budged for hours. Lyle's Dabney grabs one of her socks from the laundry basket and retires to the bed, growling disconsolately.

Other dogs take revenge. We've known those who, left home alone, have torn apart entire mattresses. A San Jose dog who asked not to be identified routinely lifts his leg on every plant in the house. Some dogs howl, others don't eat, others eat everything. A sharp-toothed mutt who frequents San Francisco's Alta Plaza Park once opened every can of Dinty Moore beef stew in the pantry.

After centuries of being told "You can't go," dogs are still complaining. Dabney and Joe have persuaded us to take them along on more and more outings. They live to hear the jingle of keys, the turn of a doorknob, the roar of an engine. Though we don't let them chase chickens or cats, we've discovered that the Bay Area is dog heaven on Earth, if you know where to go.

That's why we wrote this book. With it, you get the benefit of the exploring skills of Joe and Dabney, who've sniffed out the best places to take a dog—not just the usual beaches and parks, but restaurants that serve you outside; drive-in movies, which don't bat an eye at a dog unless he tries to eat the speaker, as Joe does; street fairs and outdoor festivals; cable car and ferry rides; special dog hikes; flea markets; good street strolls; and lodgings that welcome dogs.

If a book included all the Bay Area's parks, you couldn't lift it, so we list and describe the best, largest and handiest ones. Accessibility counted in our choice. Some counties offer so many parks that we had to narrow our listings down to the largest within each city. Other counties are so poorly supplied that for the sake of those owners who live there, we've listed parks that wouldn't otherwise be worth mentioning. If we've left out your favorite public dog-walking spot, dog activity or outdoor restaurant, please write to us at Foghorn Press and let us know.

We've included a Paws Scale that rates parks, beaches and recreation areas from a dog's point of view. Four paws means it's a peak experience *for a dog*. If it's tops for you, too, we've added a hand—meaning that it's extra enjoyable for its natural beauty, historic interest or well-designed amenities, such as picnic areas.

The Paws Scale

Four Paws 

The place has everything, or nearly so: water to swim in, good trees, good sniffing, and—in most cases—no leash requirement.

Three Paws 

A terrific place, but one element is missing—water, perhaps. Or there's a leash requirement.

Two Paws 

A rewarding outing. There's reason to drive here rather than to your neighborhood park.

One Paw 

It's better than being left at home.

Worth a Squat 

Good for a dog's immediate relief.

It's Good For People Too 

GETTING READY TO GO

Remember what the Sierra Club calls "the three L's": Lunch, Liquids, Leash. Only the first is optional, no matter what your dog may have to say about it. For a dog, we recommend the three L's and a PS—pooper scooper. Get in the habit of stuffing paper or plastic bags everywhere—pocket, backpack, purse, trunk.

For a longer car trip, you'll need leash, brush, pooper scoopers, water dish, large and portable containers of water, many towels, a first-aid kit, maps and this book. And perhaps a bag of dog biscuits for a lift during those boring waits in traffic.

If your dog loves water, remember that water equals mud. You can never take along too many towels.

It's a good idea to carry a permanent dog kit in your car trunk, since you never know when you might need the following: extra leash, bottle of water, dish, towels, brush, first-aid kit. (One of us keeps all those in her trunk along with her own earthquake kit, consisting of a suitcase with flashlight, extra batteries, blanket, heavy shoes, bottle of water, and $20 cash in small bills. Your dog might as well be prepared too.)

In the emergency section (page 300), there are some remedies for poison oak, tick, skunk and snake encounters, simple first-aid instructions and a list of 24-hour emergency animal hospitals.

We don't go into detail here about special dog products, but if you're concerned about the safety of your canine passenger on long drives, dog seatbelts are a popular new item in pet stores. If you go on a long or rough hike, consider two other specialty items: a dog backpack so she can share the weight with you, and the dog booties made of leather or synthetic fabric that are now being marketed to protect her pads on rough terrain.

Dog Etiquette

In this book we don't philosophize or argue about leash laws. We simply tell you what they are, and in some cases how strictly they're enforced. Follow your conscience and common sense. Above all, be sensitive to your surroundings. Small country towns often make their own rules; it's harder to do that in downtown San Francisco. Attitudes vary from one community to another, even from one neighborhood to another. Dog behavior that would get an indulgent chuckle in Bolinas might get you strung up in Hillsborough.

We won't tell you how to train your dog, but here's some common-sense advice: Both of you will be happier if you can trust your dog to come on command, to stay when told to and not to jump up on other people. This is the kind of dog who'll be welcome in crowds of strangers.

Now that we've said that, we have to confess that our own dogs aren't angels. So we know the kinds of trouble they can get into, and in the listings we will give you fair warning about crowds, bicycles, horses, chicken bones on the ground, dangerous surf, foxtails and poison oak.

The Poop On Scooping

Wherever you and your dog go—from sidewalk to dog park to deepest wilderness—there's a good reason to pick up after him.

- Dog poop may be biodegradable, but it's the leavings of a meat-eater, and when fresh, smells unpleasant to any living thing (except a dog).
- It may be natural, but no human being likes to step in it.
- Scooping is usually the law.
- Unscooped dog leavings are the biggest reason public officials end up barring dogs from attractive beaches and parks.

So scoop already! The cleanest, simplest way is to carry a supply of plastic supermarket bags in your pocket, your purse, your backpack and your car. If you don't believe in using plastic, use the dozens of extra paper bags that lie around your house, or pieces of newspaper. If you can't bend over easily, you can buy elegant long-handled scoopers.

Hazards Of The Trail

When sharing a trail with other hikers, horses and bicyclists, the rule is: Bicycles yield to hikers and horses, and hikers yield to horses. And always leash your dog immediately at sight of a horse unless you know he has experience with them and will treat their killer hooves with the respect they deserve.

If you're not sure what poison oak looks like, ask any ranger—or anyone who's lived in California for a while. The oil from poison oak sticks to a dog's fur and transfers itself to anything that touches your dog after that, including you.

Skunk encounters are rarer but more trouble, and we know this from experience. When Dabney once tangled with a black-and-white kitty and got the full dose of skunk defense, it was in the middle of the night on Memorial Day weekend, miles from a store and in a cabin without running water. We shut him up in our car until morning. (Advice: Don't do this. Everything Dabney lay on that night still smells of skunk.) Then we drove to the store for huge cans of tomato juice—the folk cure, but the best—and had to pump buckets of frigid water with a windmill, dump Dabney and the water into an outdoor tub and get covered with skunk and tomato juice ourselves before he got halfway clean. He came out pinkish and sticky, and he didn't lose the smell completely until he got two more real baths with dog shampoo back at home.

The emergencies section on page 300 addresses how to deal with a skunking. But the best method is prevention. Keep your dog tied or confined in the wilderness at night.

An even more serious reason to tie her up at night in the California woods is feral pigs. They're strong, mean animals with tusks. If your dog takes off into unfamiliar wilderness after one of those, she can get lost or be badly injured, even killed, by the pig.

And we won't even think about bears.

Hazards Of The Auto

The stupidest and most dangerous thing dog owners do is leave a dog in a car in warm weather. Even on a day that's cool but sunny, *always* park in the shade and leave windows open a generous amount. The temperature inside a car left in the sun can rise a lot faster than you think, and your dog is not tolerant of heat. She can overheat dangerously in minutes. Leave your dog at home if you're in doubt.

If your dog rides in the bed of an open pickup, she must be cross-tied. It's California law.

Six Feet Are Better Than Two

Running with your dog doubles the pleasure for both of you. You'll have protection and company, and your dog will love the exercise. Remember your dog's physical limitations, though. Never assume he's fine just because he's keeping up with you.

If the dog is a small breed, wait until he's eight months old to start running. Large breeds (45 to 100 pounds) should be one year old. Giant breeds (over 100 pounds) should be one and one-half years old. Some breeds are far better built for running than others. Big, short-haired dogs with long legs run best; the poorest runners are small, long-haired dogs with short legs and short noses. The maximum any dog should run in a week, depending on breed, is 15 to 35 miles. This advice comes from *Running With Man's Best Friend* by Davia Anne Gallup (Alpine Publications, Loveland, Colorado). Buy this book for more details.

Watch your dog carefully as you run, especially on warm days. Heavy panting and thickened saliva are signals to slow to a walk. And remember—he's not wearing shoes! Dogs, like people, get sore feet. Also like people, they should start with short distances and work up to greater ones; they run better on soft surfaces, not asphalt; and they prefer cool weather.

Some of the parks and beaches we recommend are pretty far off the beaten path. We tend to prefer those that allow you to be alone with your dog. But if you go alone, remember that your dog may be good at making you *feel* secure and protected, but can't always defend you in a really dangerous situation.

Restaurant Etiquette

We talked to several county health departments about dogs lying at your feet at an outdoor restaurant table. It seems that no two health officials agree. What's clear is that dogs may not go where food is being prepared or where food is being served indoors; but as for bringing a dog to your table if it's in a patio open to the air—well, the decision should be up to the restaurant proprietor. A dog is legally allowed at a table on the sidewalk, since that's a public thoroughfare—but even there, a complaint from another customer can bring a visit from the county health department.

So our advice is: Always ask the proprietor or manager of the restaurant for permission first. It's the only courteous thing to do, considering that it isn't you who will get in trouble if someone doesn't want to eat next to your dog—it's the restaurant owner.

In this book, we've listed only restaurants that have given us permission to name them as places that welcome dogs. Owners change, however, and rules change, so always ask before you sit down.

Sometimes, in our restaurant mentions, we sing the praises of one dish or another, but keep in mind that we aren't restaurant reviewers. We're only telling you where we and our dogs have had a good time.

Our ultimate subversive intent is to improve public attitudes toward dogs in public places, such as department stores and restaurants. In France and England, for example, many commercial establishments think nothing of a dog walking in the door. And dogs are seen sitting in their own chairs at tables in Parisian cafes.

Whether this last is a good idea or not—we can't imagine trying to eat soup politely next to Dabney or Joe—we do think that American attitudes could use a little loosening.

Those Awkward Moments

Because dogs are dogs, they're bound to embarrass you sooner or later. That's part of their charm. Here are some hints that may help:

- Never sit at the end of a bench in a dog park. That's dog leg-lift territory.
- We've all felt the delight of watching our dog gallop up to another dog, exchanging friendly glances with the other dog's owner. And then...our dogs meet and start sniffing each other in the most private places. Our smiles disintegrate; we start looking at the horizon, at the ground, anywhere but at our dogs, who may by now be trying to make puppies in earnest. The solution: Sunglasses. No one can see your eyes. Or bury your nose in a book and leave it there.
- And there's the unspeakable moment when your dog does a leg-lift on another human being. Do whatever your dog trainer recommends to stop this behavior. In the meantime, apologize a lot—and carry $5 bills on all your walks. When Joe was young and still figuring out what was OK to mark, Maria spent $25 on dry-cleaning bills.

Where Your Dog Can't Go

At the end of each county chapter is a separate list of public places dogs aren't allowed. (We don't list large green spots on the map that are private properties, such as golf courses and cemeteries. You should always assume private property is off limits.) Check this list before setting out. We don't claim that our lists are comprehensive; we've only included public spots where you might expect to be able to bring your dog, but can't.

Canine Correctness

In the interests of fairness to all dogs, we alternate the pronouns "he" and "she," "his" and "hers."

·Alameda County·

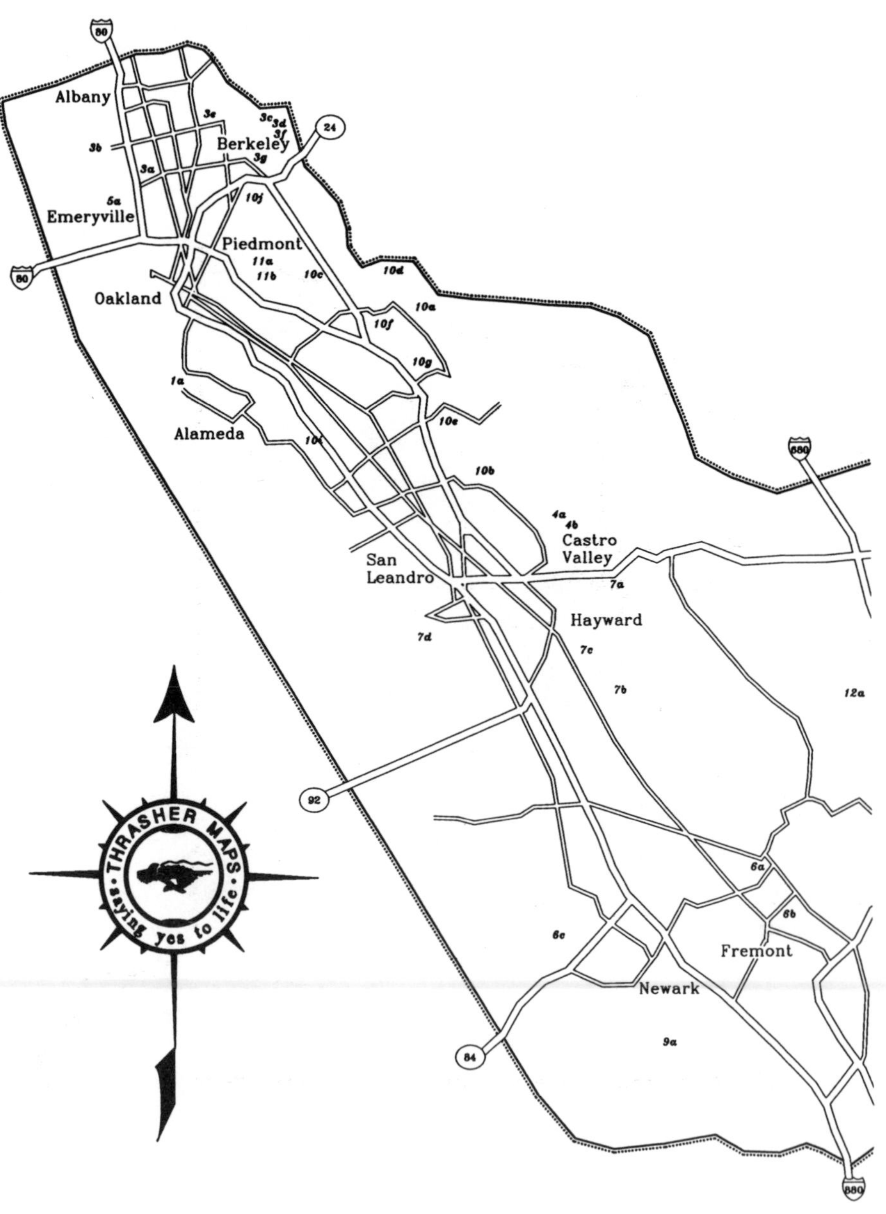
80
Albany
3b
3a
5a
Emeryville
3e
3c
3d
3f
Berkeley
3g
24
10j
Piedmont
11a
11b
10c
10d
80
Oakland
10a
10f
10g
1a
Alameda
10e
10i
10b
880
4a
4b
Castro
Valley
San
Leandro
7a
Hayward
7d
7c
7b
12a
92
THRASHER MAPS
saying yes to life
6a
6b
6c
Fremont
Newark
9a
84
880

1. ALAMEDA COUNTY (map page 22-23)

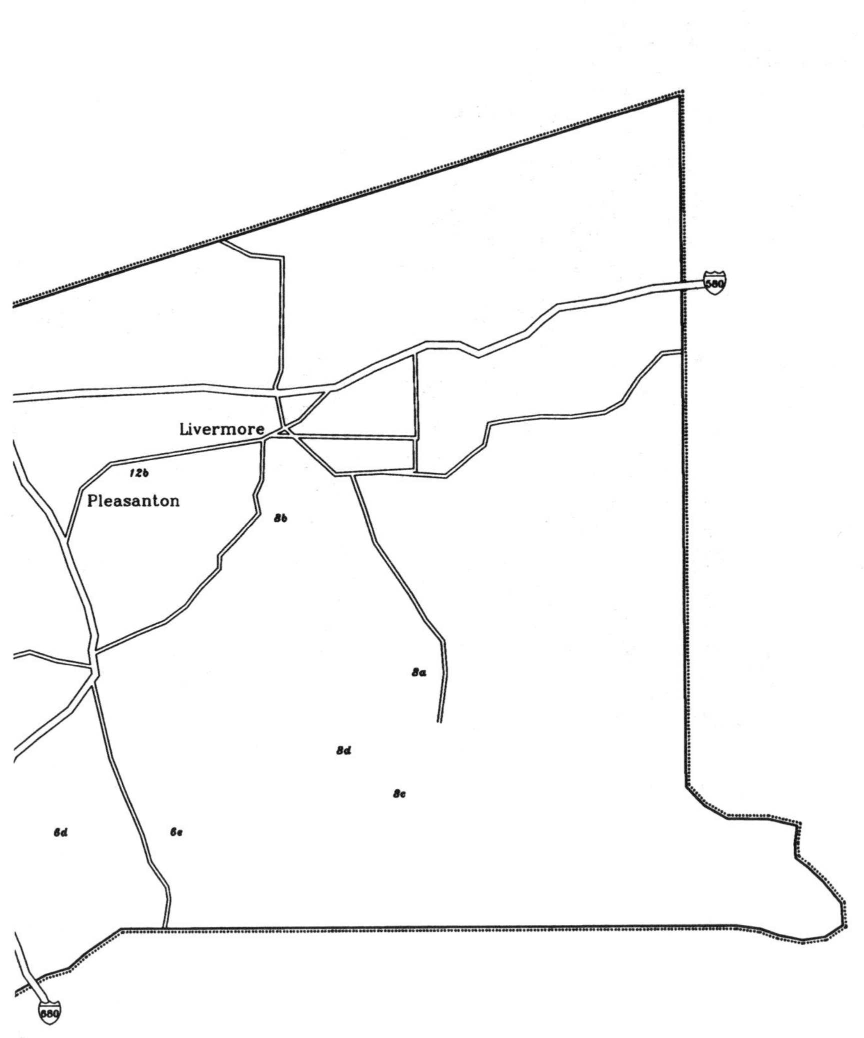

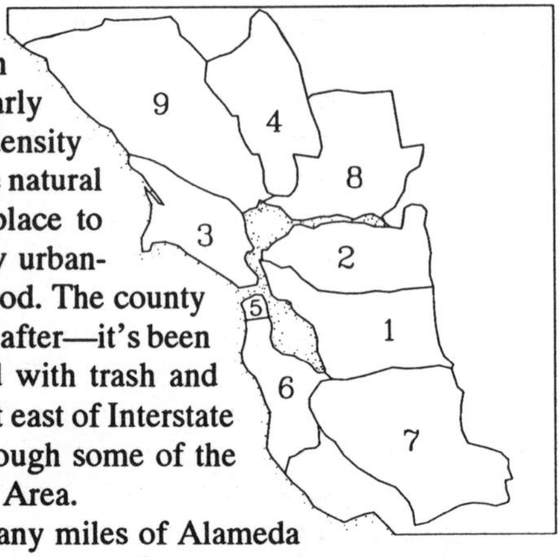

1 **Alameda County** is like California in miniature: It has nearly every level of population density and nearly every temperate natural environment. It's a fine place to own a dog, no matter how urbanized your own neighborhood. The county is like the creek it's named after—it's been lined with concrete, filled with trash and dammed into oblivion. Yet east of Interstate 680 it gushes joyfully through some of the wildest country in the Bay Area.

Our dogs have seen many miles of Alameda Creek. Between the Niles district of Fremont and the creek's mouth at Coyote Hills Regional Park runs the 12-mile Alameda Creek Regional Trail. This trail, good for dogs its entire length, runs through salt beds, farmland, rail yards, quarries, ugly industrial wastelands and pretty picnic grounds. If you were to follow the creek upstream through Niles Canyon, through miles of forest, you would see it regain its original glory in the aptly named "Little Yosemite" portion of the Sunol Regional Wilderness, where its banks are lined with willows, alders and sycamores, and it plunges over falls made by huge greenstone boulders. The creek finally meets its death in the usual California way—behind a dam at Calaveras Reservoir straddling the Santa Clara county line.

Alameda County also offers a wealth of attractive and/or laid-back city streets for wandering with your dog, and its warm and sunny weather encourages many restaurants to put out sidewalk tables.

East Bay Regional Parks

The **East Bay Regional Parks** system runs 47 parks and recreation areas and 11 regional trails in Alameda and Contra Costa counties—70,000 acres in all. Among them are the beautiful and accessible spine of parklands stretching from **Wildcat Canyon Regional Park**, above Richmond and El Cerrito, south to **Anthony Chabot Regional Park**, above San Leandro and Castro Valley. Hours vary with park and season, but they are usually open from 5 a.m. to 10 p.m. Park headquarters will give you specific information: (510) 635-0135. Be sure to call before visiting the drier parks in summer. Some of them close periodically because of high fire danger.

The most wonderful part of the park district is that dogs are allowed to run off leash on thousands of acres of undeveloped parkland. But as of press time, there is a danger that this will change: The district board is to decide in late 1992 whether to make owners tether their dogs when other visitors are nearby. They say it would make it more comfortable for those without dogs.

The rule would be a tragic blow to Bay Area dogs. In its present state, it's ambiguous (how nearby is nearby?) and unnecessarily restrictive. Dog owners can write the district at 2950 Peralta Oaks Court, P.O. Box 5381, Oakland, CA 94605.

Rangers staff the entrance kiosks during summer and on weekends; some parks will charge a $1 dog fee and a parking fee of $2 to $3.50. You can buy a $50 annual pass by calling headquarters or writing to the address listed at the end of this chapter.

If you take your dog through the kiosks often enough, it may make sense for you to buy an additional annual $50 pass for your dog. This pass covers only your dog—it doesn't cover your parking or swimming fees—but it comes with 100 disposable pooper scoopers! You can get this pass at the kiosks or from park headquarters. Many dog owners love and appreciate the regional park system so much that they gladly buy the pass to support the parks.

The park system is working on installing pooper scooper dispensers at the most heavily used areas. Rules for dogs are uniform throughout the regional parks: Dogs must be leashed in developed areas, parking lots, picnic sites, lawns, or in posted Nature Areas. They aren't permitted in swimming pools, beaches, wetlands or marshes, or in the Tilden Nature Area. They are not allowed anywhere in the three reservable picnic parks run by the EBRP system—Ardenwood Historic Farm, Little Hills Ranch Recreation Area, and Castle Rock Regional Park on Mount Diablo. Dogs (except pit bulls) may be off-leash in undeveloped areas and open spaces, provided they are "under control at all times." But the proposed changes discussed above could ruin this best feature of the park district.

To Dabney and Joe, these rules mean real freedom. To us, the East Bay Regional Parks system is the single greatest enhancer of human life east of the bay and absolutely the best deal for dogs. Use it with respect, and always carry a scooper.

Three of the regional parks have public campgrounds that welcome dogs: **Anthony Chabot** and **Del Valle** regional parks and **Sunol Regional Wilderness**. Each is described under "Lodgings" in the nearest city. Each regional park is listed under its nearest city.

East Bay Skyline National Trail

Dogs, hikers and horseback riders are welcome on the entire 31-mile length of this prodigious trail, stretching from the northern end of **Wildcat Canyon Regional Park** in Contra Costa County to the southern end of **Anthony Chabot Regional Park** in Alameda County. Bicycles are allowed on the sections that are fire trails. Dogs don't have to be leashed, but you should always use caution when you and your dog are sharing the trail with bikes or horses. Be ready to snap the leash on for his protection. You can get a brochure with a trail map, and good descriptions of seven trail segments—each of which is at least a half-day's hike—from the East Bay Regional Parks headquarters, (510) 635-0135.

East Bay Municipal Utility District (EBMUD)

- Briones Reservoir (see page 71)
- Lafayette Reservoir (see page 72)
- San Pablo Reservoir (see page 74)
- Lake Chabot
- Upper San Leandro Reservoir

A lot of beautiful East Bay trails lie within the **East Bay Municipal Utility District** (EBMUD), but the district's rules for dogs are quite strict: Dogs are allowed only in official recreation areas (San Pablo, Lafayette and Lake Chabot), and must be leashed. They aren't allowed on backcountry trails except for the **Ohlone Wilderness Trail** (see listing, page 45).

To hike the trail, you must obtain a permit from EBMUD. Call (510) 835-3000; it's $5 for one year, $10 for three years.

Most important, don't confuse EBMUD land with East Bay Regional Parks land. They come together in Las Trampas Regional Wilderness, in Contra Costa County, for example. And both EBMUD and the regional park system lease grazing rights to ranchers and need to protect cattle from dogs.

1-1

ALAMEDA

Parks, Beaches & Recreation Areas

Washington Park

The largest park in Alameda is **Washington Park**, next to Robert Crown Memorial State Beach. It has plenty of human amenities: wide green expanses, picnic areas, a marsh, bike paths and tennis courts. But since leashes are mandatory and dogs aren't permitted on the state beach at all, we can't rate it too highly.

1-1a From Alameda's Central Avenue, turn west on McKay Street to the parking lot. Open from sunup to 10 p.m. (510) 635-0135 for beach information, (510) 748-4565 for Washington Park information.

FAIRS & FESTIVALS

Alameda Park Street Fair: A family-oriented street fair. Leashed dogs who can handle crowds and kids in strollers are welcome. The usual arts and crafts, music and ethnic foods galore. It's held on the first weekend in August each year, both days, from 10 a.m. to 6 p.m. On Park Street. (510) 521-5210.

1-2

ALBANY

RESTAURANTS

Solano Avenue in Albany is a pleasant walk with a dog; people are friendly, and there are at least a couple of restaurants where you can stop for a treat at an outdoor table.

Marco Polo's Deli Cafe: sandwiches, hot dishes, salads, coffees. 1158 Solano Avenue. (510) 524-5667.

Actually in Berkeley, but just over the line from Albany is **Barney's Gourmet Hamburgers**: Just what it says. 1591 Solano Avenue, Berkeley. (510) 655-7180.

FAIRS & FESTIVALS

Solano Stroll: This community and commercial street fair on Solano Avenue, held yearly in September, is a good place for a well-behaved dog who gets along in crowds. To find out this year's date, call the Chamber of Commerce: (510) 525-1771.

1-3

BERKELEY

Berkeley is known for its eccentricity, and dog rules and practices are no exception. Like every Alameda County town, Berkeley has a leash law, and it's especially strict: Your first, second and third infraction get you a fine of $25, $40 and $60 respectively, plus a court costs assessment of $13.50 for each $10 (or fraction thereof) of the fine. That adds up to $65.50 for the first offense. For a fourth infraction, you must appear personally in court.

Then, there's an interesting technicality. If your dog is obedience trained and under absolute voice control, he needn't be leashed, but if an animal control officer sees you with your dog unleashed, he or she will cite you anyway and require you to appear in court with your dog and prove that the dog is under absolute voice control. (We can just picture Dabney or Joe sitting, lying down and rolling over in court...well, perhaps if a treat were involved...)

At the same time, more unleashed dogs can be seen in Berkeley than in any other Bay Area city.

The University of California at Berkeley campus has a leash law, too, but the place is swarming with loose dogs. The only animal you'll see leashed on that campus is a local pig whose owner walks him there.

You figure it out.

Berkeley's animal control officers clearly don't have enough manpower to enforce the laws. But in any case, they believe fervently in dog safety and freedom—and that's why Berkeley created the first official dog park in the nation, Ohlone Dog Park (see page 31). And a citizens' group is lobbying the city to set up another in the North Waterfront Park area of the Berkeley Marina.

Joe loves it here. His rasta-dog hair fits right in on Telegraph Avenue, where the '60s still reign. He gets special treatment all over town, a phenomenon I attribute to his mellow California-dog demeanor and to his bandannas, especially his red one. The last time Joe wore his red bandanna in Berkeley, he got a free slice of Blondie's pizza, an apple, and a child-sized tie-dyed T-shirt from a street vendor.

Joe and I were even invited into a clothing store while window shopping. The store clerk's boyfriend offered to watch him so I could try on a dress. "I love good dogs—good hairy dogs who wear red," he said, looking up at me and brushing his own long wisps out of his eyes.

"Well, this is a very good dog," I said, more warning Joe that's what he'd better be than telling the boyfriend that's what Joe really was.

Everything was going well until, standing with no clothes on in the tiny dressing room, I heard a cry from the boyfriend. "Oh my God! Not the silk pants!"

I was trapped, but I think I preferred it that way to facing the scene that lurked outside my curtain. I prayed fervently that perhaps the boyfriend was answering a question about what looked good on a customer. But with his next words, I knew the truth, and it was not good.

"Bad dog. Bad, bad dog!"

Eventually, I slithered out of the dressing room and surveyed the damage. A pair of purple silk pants, one leg slimy wet and dented from Joe's fangs. I apologized and drew out my checkbook, but the clerk said, "Don't worry. We get a lot of shoplifters here. We'll hide it, and the manager won't know the difference."

With that, the clerk cut off the unscathed leg and tied it in a bow around Joe's neck.

Several doors down, a shopkeeper watched Joe from the doorway of her clothing store. "Oh, come in!" she said. "He looks soooo good in purple. Come take a look inside if you want, and I'll watch him for you."

I smiled, nodded my head in thanks, and walked on. Even in Berkeley, tolerance must have its limits. —M.G.

PARKS, BEACHES & RECREATION AREAS

Aquatic Park

Aquatic Park, a Berkeley city park, is good for a quick stroll by the water and convenient to Interstate 80. The spot's neatness and peacefulness are somehow enhanced by its location, smack between Interstate 80 and Amtrak tracks, with power boats whizzing by on the lagoon dragging water skiers. The banks of the lagoon are planted with grass, willows, cypresses and eucalyptus.

Since it's an oasis in an industrial district, birds are plentiful. The concrete paths are popular with joggers and parents pushing strollers, and there's a parcourse, picnic tables and plenty of trash cans. There is no fresh water for dogs, but Dabney doesn't seem to mind lapping at the brackish lagoon water as he's splashing about on his mandatory leash. Dogs who like shallow, calm water will love this park.

1-3a From Interstate 80, take the Ashby exit and turn north on Bay Street. There's a small parking lot and no fee. Open from sunup to 10 p.m. (510) 644-6530.

Berkeley Marina Park 

In the marina, right off Interstate 80 near the Bay Bridge, you can walk your dog before work, grabbing breakfast on the way (see Sea Breeze Market and Deli, page 34), or spend an afternoon. Parking is plentiful, including some shady spots. Dogs must be leashed. There's an athletic course, and swings and jungle gyms for kids. Most of the shoreline is rocky, but there's one tiny sand beach where you, children and dogs can swim (but no lifeguard). In the small but pleasant wild area of grassy hills, pines and scrub, you can watch windsurfers or picnic looking east across an inlet toward the Oakland skyline.

A plan is afoot to create a leash-free dog run, similar to Ohlone Park (see page 31), in the North Waterfront Park section of the marina. A citizens' coalition called Area for Animals to Run Free (AARF) is lobbying the city for 20 acres of space. If it happens, this will become a four-paw experience for sociable dogs and good fetchers.

1-3b Go west on University Avenue, past the Interstate 880 interchange, and follow signs. Open from sunup to 10 p.m. (510) 644-6530.

Charles Lee Tilden Regional Park 

Tilden is probably the most appreciated of the incomparable East Bay Regional Parks. From Tilden's breezy western border, the entire bay, the mountains of Marin and the skyline of San Francisco lie at your feet.

Dogs aren't permitted in the large Nature Area at the northern end, or in the swimming area of Lake Anza. They must be leashed in the developed areas—picnic grounds, tennis courts, ball fields, golf courses, recreational steam trains and pony rides. So your best bets are the trails leading east from South Park Drive that connect with the **National Skyline Trail**. But watch out for ticks here!

One excursion begins at the Big Springs sign, where you can take the **Arroyo Trail** up to the ridgetop. There's an inviting stream at the trailhead. As you follow the stream in a gentle ascent through laurel, pine, toyon and scrub, you may hear the mournful whistle of Tilden's steam trains, the scream of a redtail hawk, a horse clopping by (always yield to horses, especially when you're with a dog), but little else.

Soon the trail leaves the stream, steepens and enters rounded meadows studded with cypress and eucalyptus groves. Even before you reach the **Skyline Trail**, which is the same as the **Sea View Trail**, you'll see the bay with the Richmond-San Rafael Bridge crossing to the Marin headlands.

When you come back down, your dog can refresh herself at the trailhead stream. This is a beautiful part of the park that doesn't seem too heavily used. Step carefully in the big dog-use areas, though. Many dog owners here are negligent, and patties abound.

For a real treat for both of you, take your dog along with you on Tilden's miniature steam train (see Diversions, page 35).

1-3c From Highway 24, take the Fish Ranch Road exit north (at eastern end of the Caldecott Tunnel). At the intersection of Fish Ranch, Grizzly Peak Boulevard and Claremont Avenue, take a right on Grizzly Peak and continue north to South Park Drive. One more mile north brings you to Big Springs Trail. Open from 5 a.m. to 10 p.m. (510) 635-0135.

Claremont Canyon Regional Preserve

Just south of the Berkeley campus, this is an accessible and refreshing park, alive with the bracing scent of eucalyptus. That and its steep hillside trails are sure to wake you up on a morning jaunt. It's easy to enter from Stonewall Road or several fire trailheads off Claremont Boulevard, or from the east end of Dwight Way. From the preserve's crests, if you make it, views are spectacular. There are no developed facilities; your dog will love it here—it's an East Bay Regional Park (no leash required). On a warm day, carry water for your dog. Carry a jacket, too, in case a cold fog blows in.

1-3d From Highway 13 (Ashby Avenue), drive north on College Avenue; turn right on Derby Street, past the Clark Kerr Campus. The trailhead is at the southeast corner of the school grounds, near the beginning of Stonewall Road. Open from 5 a.m. to 10 p.m. (510) 635-0135.

Ohlone Dog Park

Ohlone is the dog park that other dog parks try to be. It's believed to be the first officially leash-free dog park in the nation, and has served as a model for experiments in other cities since it opened in 1979. The fences are high, the other dog owners are friendly and the grass is usually green, despite years of constant use. The park upkeep committee furnishes plenty of plastic bags for cleaning up after your dog, and there's even a water faucet with its own dog bowl set in concrete. The park has two picnic tables for owners who want to read and relax or dare to eat in front of dogs who have worked up an appetite.

1-3e At Martin Luther King Jr. Way and Hearst. Open from 7 a.m. to 10 p.m. (510) 644-6530.

Strawberry Canyon 

This canyon is actually in Oakland, but we've listed it under Berkeley because it lies within the University of California campus, between Claremont Canyon and Tilden Park. It's owned by the University of California and is termed an Ecological Study Area; with your dog, you must avoid the Botanical Gardens, and keep him leashed. This leash rule, though, as in much of anarchic Berkeley, is often honored in the breach. These trails see heavy use. Be sure to scoop.

One good bet is the **Grizzly Peak Trail**, which you can pick up just below the Botanical Gardens. It crosses three small creeks that join to become Strawberry Creek farther down.

1-3f From the Berkeley campus, follow Centennial Drive to the gate near the Botanical Gardens. Open 5 a.m. to 10 p.m. (510) 643-6720.

Willard Park 

At first glance, just another pleasant but ordinary neighborhood park. But if you go mornings before people start their commute or on weekends, your dog can enjoy quite a crowd of congenial friends and their owners. There's a water fountain, restroom, children's sandbox area (no dogs) and tennis courts. Dogs are supposed to be leashed. There's been some understandable tension between owners of messy dogs and parents of small children, and if you don't scoop, one of the vigilant park regulars, such as Dabney's owner, may scalp you.

1-3g At Hillegass Avenue and Derby Street. Open from 7 a.m. to 10 p.m. (510) 644-6530.

RESTAURANTS

Shattuck Avenue north of University Avenue is the place to go with your dog if you just can't decide what you're in the mood for. Within three blocks, there are several restaurants with outdoor tables.

Bubi's After Hours: Light Armenian fare with a large selection of desserts and lots of outdoor tables, some with umbrellas. Joe loves the creamy Armenian rice pudding. 1700 Shattuck Avenue. (510) 549-1759.

Cafe Ariel: Specializes in Israeli food. Its raised deck is good for getting your dog off the sidewalk and away from passing feet. The perfect place for an obedient but distractable puppy. 1600 Shattuck Avenue. (510) 845-4300.

Clarinet Cafe: No clarinets here, but great croissants and lattes. 1908 Shattuck Avenue. (510) 644-1070.

The French Hotel Cafe: European-style coffee house. Someone gave Joe a saucer of espresso, and he barked at feet for the rest of the day. It's the real stuff—good and strong. 1540 Shattuck Avenue. (510) 548-9930.

Mama's Bar B-Q: The motto here is "Walk in, pig out." This tiny restaurant with only two little outdoor tables dishes out huge helpings of ribs, chicken, burgers and baked beans. Prices are extra low. 1686 Shattuck Avenue. (510) 549-2316.

Smokey Joe's Cafe: Our last waiter wore tie-dye and dreadlocks. The menu lists the address as Berzerkley. Famous for its Mexican breakfast and matzoh brie. 1620 Shattuck. (510) 548-4616.

Elsewhere In Berkeley

Auntie Pasta and **Euromarket** (two businesses open under the same roof): Heavenly, and pricey, pasta and deli food of every description. 1601 Martin Luther King Way. (510) 843-4338.

Burnaford's Produce: A friendly store and cafe that sells groceries, espresso coffee and pastry. Begging is good at the six sidewalk tables, but there's lots of foot traffic and it can get quite sunny after 10 a.m. 2635 Ashby Avenue at College. (510) 548-0348 or (510) 548-7720.

College Avenue Delicatessen: Sandwiches, salads, soups. No liquor may be served at outside tables (California state law). 3185 College Avenue. (510) 655-8584.

La Mediterranee: Cheap and good Middle Eastern food. Lines are usually out the door on weekend nights when Cal is in session. Dogs are welcome to sit quietly at your feet at the outdoor tables, which even get an outdoor heater on chilly nights. If it's very crowded, it's better to tie your dog up on the sidewalk right outside the fence separating the tables. 2936 College Avenue. (510) 540-7773.

Noah's New York Bagels: It has no tables—only a couple of benches on the sidewalk—but it's such a mecca we should mention it. Sells bagels and everything that goes with them. There's lots of foot traffic, especially on Sunday mornings. 3170 College Avenue. (510) 654-0944.

Peet's Coffee: Not only Peet's but the **Bread Garden Bakery** and various other cafes and shops encircle a sunny patio with benches in the small **Village Square** shopping center. Nearly every morning, crowds of hungry bicyclists and amblers congregate to sit in the sun, argue (this is Berkeley), eat pastries and sip Peet's coffee, which many call the best in the Bay Area. Dogs' noses don't stop quivering, and they can often meet other frustrated dogs. 2916 Domingo Avenue off Ashby. Peet's: (510) 843-1434. Bread Garden: (510) 548-3122.

Sea Breeze Market and Deli: Smack in the middle of the Interstate 880 interchange, you won't even notice the traffic as you and your dog bask at sunny picnic tables, where crab claws crunch underfoot and begging is outstanding. Dogs are perfectly welcome so long as they don't wander into the store itself. You can buy groceries, beer, wine, classy ice cream or a meal from the deli: fresh fish and chips, calamari, prawns, scallops, chicken and quiche. The deli serves croissants and coffee early; if you live in the East Bay, you can zip in for a quick croissant and dog walk in the Marina before work. At the foot of University Avenue, past the Interstate 880 entrance—598 University Avenue. (510) 486-8119.

Lodgings & Campgrounds

Berkeley Marina Marriott: At Berkeley Marina, one-half mile west of University Avenue exit off Interstate 80. 200 Marina Boulevard, Berkeley, CA 94710. A double room costs around $150. (510) 548-7920.

Golden Bear Motel: Gilman Street exit, east off Interstate 80, three-fourths mile south on Highway 123. 1620 San Pablo Avenue, Berkeley, CA 94702. A double is around $40. Small dogs only. (510) 525-6770.

Fairs & Festivals

Juneteenth: Each year sometime in late June, the "Juneteenth" festival commemorates June 19, 1865, the day news of the Emancipation Proclamation reached the slaves of Galveston, Texas. In Berkeley, Juneteenth is everything a street fair should be: good jazz and other music, Ferris wheel rides, delicious food and smells, arts and crafts, and great fun for leashed dogs who don't have a weakness for sniffing out chicken bones. On Adeline Street between Ashby

Avenue and Alcatraz Avenue (near Ashby BART station). Call for date: (510) 655-8008.

DIVERSIONS

Ride the Tilden Park steam train: If your dog's not a wiggler or an escape artist, he's welcome to ride with you on Tilden's miniature train. He'll be a hero with the kids taking the ride. Dabney stood in line with us for tickets. "Two people and a dog, please," we told the ticketmaster. "Well, let's see...how much shall we charge him?" he said with a twinkle. It turns out that dogs ride free. The open-car train takes you for a 15-minute ride through woods with brief glimpses of view, toots its whistle and rumbles past a miniature water tower, a car barn and other train accoutrements. It may be the most fun you can have for $1.25 per person. Dabney's ears were cocked every second, his nose to the wind. After all, he was in the woods...yet he wasn't in the woods. It was a tantalizing puzzle for him.

The Redwood Valley Railway Company runs trains between 11 a.m. and 6 p.m. weekends and holidays only, except during spring and summer school vacations, when it runs daily, 12 noon to 5 p.m. Tickets are $1.25; kids under two and dogs ride free. You must keep the dog on a tight leash and make sure he doesn't jump out. In the southeast corner of Tilden Park, Berkeley. From the intersection of Grizzly Peak Boulevard and Lomas Cantadas, follow signs. (510) 548-6100.

Shop for fleas: Taking a dog to a flea market can be as crazy as it sounds, but if your dog knows not to do leg-lifts on furniture even when it's outdoors, you can have a relaxed time at the Ashby Flea Market. Crowds will be tolerant, but keep him on a short leash and watch out for chicken bones and abandoned cotton candy. Dabney, for instance, is a dog who knows how to shop for scraps, nose to the ground for hours. He's been to his last flea market.

Good dogs love the easy camaraderie you'll find here. If it's hot, though, keep it short. This market is held every Saturday and Sunday at the Ashby BART Station parking lot.

From Interstate 80, take the Ashby exit and drive about 1.5 miles east to the intersection of Adeline.

Shop on the sidewalk: Telegraph Avenue near the UC Berkeley campus is what any dog would call urban paradise. The smells from the restaurants and some of the people are heavenly to dogs.

The street vendors seem to love our puppies, lavishing them with attention and an occasional snack. (If you don't want your dog to take treats from strangers, better stay away from Telegraph.)

Some dogs—and humans—may find the weekend crowds a sensory overload, and you will be asked for money. But you can shop the outside street merchants with your dog the whole afternoon if you like earrings, crystals, pottery and T-shirts with clouds. There are usually a few street musicians out on weekends, and you can even have your palm read.

From Interstate 80, take the Ashby exit, go about two miles east to Telegraph and turn left (north). The street-merchant part begins around the intersection of Dwight Way. On weekends, parking is challenging.

1-4

CASTRO VALLEY

PARKS, BEACHES & RECREATION AREAS

Cull Canyon Regional Recreation Area

This is one of those developed East Bay Regional Parks where you must keep your dog on-leash in the areas designed for human fun. In summer, fishing and swimming are popular here. Dogs may not go near the swimming complex, which includes an attractive pavilion and sandy beach. But you may bring them on-leash into picnic areas, along Cull Creek and around the willow-lined reservoir with a wooden bridge and its complement of ducks and coots. Up on the grassy slopes with their eucalytus stands, dogs may come off the leash.

1-4a From Interstate 580, take Crow Canyon Road, then a left (north) on Heyer Avenue. Gates are open between 10 a.m. and 8 p.m.; Open from 7 a.m. to 10 p.m. (510) 635-0135.

Greenridge Park

This is a small, very pleasant neighborhood park in the hills above the city. Its only drawback is that it isn't very accessible. It's managed by the Hayward Area Recreation and Parks District. From the green ridge that gives it its name (at least in the rainy season), you can see the bay on one side, suburbs and hills on the other. There are basketball courts, swings and a slide for children, and a stream at the eastern end. Dogs must be on-leash. You could take a dog and a child in a stroller on the paved paths through the hills.

1-4b Take the Crow Canyon Road exit off Interstate 580 and turn left (north) on Cold Water Drive. Hours vary with season: 6 a.m. to 7 p.m., 6 a.m. to 9:30 p.m. during Daylight Savings Time. (510) 881-6715.

Lodgings & Campgrounds

Anthony Chabot Regional Park, Chabot Family Campground: Trailer, tent and walk-in campsites with hot showers. Dogs are admitted for $1 and must be leashed or confined to tents at all times. Reserve by calling the East Bay Regional Parks reservations department: (510) 562-CAMP. Gates are locked at 10 p.m. No reservations are taken between October 1 and March 31, when sites are first-come, first-served.

From the intersection of Redwood Road and Skyline Boulevard in Oakland, go 6.5 miles east on Redwood to Marciel Gate, one entrance to the regional park. Or from Castro Valley, go from the intersection of Redwood Road and Castro Valley Boulevard north on Redwood about 4.5 miles to Marciel Gate. The campground is about two miles inside the gate.

1-5 EMERYVILLE

Parks, Beaches & Recreation Areas

Emeryville Marina Park 

This is an accessible spot, but it's designed for people, not dogs. A concrete path follows the riprap shoreline through well-kept grass and cypresses. Runners and exercise walkers use the path; a quick and scenic stroll is down the north side, where there's a view of the marina and a miniature bird refuge where egrets, sandpipers, blackbirds and doves inhabit a tiny marsh. At the end is the fishing pier (no dogs). You might picnic at the tables, with views of the Bay Bridge and city. Dogs must be leashed.

1-5a From Interstate 80, take the Powell Street exit at Emeryville and go west on Powell to the end of the marina. There's lots of free parking. Open 7 a.m. to 9 p.m. (510) 596-4340.

Lodgings & Campgrounds

Holiday Inn—Bay Bridge: Powell-Emeryville exit off Interstate 80; one mile north of Bay Bridge. 1800 Powell Street, Emeryville,

CA 94608. A double room costs about $100. Dogs on second and third floors only. (510) 658-9300.

1-6

FREMONT

PARKS, BEACHES & RECREATION AREAS

Alameda Creek Regional Trail

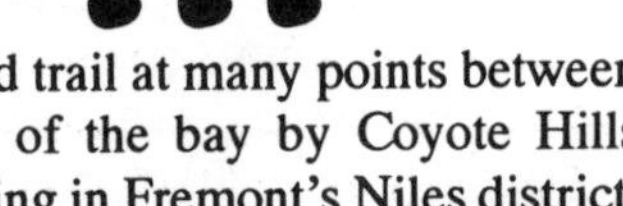

You may enter this 12.4 mile paved trail at many points between the creek's mouth—in the salt flats of the bay by Coyote Hills Regional Park—and the trail's beginning in Fremont's Niles district, at the intersection of Mission Boulevard (Highway 238) and Niles Canyon Road (Highway 84).

Although the East Bay Regional Park District's usual liberal leash rules apply here, it has posted a good many areas with "leash up" symbols. If you see one, do so. On this trail, as on any you share with other hikers, horses and bicycles, just use common sense.

A scenic stretch of the trail is the Niles Canyon end, especially in winter after a storm, when the creek is full. After a big deluge, we've seen ducks and coots struggle against a rushing muddy current. More commonly, the creek is a mere trickle in the center of its concrete lining. There is an attractive picnic area at the Niles staging area.

At the bay end, there's access from the south side of the trail to Coyote Hills and a 3.5 mile loop trail equipped with markers for long-distance runners. You can't get into the park from the north side of the trail, which is the side recommended for horseback riders; the south side is recommended for joggers, runners and bicyclists. Choose your dog hazard! It's a fine hike to take with a child in a stroller, since it's paved and flat and passes through a cross-section of the county: salt flats, farmland, rail yards, industrial lots and quarries.

1-6a Open 5 a.m. to 10 p.m. (510) 635-0135.

Central Park

This is a city-owned park where, as usual, dogs must be leashed. It's largely a sports complex, with six softball fields, 10 soccer fields, tennis courts and a football field, but there are also picnic areas and a playground. Lake Elizabeth and the swim lagoon are off-limits to dogs.

1-6b At Stevenson Boulevard and Paseo Padre Parkway. Open 7 a.m. to 10 p.m. (510) 791-4340.

Coyote Hills Regional Park 

This park is a paradox—a working research project on Ohlone Indian history, a teeming wildlife sanctuary and a family picnic and bicycling mecca, all in 966 acres.

The smooth paths and boardwalks are wonderful for wheeling small children. Its freshwater and saltwater marshes are peaceful and mysterious; sit quietly on a boardwalk and a muskrat may pop out of the water only a few feet away. And the park offers excellent organized nature tours and demonstrations of Ohlone life.

But to enjoy all these, you must leave your dejected dog behind. (We once tried leaving Dabney tied to a tree while we toured the marshes, and his yowls echoed all over the hills.)

You and dog may, however, run loose in the small hills that give the park its name. Though they're only 200 or 300 feet high, they give you that familiar East Bay wide-open feeling, and you'll see redtail hawks, vultures and the magical white-tailed kites that hover like vibrating light above the grass, suddenly plunging down after ground squirrels.

The **Bayview Trail**, for example, climbs quickly up behind the Visitors Center (aided by wooden steps, so no strollers here). From the crest of Red Hill—green even in the dry season because its ground cover is drought-tolerant—you look down on varied colors of marsh grasses, waterfowl and wading birds, and the shallow salt ponds in the bay.

Picnic tables on the lush lawn around the Visitors Center are off-limits to dogs, and most of the park is a fragile sanctuary. But take your dog for a romp in the hills.

1-6c From Interstate 880, take the Decoto Road/Highway 84 exit in Fremont. Go west on 84 to the Thornton Avenue/Paseo Padre Parkway exit. Go north on Paseo Padre about one mile to Patterson Ranch Road/Commerce. A left on Patterson Ranch Road brings you to the entrance. When the kiosk is staffed, the parking fee is $2.50; dog fee is $1. Open 5 a.m. to 10 p.m. For information on tours and activities, call (510) 795-9385. General information, call (510) 635-0135.

Mission Peak Regional Preserve 

This regional park is where many Fremont dwellers take their dogs. It's a huge expanse of grass, dotted with occasional oak groves and scrub. Unfortunately for humans who get short of breath, the foot trails head straight up: Trails to the top rise 2,500 feet in three miles.

The entrance at Stanford Avenue offers a gentler climb than the entrance from the Ohlone College campus. You'll pass Caliente Creek if you take the **Peak Meadow Trail**, but in hot weather, there won't be much relief from the sun. Be sure to carry water for yourself and dog. The main point of puffing up Mission Peak is the renowned view stretching from Mount Tamalpais to Mount Hamilton (on *very* clear days to the Sierra's snowy crest), but your dog will appreciate the complete freedom of those expanses of pasture. No leash necessary.

1-6d From Interstate 680, take the southern Mission Boulevard exit in Fremont (there are two; the one you want is in the Warm Springs district), go east on Mission to Stanford Avenue, turn right (east), and in less than a mile, you'll be at the entrance. Open 8 a.m. to sunset. (510) 635-0135.

Sunol Regional Wilderness

Probably because it lies in the middle of nowhere in particular, this gorgeous treasure of a wilderness, run by the East Bay Regional Park District, is nearly deserted. You and your dog will rejoice that you made the drive.

We recommend taking your dog to the main park entrance via Geary Road and then walking along the **Camp Ohlone Trail** to the area called **Little Yosemite.** Like its namesake, Little Yosemite really is magnificent: a steep-sided gorge with a creek at the bottom; lofty crags and outcrops of greenstone, schist, metachert and basalt that reveal a turbulent geological history; huge boulders that throw Alameda Creek into gurgling eddies and falls. (No swimming here!)

You can return via the higher **Canyon View Trail**, or head for several other destinations: wooded canyons, grassy slopes, peaks with views of Calaveras Reservoir or Mount Diablo. The park brochure offers useful descriptions of each trail. Dogs may run free on trails except for the Backpack Loop.

Unfortunately, you may not camp with a dog at the campsites farther in. They're allowed overnight only at Family Campground. Watch for poison oak here.

1-6e From Interstate 680, take the Calaveras Road exit, then go left (east) on Geary Road to the park entrance. Open 7 a.m. to dusk. The park may be closed or restricted during fire season, June to October. (510) 635-0135.

RESTAURANTS

Big Daddy's: On your way back from Coyote Hills, or after a trek along the Alameda Creek Regional Trail, or an appetite-arousing hike through the Sunol Regional Wilderness or up Mission Peak, here's where you and your dog can eat together year round at the outdoor tables—a cheerful, old-fashioned cafe that serves all-American cafe food. Big Daddy's boasts painted murals featuring Niles street scenes on the walls and water birds on the ceiling.

At Mission Boulevard (Highway 238) and Niles Canyon Road (Highway 84). Open 24 hours, whenever your dog's hungry. (510) 790-9155.

LODGINGS & CAMPGROUNDS

Sunol Regional Wilderness: Dogs are allowed only at the Family Campground site at headquarters (see page 40), and not at the backpacking campsites farther in. Dog fee is $1. Dogs must be leashed in the campground or confined to your tent (anyone whose dog has ever chased off after a wild boar in the middle of the night understands the reason for this rule, and this park has plenty of boars). No recreational vehicles are allowed. No food, firewood or ice is available. Call (510) 636-1684 to reserve. Reserved sites are held until 5 p.m.

FAIRS & FESTIVALS

Fremont Festival of the Arts: This street fair, usually held in July, features arts and crafts booths, 5K and 10K runs, music and food. And you can watch artists and craftspeople at work. Just make sure your dog is firmly leashed and appreciates the art properly.

On Paseo Padre Parkway between Mowry Avenue and Walnut Avenue. Free. For this year's date, call (510) 657-1355.

1-7

HAYWARD

PARKS, BEACHES & RECREATION AREAS

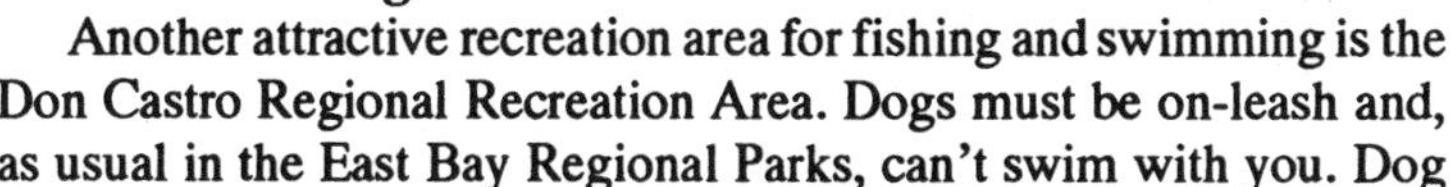

Don Castro Regional Recreation Area

Another attractive recreation area for fishing and swimming is the Don Castro Regional Recreation Area. Dogs must be on-leash and, as usual in the East Bay Regional Parks, can't swim with you. Dog fee is $1, parking fee is $2 (charged on summer weekends).

1-7a The park is just off Interstate 580, just over the line from Castro Valley. Exit at Grove Way; bear left on Center; left on Kelly; left on Woodroe. Open from 8 a.m. to 10 p.m. (510) 635-0135.

Garin Regional Park & Dry Creek Regional Park (contiguous)

Garin is a good place to learn about Alameda County farming and ranching. The parking lot next to Garin Barn—an actual barn, blacksmith's shop and tool shed that is also Garin's Visitor Center—is strewn with antique farm machinery.

Some trails near the Visitor Center are smooth enough for strollers. Tiny **Jordan Pond** is stocked with catfish. A total of 20 miles of trails, looping among the sweeps of grassy hills, beckon you and your dog. Off-leash is fine once you've left the Visitor Center. **Dry Creek**, which runs near the Visitor Center, was a delightful small torrent one day when we were there after a March storm. There isn't much shade on hot days, though.

1-7b From Highway 238, Tamarack Drive takes you quickly up the hill to Dry Creek Regional Park; Garin Avenue takes you to Garin, or you can enter Garin from the California State University, Hayward campus. Open 8 a.m. to dusk. Parking fee is $2 on weekends and holidays, dog fee is $1. (510) 635-0135.

Hayward Memorial Park Hiking & Riding Trails

This is a greenbelt run by the Hayward Area Recreation and Parks District. You can enter through Hayward Memorial Park, at Mission Boulevard (Highway 238) just south of the intersection of Highway 92.

Memorial Park offers parking space and an indoor pool, the Hayward Plunge, and tennis courts, kids' swings and slides, picnic tables, a band shell, and even a slightly funky cage full of doves.

The fun for a dog begins, though, when you get on the **Wally Wickander Memorial Trail** and enter the greenbelt portion of the park, laced with dirt fire trails designed for hikers and horses. Unfortunately, dogs must remain on-leash, but the trail follows a steep-sided creek lined with a thick tangle of oak, laurel, maple and lots of noisy birds. The trash pickup is a little slovenly, but if you're looking for solitude in a city park, you'll find it here.

1-7c You can enter these trails from parking lots on East Avenue, through East Avenue Park on the north end; or on Highland Boulevard through Old Highland Park on the south end. Open from 6 a.m. to 7 p.m. (to 9:30 p.m. during Daylight Savings Time). (510) 881-6715.

Hayward Regional Shoreline 

This is the largest marsh restoration project on the West Coast, overseen by the East Bay Regional Park District, and like all wetlands, it is ecologically delicate. Dogs aren't permitted south of Winton Avenue, so the best access point for a dog run is from Grant Avenue. Unfortunately, it's an isolated place, and the restored sections—the only ones worth looking at for natural beauty—are off-limits. The restoration-in-progress north of Winton Avenue is bleak, featureless and often windy. It's good for biking, however, and for a dog who really loves to stretch out and run. Leash is required only in areas you could call developed.

Store this place away for the future; it should grow marshier and more attractive year by year.

1-7d From Interstate 880, take the Washington Avenue exit and go south on Washington to Grant Avenue. Go right on Grant. The entrance is on the right about 100 yards from the end of Grant. Open 5 a.m. to 10 p.m. (510) 783-1066.

LODGINGS & CAMPGROUNDS

Motel Orleans: West of Interstate 880; exit southbound Industrial Parkway, northbound Whipple/Industrial Parkway. 2286 Industrial Parkway, Hayward, CA 94544. Around $40 for a double. Small dogs only. (510) 786-2844.

Vagabond Inn: One-half mile west off Interstate 880 via West A Street. 20455 Hesperian Boulevard, Hayward, CA 94541. Around $70 for a double. $6 extra for dog. (510) 785-5480.

1-8 LIVERMORE

PARKS, BEACHES & RECREATION AREAS

Del Valle Regional Park

This popular reservoir is best known for swimming, boating, fishing and camping. Like Anthony Chabot Regional Park, it's primarily a manicured and popular human recreation area, with neat lawns and picnic tables (where dogs must be leashed), but there are several unspoiled trails for hiking and riding in the surrounding hills. And, unlike on Lake Chabot, here you're permitted to take a dog on a rented boat.

From this recreation area, you can enter the **Ohlone Wilderness Trail**—29 miles of gorgeous trail through four regional parks (see Ohlone Regional Wilderness, below). Del Valle's Family Campground allows dogs (see Lodgings, page 45).

1-8a From Interstate 580, take North Livermore Avenue from downtown Livermore. It will become South Livermore Avenue, then Tesla Road. Take a right (south) on Mines Road, then right on Del Valle Road. Hours vary seasonally. Parking fee is $2.50, $3.50 from March through October. Dog fee is $1. (510) 635-0135. For boat rentals: (510) 449-5201.

Sycamore Grove Regional Park 

An unusual and attractive streamside park for bicycles, horses and hikers. In rainy times, it can look semi-swampy, as most of the Central Valley used to look. In fact, it is Lake Del Valle's flood plain, and federal flood controllers occasionally send run-off into this park's stream, Arroyo Del Valle, when Lake Del Valle rises too high.

With its low hills, tall grass and loud sounds of birds and squirrels, it's almost an African savanna. Blackbirds and swallows swoop over the stream and marshy spots, grabbing insects. Poppies and blue dicks are plentiful in spring. Kids wade in the stream pools near the picnic tables (and so may dogs, but technically they must be on-leash). Follow the paths far enough, though, and the place becomes satisfyingly wild.

The bike trails are wide and smooth enough for a stroller, and the whole park is quite level. You can rent a horse from **Sycamore Grove Stables**. The horse paths are dirt. The park belongs to the Livermore Area Recreation and Park District, which provides naturalist programs. There's no fee.

1-8b Take Interstate 580 to Livermore; exit to North Livermore Avenue; go south to College Avenue (it's in about two miles) and turn right. At Arroyo Road, turn left, and then right on Wetmore Road. Open from 8 a.m. to sunset. (510) 373-5700.

Ohlone Regional Wilderness 

To enter this wild and beautiful area east of Sunol Regional Wilderness, you must pick up a permit (which includes a detailed trail map and camping information) for $1 at East Bay Regional Park Headquarters or the Del Valle, Coyote Hills or Sunol kiosks.

The regional parks system shares the wilderness with the San Francisco Water District, which wants to limit human contact. The dog rules are surprisingly liberal: Dogs may not stay overnight in the campgrounds, but during the day, they're subject only to the usual regional park rules, "on-leash or under control."

Any part of this vast area you can cover in one day will be a bit of heaven for your dog. Be sure to carry water, though.

1-8c (510) 635-0135.

Ohlone Wilderness Trail 

This daunting trail stretches 29 rugged miles from Mission Peak, east of Fremont, through Sunol Regional Wilderness and Ohlone Regional Wilderness to Del Valle Regional Park, south of Livermore. The same permit is required, and the same dog rules apply—so you won't be able to do all 29 miles at once with your dog. That's okay.

1-8d (510) 635-0135.

Lodgings & Campgrounds

Del Valle Regional Park campground: Family Camp allows dogs, but only on-leash or confined to your tent. One-hundred-fifty sites, 21 with water and sewage hookups, but no electrical. Showers. $12 a night for a tent or drive-in site; $15 or $18 for sites with additional trailer hookups. $5 for each additional vehicle. Reserve through the East Bay Regional Parks reservation number: (510) 562-CAMP. From November 1 through January 31, though, sites are first-come, first-served. The entrance gate closes at 10 p.m.

Holiday Inn—Livermore: One block north adjacent to Interstate 580, exit Springtown Boulevard. 720 Las Flores Road, Livermore, CA 94550. A double room is around $65; $7 extra for dog, rooms on first floor only. They have a very friendly attitude. (510) 443-4950.

1-9

NEWARK

Parks, Beaches & Recreation Areas

San Francisco Bay National Wildlife Refuge 

This refuge offers a sanctuary for countless waterfowl and protects a huge portion of the bay's marshes and mudflats from civilization's insults. Unfortunately, one of the most damaging creatures to delicate wetlands ecosystems is...the dog. Whether or not your dog would actually chase wild birds, birds are terrified by the mere sight of him. So dogs are banned from most marshy refuges. But this one permits leashed dogs on its **Tidelands Trail** right at the Visitor Center, located near the toll plaza on the Newark side of the Dumbarton Bridge (Highway 84).

1-9a Open during daylight hours. (510) 792-0222.

1-10

OAKLAND

Oakland, the most urban city in the East Bay, is also blessed with the best collection of generous and tolerant city parks. Unfortunately, what we call the "white gloves" part of Oakland—the parklands ringing Lake Merritt and the Oakland Museum—is off-limits to dogs. But read on!

Parks, Beaches & Recreation Areas

Anthony Chabot Regional Park 

Since cattle no longer graze this park, many of its hillsides have been overgrown by brush and eucalyptus. The **Goldenrod Trail**, starting at the southern terminus of Skyline Boulevard and Grass Valley Road, can connect you with the **East Bay Skyline National Trail**, which winds through Grass Valley and climbs through eucalyptus forests. Unfortunately, shots from the nearby firing range can be heard nearly throughout the park. But these trails have everything a dog could want, except much stream access. Dogs may be off-leash everywhere, except in developed areas. Carry water with you in hot weather.

1-10a The park has several main entrances. To reach the Goldenrod Trail, exit on Golf Links Road from Interstate 580 and travel south on Golf Links. Bear west on Grass Valley Road and park at the small lot at the intersection of Grass Valley Road and Skyline Boulevard. Open from 7 a.m. to 10 p.m. (510) 635-0135.

Lake Chabot Marina area 

The Lake Chabot Marina area of the park is popular with picnickers, fisherpeople and boaters on weekends, and dogs must be leashed as in all developed areas in the East Bay Regional Parks. So it's a qualified pleasure for dogs, unless you're there on an uncrowded day. The lake is a reservoir, so no swimming for people or dogs; dogs aren't allowed on the rented boats; and the park is extremely well kept, but a bit artificial for our taste.

There are plenty of toilets, scoop dispensers and water fountains for people and dogs, and all the usual recreation area amenities: marina, cheerful ducks, picnic tables, parcourse, bike trails. Dabney doesn't like to share paths with many bikes, however. The hillside trails are forbiddingly steep and given to erosion.

1-10b Bring quarters to pay the parking fee machine—$1. From Interstate 580, take the Fairmont Drive exit east; Fairmont becomes Lake Chabot Road. Continue south to the Lake Chabot entrance. Hours for the marina area vary seasonally. (510) 635-0135.

Dimond Park

In this small jewel of a canyon, dense and wild in the midst of the city, you must follow the city rules and leash your dog, even though you may not see another person on the trail. The **Dimond Canyon Hiking Trail** begins to the east of El Centro Avenue. There's a small parking lot at El Centro where it bisects the park. A short foot trail goes off west of El Centro, ending quickly at the **Dimond Recreation Center** and an attractive jungle gym for children.

The main trail, wide and of smooth dirt, starts on the east side and follows Sausal Creek about one-quarter mile up the canyon. At that point, the trail becomes the creekbed, so you can continue only in dry season. But what a quarter-mile! The deciduous tangle of trees and ivy make the canyon into a hushed, cool bower, and the creek is wide and accessible to dogs longing for a splash. When the water level is high enough, there are falls, and except in the driest months, there's enough for a dog pool or two.

After the trail goes into the creekbed, the going is a little rougher, but you can follow it all the way to the ridge at the eastern end.

1-10c From Interstate 580, take the Fruitvale Avenue exit north to the corner of Fruitvale and Lyman Road, the eastern entrance. Or, to park at the trailhead, take the Park Boulevard exit from Highway 13 and turn left (south) on El Centro Avenue. Hours are 7 a.m. to 10 p.m. (510) 531-2205.

Joaquin Miller Park

This large, beautiful city park nestles at the western edge of the huge **Redwood Regional Park**, where dogs run free legally. If it weren't for the Oakland city parks' rule that dogs must always be leashed, Joaquin Miller would be dog heaven.

Dogs can't even enter some of the landscaped areas, such as around Woodminster Amphitheatre. On the deliciously cool and damp creek trails below, however, you and your dog will feel like you own the place.

The **West Ridge Trail**, reachable from Skyline Boulevard, is popular with mountain bikers. It's waterless, but a good run. The best trails can be entered from the Ranger Station off Joaquin Miller Road; the Sunset Trail, for example, smooth enough for a stroller, descends about one-eighth mile to a cool, ferny stream winding through second- and third-growth redwoods, pines, oak and laurel, then ascends to a ridge overlooking cities and bay, and peppered in spring with wildflowers.

Throughout the park are plenty of picnic tables and water fountains.

> ***1-10d*** From Highway 13 in Oakland, take the Joaquin Miller Road exit and go one-half mile east to the ranger station. No parking fee. Open 6 a.m. to sundown. (510) 531-2205.

Knowland Park 

Behind Oakland's Knowland Park Zoo are wild hillsides criss-crossed by fire trails. Dogs are welcome there on-leash. The best entry for a fairly flat, circular walk is from one of the suburban streets running off Malcolm Avenue at the park's southern edge. You'll find gentle hills covered with scattered brush and pine trees, offering unofficial picnicking spots, hawks and vultures, and panoramic views of the bay, San Francisco, Oakland and Marin. At some crests, you can see three bay bridges.

This park gives you that fine feeling you get from wide-open country. It puts you in touch with everything in the local sky, including air traffic around Oakland Airport. We wouldn't recommend it on a hot or very windy day, and your dog won't find any water. Carry some with you.

> ***1-10e*** Exit Interstate 580 at Golf Links Road; drive south just past Elysian Fields Drive, where one fire trail starts. Or drive south all the way through the park to Caloden Street. Take a right, then another right on Malcolm Avenue. Several residential streets running off Malcolm lead to the park. Open from 7 a.m. to 5 p.m., to 7 p.m. in summer. (510) 632-9525.

Leona Heights Park

This park is a miniature version of the incomparable Redwood Regional Park (page 50), our idea of dog Nirvana. If it weren't for the Oakland city parks' leash requirement, we'd rate it among the best. Another flaw is a distinct lack of trail maintenance. Several spots on the **York Trail** are downright dangerous, and the lack of railings next to steep creek banks and slippery boulders rules out bringing a young child along.

Park at the entrance on Mountain Boulevard; there are lots of paths on both sides, but we recommend walking east on Oakleaf Street, past Leona Lodge. The street is actually the **York Trail**, which follows boulder-lined **Horseshoe Creek**, with falls and plentiful dog pools. The dirt path is passable for about one-quarter mile, over wooden bridges and through glades of eucalyptus, ferns, oaks, pines, redwoods, bay and French broom. No strollers here, though, and when you reach the stream crossing lacking a bridge, don't continue unless you're prepared to clamber, slide and grab trees on this ill-maintained portion of the trail.

It isn't a user-friendly park, but there are advantages for the dog owner looking for solitude. No bikes could possibly negotiate this trail, and the park is nearly deserted, even on weekends.

1-10f Take the Redwood Road exit from Highway 13 and go south on Mountain Boulevard. Park when you see the sign for Leona Lodge. There is also a fire trail starting behind Merritt College's recycling center—at the first parking lot on the right on Campus Drive (off Redwood Road). A new hiking trail will soon be open leading down into the park from this lot. Open 8 a.m. to 10 p.m. (510) 238-3866.

Leona Heights Regional Open Space

Unmarked on most maps, this open space stretches from Merritt College south to Oak Knoll, and from Interstate 580 east to Anthony Chabot Regional Park. Since it's part of the East Bay Regional Parks system, your dog need not be on-leash. A bumpy fire trail goes from Merritt College downhill to the southern entrance, just north of Oak Knoll.

The best way to enter is to park at a lot off Canyon Oaks Drive, next to a condominium parking lot. Right at this entrance is a pond, but you won't see any more water as you ascend. It's a dry hike in warm weather, so be sure to carry water for your dog.

The fire trail leads gently uphill all the way to Merritt, through coyote brush and oak woodland and, in spring, plentiful wildflowers and the loud hum of bees. Watch out for poison oak.

1-10g From Interstate 580, exit at Keller Avenue and drive east to Campus Drive. Take a left (north), then a left on Canyon Oaks Drive. Open 24 hours. (510) 635-0135.

Redwood Regional Park 

This is Dabney's all-star, four-paw park. It's less frequented than Tilden Park, and our favorite spots are easy to find. The cool redwood canyons are filled—even through most summers—with ferny pools for dog swims. We've seen the larger pools hold three or four blissed-out golden retrievers at once. Off-leash once we leave the parking lot, Dabney spends hours on the trails, sniffing, swimming and gathering burrs.

This is also one of the most naturally beautiful and varied of the regional parks, with its majestic redwood, pine, eucalyptus, madrone and flowering fruit trees. A human being won't want to go home from here, either.

Mud is inevitable if you follow the **Stream Trail** and stop at the pools, but fortunately it dries quickly and falls off. The only real hazards on these trails are ticks and poison oak.

No parking fee is charged at Skyline Gate at the north end (in Contra Costa County; the park straddles Contra Costa and Alameda counties). Entering here also lets you avoid the tempting smells of picnic tables at the south end. The Stream Trail takes you steadily downhill, then takes a steep plunge to the canyon bottom. It's uphill all the way back, but worth it.

1-10h Take the Carson Street-Redwood Road exit from Highway 13. Go straight, and turn right onto Redwood Road. Follow it to the park entrance. Some entrances charge a parking fee ($2) and a dog fee ($1). Open from 5 a.m. to 10 p.m. (510) 635-0135.

San Leandro Bay Regional Shoreline 

The Oakland shoreline hasn't much to offer a dog besides this park, well-maintained by the East Bay Regional Park system. And it has a major flaw: The parks system classifies the whole thing as a developed area, so you must leash. The kinds of fun that a dog most wants—running full-out across grass, swimming in the bay or chasing ground squirrels—are illegal.

But you can have a genteel good time on a sunny day that's not too windy, ambling along the extensive paved bayside trails with a child in stroller, or giving your dog a workout while you ride a bike. Amenities for people are plentiful: picnic tables, a few trees, fountains, a parcourse, a tiny beach and a huge playing field.

Dabney once watched a cricket game there, but he would much rather have been chasing the piping ground squirrels who taunted him from the riprap lining the shore. (If you do unleash, your dog can have the time of his life chasing them and will almost certainly never catch one.)

There's a wooden walkway over some mudflats for watching shorebirds and terns fishing, but remember that a dog will always cut down on the number of birds you'll see. For birdwatching, go at low tide. Keep your dog firmly leashed and held close to you and hike along the **San Leandro Creek Channel** to **Arrowhead Marsh**, or (if you enter from Doolittle Drive) walk along the **Doolittle Trail**. There's a small sandy beach here, but dogs aren't allowed to swim. (Usual East Bay Regional Park rules: no dogs on beaches.)

> *1-10i* From Interstate 880, exit at Hegenberger Road in Oakland. Go west on Hegenberger and turn on Edgewater Drive, Pardee Drive or Doolittle Drive. Parking is free at all these entry points. Unless your dog can drink from your cupped hands, carry a water dish. Open from 5 a.m. to 10 p.m. (510) 635-0135.

Temescal Regional Recreation Area 

Lake Temescal, a small, natural-looking reservoir in North Oakland, is popular for swimming, fishing and picnicking, and in warm weather is swarming with happy families from every part of the world, cooking up smells that will drive your poor leashed dog wild. We've seen Japanese group games, outdoor church services and piñata parties.

Our dogs love the paths through woods around the lake. Because this is a regional recreation area and not a park, they're supposed to be on-leash even on the trails, and park staff are strict about dogs in the water. In winter, however, you may have the park nearly to yourself. One drawback is a low-key whoosh of traffic noise from Highways 13 and 24. The pine and willow trees on the steep-sided hills on a misty winter day can remind you of a Japanese watercolor.

The terrible fire of 1991 burned about 20 acres of trees on the western hillside, but they are coming back quickly.

The usual seasonal and weekend East Bay Regional Park fees are charged for parking and swimming.

1-10j From Highway 24, take the Broadway exit and follow signs to Highway 13. You'll see the parking area on the right. Or, from Highway 13, take the Broadway Terrace exit and drive west a short distance to the park entrance. Open 8 a.m. to 6 p.m., November through March; 8 a.m. to 10 p.m., April through October. (510) 635-0135.

RESTAURANTS

Oakland's College Avenue, in the Rockridge District, has a tolerant family atmosphere. Lawyers with briefcases buy flowers on the way home from the BART station, and students flirt over ice cream. We've never seen anyone in that neighborhood who didn't love dogs. Even so, you should leash for safety on this busy street.

The avenue is known to be a food lover's paradise, and among the attractions are a string of restaurants with outdoor tables.

Cactus Taqueria: Tacos, burritos, beer and wine served cafeteria-style. Yup-Mex decor. Eight tables in a tiled space set off from the sidewalk are inviting to dogs, no Spanish necessary—but since health departments are ambivalent about dogs in any enclosed space, you'll do the owners a favor if you tie your dog up on the sidewalk. 5525 College Avenue. (510) 547-1305.

Cafe Rustica: Elegant pizza, desserts, beer and wine. 5422 College Avenue. (510) 654-1601.

Dave's Newsstand: Newspapers and magazines from everywhere. Lounge at sidewalk tables with Corriere Della Sera or Le Monde, coffee, pastry and your dog. The folks who run Dave's are so much in favor of dogs that they are planning to install a water trough outside. They even welcome your dog inside the store if she's well-behaved. 5820 College Avenue. (510) 654-8200.

Oliveto Cafe: This cafe and Peaberry's, next door, share a building with the Market Hall, God's own food emporium. The food's the best, but for a dog, the atmosphere is congested. It's not for nervous dogs. Oliveto serves very classy pizza, tapas, bar food, desserts, coffees and drinks, but alcohol is not allowed at the sidewalk tables. 5655 College Avenue, just south of Rockridge BART. (510) 547-5356.

Peaberry's: Serves coffees, pastries and desserts. A favorite with BART commuters. 5655 College Avenue. (510) 653-0450.

Royal Coffee: A cheery and popular place with very good coffee and tea, in the bean or in the cup, and supplies. On weekend mornings, it's dog central. 307 63rd Street at College Avenue. (510) 652-4258.

Lodgings & Campgrounds

Holiday Inn—Oakland Airport: Two and one-quarter miles east of Oakland Airport; east of I-880, exit Hegenberger Road. 500 Hegenberger Road, Oakland, CA 94621. Around $100 for a double. (510) 562-5311.

Oakland Airport Hilton: One and one-quarter mile east of Oakland Airport; west of I-880, exit Hegenberger Road. One Hegenberger Road, PO Box 2549, Oakland, CA 94614. $120 to $140 for a double. Small dogs only; $10 extra. (510) 635-5000.

1-11

PIEDMONT

Piedmont, the incorporated town in the midst of Oakland, is almost entirely residential and very proper and clean. This means you won't be able to find a stray scrap of paper to scoop with, so be prepared. Its quiet streets are delightful for walking, offering views from the hills.

Piedmont has no official park curfews. "We don't have the kind of parks people would be in after dark," says a woman at the city recreation department, and it's true.

Parks, Beaches & Recreation Areas

Dracena Park

A woodsy oasis for a 15-minute walk and sniff. Signs say you must pick up after your dog, and they mean it. But it's an official off-leash dog run.

1-11a At Blair Avenue and Dracena Avenue. (510) 420-3070.

Piedmont Park 🐾🐾🐾

Enter this elegant urban park at the main gate, on Highland Avenue. (You can also enter through the Piedmont High School playing fields, but the school would rather you didn't bring your dog that way during school hours.) Be sure to keep your dog leashed at either end: The city animal control headquarters and a police station flank the main entrance, and Piedmont is strict! Police make periodic sweeps and cite owners who've forgotten that they aren't in Berkeley.

The city is restoring Piedmont Park to its 19th century elegance after years of neglect, clearing and re-lining the creekbed and building attractive new salmon-pink concrete pathways, good for pushing a stroller. There's a fine jungle gym for children, too. The stream, fed year-round by a spring higher in the hills, creates a cool canyon of ivy and redwoods, pines, eucalyptuses and acacias. Even in the driest summer, you and your dog can enjoy a genteel stroll past pools and waterfalls.

1-11b The park's main entrance is at Highland Avenue and Hillside. (510) 420-3070.

FAIRS & FESTIVALS

Piedmont Fourth of July: Well-behaved dogs are welcome to watch Piedmont's old-fashioned parade, but—as with all Fourth celebrations—leave your dog at home if he's afraid of firecrackers and other loud noises. Dabney and Joe, for instance, celebrate our nation's birth from under the bed. The Piedmont parade begins with a cannon shot and a fire truck siren. (510) 420-3040.

1-12 PLEASANTON

PARKS, BEACHES & RECREATION AREAS

Pleasanton Ridge Regional Park 🐾🐾🐾🐾

This recent and beautiful addition to the East Bay Regional Park system is a treat, though isolated unless you live in Dublin or Pleasanton. Dogs may run off-leash on trails as soon as you leave the staging area.

At this time, access to Pleasanton Ridge is only from the entrance on Foothill Road. There are fine picnic sites at the trailhead. Climb up on the **Oak Tree** fire trail to the ridgeline, where a looping set of trails goes off to the right. The incline is gentle, through pasture (you share this park with cattle) dotted with oak and—careful—poison oak.

Wildflowers riot in spring; it's a hot place in summer. At the bottom of the park, however, is a beautiful streamside stretch along **Arroyo de la Laguna.** There's no water above the entrance, so be sure to carry plenty.

1-12a From Interstate 680, take the Castlewood Drive exit and go left (west) on Foothill Road to headquarters. Open from 5 a.m. to 10 p.m. (510) 862-2963.

Shadow Cliffs Regional Recreation Area 

Shadow Cliffs is one of the East Bay Regional Parks. Its lake (an old Kaiser Industries gravel quarry) and water slide are understandably popular with people on hot summer days, but dogs aren't allowed on the beaches here or in the picnic area. So there's not much point in bringing her, unless you're going fishing from the bank or launching your own boat. You can rent a boat here, but the dog isn't allowed on it. If you launch your own (electric motors only), the park charges a boating fee.

Or you can fish in the quieter Arroyo area, where swimming and boating aren't allowed. Keep your dog leashed in the developed areas and near the marshy spots, where birds nest.

1-12b Off Stanley Boulevard, one mile east of Pleasanton. Gates are open 6 a.m. to 9 p.m. Parking fee in summer is $3.50. (510) 635-0135. For boat rentals: (510) 846-9263.

LODGINGS & CAMPGROUNDS

Doubletree Hotel: One-half mile southwest of the junction of Interstate 580 and 680; exit 580 at Foothill Road; one-quarter mile south, then one-quarter mile east on Canyon Way. 5990 Stoneridge Mall Road, Pleasanton, CA 94588. A double room goes for around $95; $15 extra for dog. (510) 463-3330.

Holiday Inn: Exit Interstate 580 at Foothill Road, one-quarter mile south on Dublin Canyon Road. 11950 Dublin Canyon Road, Pleasanton, CA 94588. $70 to $90 for a double. Dogs on first floor only; credit card payment or refundable $100 cash deposit required. (510) 847-6000.

FAIRS & FESTIVALS

Heritage Days: Pleasanton holds Heritage Days each year on the second weekend in June. It's the usual fair on Main Street, with arts and crafts good and bad, cotton candy and cheerful crowds. Heritage Days really goes all out for an old-fashioned, small-town atmosphere, though, with band concerts, magicians, square dancing and barbershop singing. And in a small town like this, everyone shows up. Someone tried to sell Dabney a special sun visor for dogs.

From Interstate 680, take the Bernal Avenue exit east and turn left (north) on Main Street; or take the Sunol Boulevard exit east, jog left (west) at Bernal Avenue and turn north on Main. (510) 484-2199.

1-13

SAN LEANDRO

DIVERSIONS

Wag your tail for a good cause: Each October, the Oakland Society for Prevention of Cruelty to Animals holds a fundraising dog run. You and your dog can do a 2-mile run or a scenic 1-mile walk, watch the World Canine Frisbee Champs perform, or enter contests—goofy pet tricks, tail-wagging, that sort of thing. It's held in the San Leandro Marina. For this year's date and info on fees, call the Oakland SPCA: (510) 569-0702.

MORE INFO

WHERE YOUR DOG CAN'T GO

- Alameda Penny Market
- Ardenwood Regional Preserve, Fremont
- Berkeley Marina Fishing Pier
- Botanic Garden in Tilden Regional Park, Berkeley
- Castro Valley Community Center Park
- Centennial Park, Hayward
- Crow Canyon Park, Castro Valley
- Emeryville Marina Fishing Pier
- Fairmont Terrace Park, Castro Valley
- George E. Weekes Memorial Park, Hayward
- John F. Kennedy Park, Hayward
- Lakeside Park (and all parkland surrounding Lake Merritt), Oakland
- Marshlands of Coyote Hills Regional Park, Fremont
- Meek Park, San Lorenzo

1. ALAMEDA COUNTY (map page 22-23)

- Nature Study Area of Tilden Regional Park, Berkeley
- Robert Crown Memorial State Beach, Alameda
- South Shore Beach, Alameda
- Ohlone Regional Wilderness backcountry campgrounds (Family Campground only)

USEFUL PHONE NUMBERS & ADDRESSES

East Bay Municipal Utility District: (510) 835-3000; questions about trails: (510) 254-3798. 500 San Pablo Dam Road, Orinda, CA 94563. Hiking permit available for $5 for one year, $10 for three years.

East Bay Regional Park District: (510) 635-0135; camping reservations: (510) 562-CAMP. 2950 Peralta Oaks Court, Oakland, CA 94605.

·Contra Costa County·

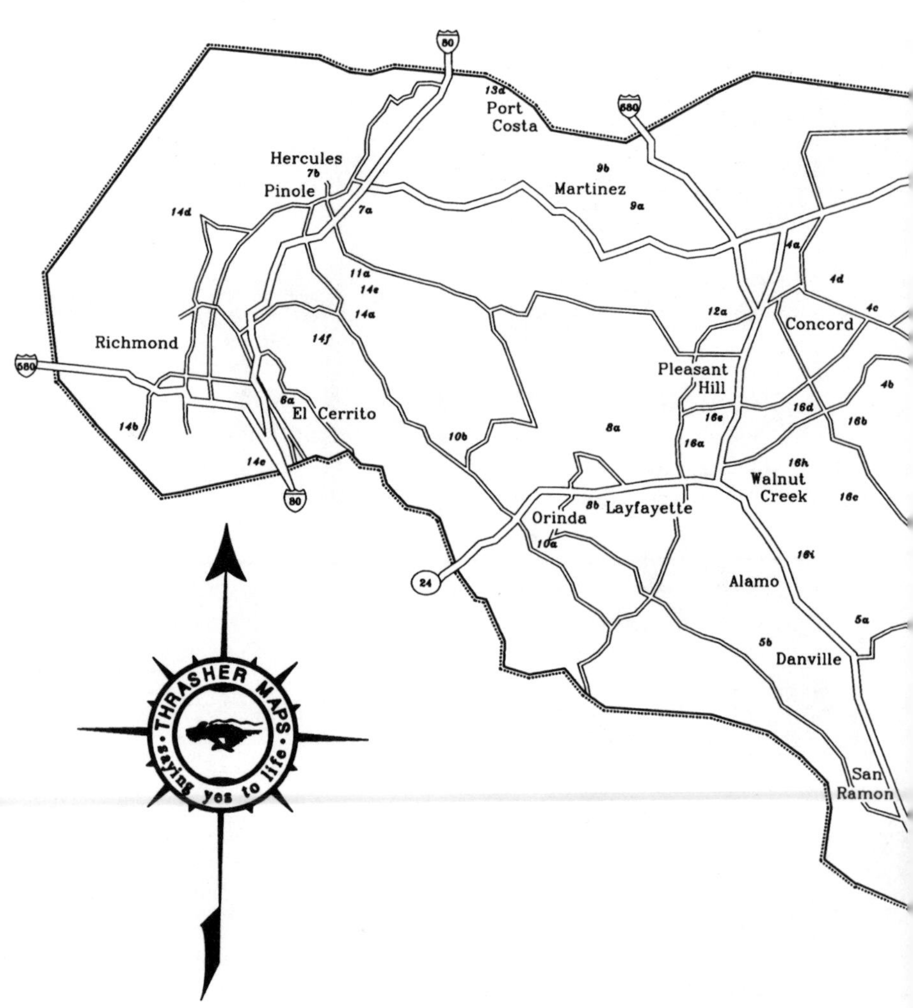
80
13a
Port
Costa
680
Hercules
7b
Pinole
9b
Martinez
9a
7a
14d
4a
4d
11a
14a
12a
4c
Concord
Richmond
14f
580
Pleasant
Hill
4b
8a
El Cerrito
16d
16b
14b
8a
10b
16a
14c
16h
Walnut
Creek
16c
80
8b Layfayette
Orinda
10a
24
Alamo
5a
5b
Danville
THRASHER MAPS
saying yes to life
San
Ramon

2. CONTRA COSTA COUNTY (map page 60-61)

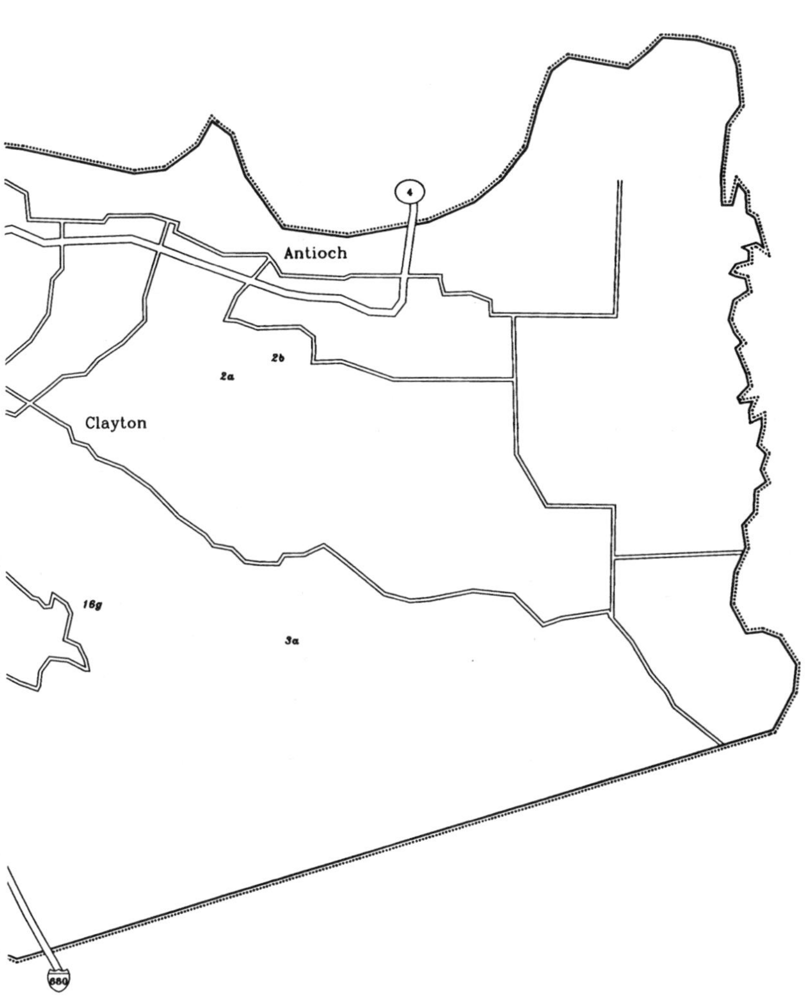

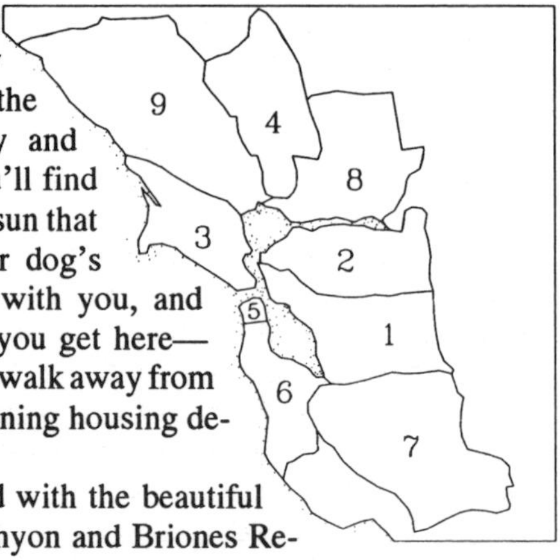

2 The interior of **Contra Costa County** feels like a piece of the Old West. It's open, dry and horsy, and in summer, you'll find it's home to a magnificent sun that will cook an egg on your dog's forehead. So carry water with you, and relish the frontier feeling you get here—even though it's just a short walk away from any of the county's burgeoning housing developments.

Contra Costa is blessed with the beautiful and accessible Wildcat Canyon and Briones Regional Parks and even wilder outposts such as Black Diamond Mines, Las Trampas and Morgan Territory. For a cooler, breezy coast walk, nothing beats Richmond's Point Pinole. For socializing off the leash with other dogs and their owners, Point Isabel is renowned throughout the Bay Area.

Even in town, it's good to be a dog. Ten long regional trails—thanks to the East Bay Regional Parks District—lace Lafayette, Walnut Creek and the other urban areas of the Diablo Valley. There are 60 miles of trails in all. Two of the more delightful segments are described below. Remember: Bicycles yield to horses and hikers, and hikers yield to horses—hikers with dogs, especially. Dogs must be leashed on these trails. For information and a trail map, call: (510) 635-0135.

Regional Trails

Briones to Diablo Regional Trail

A little more than 12 miles of trail and six parks snake through Lafayette and Walnut Creek between Briones Regional Park and Mount Diablo State Park (where you must stop at the border, since dogs aren't allowed). Some portions are paved, some dirt. Lafayette Staging Area is the entrance to the Briones end on Pleasant Hill Road, just north of Acalanes High School. The trail then goes through **Acalanes Ridge Open Space Recreation Area, Larkey Park**—home of the sweet **Alexander Lindsay Museum**, with its live samples of local wildlife—**Walden Park Land Bank, Heather Farms Park, Shell Ridge Open Space** and the historic **Borges Ranch**, and **Diablo Foothills Regional Park**.

This trail is popular with cyclists and equestrians, so be cautious and leash your dog (the law), unless you're confident that you have the trail to yourself. Wear rugged shoes, and remember that your poor dog's unprotected feet may wear out before yours do. Carry plenty of water, of course.

Contra Costa Canal Regional Trail

The Contra Costa Canal Regional Trail is a 12-mile greenbelt and paved trail that winds through Concord, Pleasant Hill and Walnut Creek, following the canal. A dog will enjoy going along on a hot bike ride or hike with you—if he can jump into the water along the way. Don't let him jump in where the banks are steep, though, as he may not be able to scramble back out. Leash where rules are posted. And no, we doubt that dog swims are encouraged by the Contra Costa Water District; human swimming and fishing are prohibited in the canals. On the other hand, the water *is* treated before it goes into people's taps in Martinez. Let your conscience be your guide.

East Bay Municipal Utility District Lands

For a general description and rules for dogs within East Bay Municipal Utility District Lands, please see Alameda County (page 26). These parklands are listed under their closest city:

- Briones Regional Park (page 71)
- Lafayette Reservoir Recreation Area (page 72)
- San Pablo Dam Reservoir (page 74)

East Bay Regional Parklands

See the general description under Alameda County (page 24).

2-1

ALAMO

Fairs & Festivals

Alamo Plaza Music Festival: This musical good time is held every year in early September. Dog and human ears are treated to folk, country-western and jazz. It's all held outdoors, so leashed dogs who don't howl are welcome. Arts and crafts and a barbecue dinner are included.

At the Alamo Shopping Center, Danville Boulevard and Stone Valley Road. For date and information: (510) 831-1122.

2-2

ANTIOCH

Antioch is pretty much a desert for dogs, but south of town are two charming spots of relief.

PARKS, BEACHES & RECREATION AREAS

Black Diamond Mines Regional Preserve

The only reason this preserve doesn't get a four-paw rating is its lack of water. That aside, it's a delight for human and beast. You can walk into this East Bay Regional Preserve from the Contra Loma Regional Park just below it (see listing, page 65). But from that direction, the trails are too hot and dry for a dog in summer. Instead, enter from the north by car via Somersville Road and park in the last lot, which has some shade trees.

The coal miners who worked and lived here in the 1860s and 1870s planted a variety of drought-tolerant trees not usually found in the East Bay: black locust, tree of heaven, pepper tree and almond. Dabney once surprised a lazing garter snake here. Fortunately, he did not regard it as a creature to chase. You should be alert in warm seasons for rattlers, although any rattler not actually snoozing will probably get out of your way before you even know he's near.

The hills of Black Diamond Mines are jumbled and ragged, looking a lot like the Sierra foothills—mining country. From the parking lot, it's a moderate climb to the **Rose Hill Cemetery**, where Protestant Welsh miners (the tombstones bear the names Davis, Evans, Jenkins) buried victims of mine accidents and many of their children, who died of diphtheria, typhoid and scarlet fever.

Plenty of tunnel openings and piles of tailings have been preserved by the parks service for walkers to examine. The brochure marks mine sites.

2-2a From Highway 4 at Antioch, exit at Somersville Road and drive south to the park entrance. Keep driving for a bit more than one mile if you want to park in the lot farthest in. You'll pass wonderful old mining-era houses and barns, now used as park headquarters and offices. Gates are open between 8 a.m. and 8 p.m. A parking fee of $2 is seldom charged. (510) 635-0135.

Contra Loma Regional Park 

Well-hidden amid barren hills north of Black Diamond Mines—you'd never know it was there—this park is a clean, green oasis for swimming, fishing and picnicking. Windsurfing is popular here, and you may launch your own boat (electric motors only). It's a reservoir, mostly lined with tules and trees, and with a few attractive trails rising into the surrounding hills, including a trail leading into Black Diamond Mines Regional Preserve (see previous listing).

Unfortunately, as in all regional parks, your dog may not accompany you in the swimming area. Nor can he take an informal swim himself in the fishing areas, since the park managers want to protect his feet from stray fishhooks. It's probably better not to take your dog to Contra Loma on a hot day. Instead, save it for winter or spring, when the wildflowers congregate.

2-2b From Highway 4, take the Lone Tree Way exit, go south on Lone Tree, then turn west on Fredrickson Lane to the entrance. Fee for parking is $2.50 or $3.50, depending on season; dog fee $1. Gates open 7 a.m. to 9 p.m. (510) 635-0135.

2-3

CLAYTON

Stop in Clayton on the way to Morgan Territory and walk through its Old Town. You'll discover quite a few old Victorian buildings around Main Street. If you're lucky enough to be free on Wednesdays during the summer, the town holds a farmers' market from May through October on Main from 3 p.m. to 8 p.m. where you can listen to music and buy fresh produce and flowers.

PARKS, BEACHES & RECREATION AREAS

Morgan Territory 

One way to approach this faraway place with the strange-sounding name is through Clayton, but it doesn't really lie near anywhere. As the crow flies, it's equidistant from Clayton, Danville, San Ramon, Livermore, Byron and Brentwood. And "distant" is the key word. Morgan Territory, named after a farmer who owned the land long before it became part of the East Bay Regional Parks system, is as far away from the Bay Area as you can get. From its heights, on a rim above the Central Valley, you see the San Joaquin River, the delta, the valley, and on a clear day, the peaks of the Sierra as well. Morgan Territory is close to the end of the Earth, but well worth the journey.

Best of all, several trails lead to views of the Central Valley without much uphill climbing. For example, try the **Blue Oak Trail** that starts at the entrance. You'll see the "backside" of Mount Diablo, unusual for Bay Area folk. There are lichen-covered sandstone outcroppings, ancient and twisted old giant oaks and copses of blue oak, chaparral and manzanita, as well as many subtly varied shades of grass. But be careful—there's also some poison oak. The only sounds you will hear are the wind, the grinding of crows and the ticking of insects.

There is no shade in the parking lot. In summer, fill up your water bottle here, for most of the creeks are dry as a bone, though your dog can splash into cattle ponds, if he's so inclined. No leash is necessary, but watch for wicked foxtails in these grasses. Poor Dabney was once made to pose for a photo in long grass in front of a picturesque oak, and came away bristling with them.

2-3a The easiest access is from Livermore in Alameda County: From Interstate 580 take the North Livermore Avenue exit and drive north on North Livermore; go left (west) on Manning Road, then right (north) onto Morgan Territory Road to the entrance. Or, for a longer but more picturesque drive: From the intersection of Highway 24 and Interstate 680 in Concord, exit at Ignacio Valley Road, go east on Clayton Road to Clayton and continue east on Marsh Road. Take a right (south) on Morgan Territory Road to the entrance. Hours are 8 a.m. to dusk. (510) 635-0135.

RESTAURANTS

Skipolini's Pizza: Serves New York-style pizza, salads and sandwiches, and welcomes dogs at its outdoor tables—including groups such as Guide Dogs for the Blind and their canine employees. Main Street and Diablo Road. (510) 672-5555.

2-4 CONCORD

Most of Concord's city parks are just run-of-the-mill, and dogs must stay on-leash except in Lime Ridge Open Space Recreation Area. But a city park is a park, so we've listed the largest ones. For a good free run with your dog, though, go to Lime Ridge, which has an entry point on Treat Boulevard west of Cowell Road (see listing).

PARKS, BEACHES & RECREATION AREAS

Hillcrest Community Park 

This one is the cleanest of those we visited; it's mostly lawn and playing fields. Its creek is attractive, although dry in summer. There are no trails, and dogs must be leashed, as in all of Concord's city parks.

2-4a At Olivera Avenue and Grant Street. Open 6 a.m. to 11 p.m. (510) 671-3165.

Lime Ridge Open Space Recreation Area 

This open space reserve, run by the cities of Walnut Creek and Concord, along with Contra Costa County and a private developer, is huge, sprawling across parts of both cities. It's undeveloped and open, and unless you find a creek, it can be hot and dry. But at least it's there, and your dog can run off-leash to her heart's content.

2-4b The only entry point at this time from Concord is from the parking lot on Treat Boulevard west of Cowell Road. The space is open during daylight hours and charges no fees. As yet, there are no legal access points in Walnut Creek. (510) 256-3560.

Newhall Community Park 

A large park with a generous parking lot, this park has picnic tables, a pond, playing fields and only scattered trees. It's a bit trashy, and Dabney found his quota of chicken bones. There's a creek off Wharton Drive, but it's dry in summer. There are no trails. Dogs on-leash only.

2-4c Off Clayton Road and Treat Boulevard. Enter from Turtle Creek Road or Wharton Avenue. Open one-half hour before sunrise to one-half hour after sunset. (510) 671-3165.

Willow Pass Community Park 

This is very much a sports park, with at least three softball fields, tennis courts and picnic and party sites. There's some shade in the parking lot, a creek and a pond, but no trails—and too much broken glass for comfort. Dogs on-leash only.

2-4d At Willow Pass Road and Olivera Road. Open 6 a.m. to 11 p.m. (510) 671-3165.

LODGINGS & CAMPGROUNDS

Best Western Heritage Inn: Three miles east of Highway 242 on Clayton Road at Wharton Way. 4600 Clayton Road, Concord, CA 94521. Around $60 for a double. There's a $50 deposit for the dog. (510) 686-4466.

Holiday Inn Concord: Exit Interstate 680 at East Concord Avenue. Go south on Diamond Avenue, west on Burnett Avenue. 1050 Burnett Avenue, Concord, CA 94520. (510) 687-5500. Between $60 and $95 for a double. $75 cash or credit card deposit for dog.

Sheraton Hotel & Conference Center: From Interstate 680, exit at Concord Avenue and drive east to John Glenn Drive. 45 John Glenn Drive, Concord, CA 94520. (510) 825-7700. Around $130 for a double. Dogs may stay on first floor only.

The Trees Inn: One-half mile east of Interstate 680, northbound exit Monument Boulevard; southbound exit Gregory Lane. 1370 Monument Boulevard, Concord, CA 94520. (510) 827-8998. Between $47 and $85 for a double. You shouldn't leave the dog alone in the room.

2-5 DANVILLE

PARKS, BEACHES & RECREATION AREAS

Oak Hill Park 

Here's a very clean, beautiful park run by the city of Danville. It's about as nice as a park designed for people can get, offering picnic tables, a pond with ducks and geese and waterfalls, volleyball and tennis courts, and an unusually attractive children's play area with swings, slide and its own waterfall. The rest of the park is natural oak-studded hillside laced by an equestrian/hiking/exercise dirt trail, from which there is a fine view of Mount Diablo. Dogs will enjoy this path, but must remain on-leash. No wading in the pond, either.

2-5a At Stone Valley Road and Glenwood Court. The gate is locked at nightfall. (510) 820-6074.

Las Trampas Regional Wilderness 

This regional wilderness is remarkable for its sense of isolation from the rest of the Bay Area. You can hear utter silence here, and the views from the ridgetops are breathtaking. Mount Diablo, says Malcolm Margolin in his wonderful walking guide, *East Bay Out*, looms "like a huge mother hen brooding over her flock of little chick hills." Centuries of wind have formed weird rock outcroppings.

Rocky Ridge Trail (from the parking lot at the end of Bollinger Canyon Road) leads up a fairly steep three-fourths of a mile to the top of the ridge, where you enter the East Bay Municipal Utility District watershed and must have a permit to continue (and *sans* dog, in any case). It's better to head west, on any of several trails climbing the sunny southern flanks of Las Trampas Ridge.

Creeks will be running low or dry by June, so bring plenty of water. Your dog should know how to behave around cattle, deer and horses.

2-5b From Interstate 680 about six miles north of the intersection with Interstate 580, take the Bollinger Canyon Road exit and head north on Bollinger Canyon Road to the entrance. (Go past the entrance to Little Hills Ranch Recreation Area, where dogs aren't allowed.) Open 9 a.m. to 7 p.m. (510) 635-0135.

Dabney is usually sensible about cattle, but one day in Las Trampas he decided to charge after a lone calf on a ridgetop. I ran shouting after him, crested the ridge, and discovered the calf had company—angry company! A hillside full of grown cattle began breaking into indignant bellows and lowering their heads at us. Fortunately, Dabney knew it was time to lose interest in that little chase. And fortunately again, no bull was around.—L.Y.

LODGINGS & CAMPGROUNDS

Sycamore Inn: From Interstate 680, exit east via Sycamore Valley Road. 803 Camino Ramon, Danville, CA 94526. (510) 838-8080. Around $55 for a double. Don't leave the dog unattended in your room.

2-6

EL CERRITO

PARKS, BEACHES & RECREATION AREAS

Hillside Park

The city of El Cerrito has a great amenity: Hillside Park is an official dog run—no leash required. It's not the prettiest park around. The southern end is mostly an eroded hillside of scrubby grass with power lines. But off Schmidt Lane is the much nicer **El Cerrito**

Foundation Memorial Grove. A bumpy dirt path leads up through coyote brush to eucalyptus groves at the hilltop, overlooking El Cerrito, the Golden Gate and Bay bridges and Mount Tamalpais. The trail doesn't go far into the open space. It's a good neighborhood running spot, and you might take your dog along for a visit to the city recycling center, at the end of Schmidt.

2-6a Enter off Schmidt Lane, which runs north off San Pablo Avenue. The park is closed after dark. (510) 215-4300.

2-7

HERCULES

PARKS, BEACHES & RECREATION AREAS

Refugio Valley Park

This is a well-groomed, but not very doggy, city park. At the western end, the official entrance, there are beautiful lawns, a pond, tennis courts, picnic tables and a jungle gym. Dogs must be on-leash. You can walk east on paved bike paths that parallel Refugio Valley Road and **Refugio Creek**, a particularly lovely creek that your dog will enjoy on a hot day. You can also get onto these paths from turnouts off Refugio Valley Road or from the Community Center and Swim Center at the eastern end.

2-7a From Interstate 80, exit at Sycamore Avenue and go east. You'll shortly take a right (south) on Refugio Valley Road, and you'll be at the park entrance. Open from sunrise to 9:30 p.m. (510) 799-8291.

San Pablo Bay Regional Park 

This tiny, undeveloped East Bay Regional Park shoreline can't hold a candle to Point Pinole, but if you're in Hercules exploring the old **Santa Fe Railroad yard**, take a look. A paved trail runs about one-eighth of a mile along the tracks, which may be loaded with freight. New housing developments and interesting restored Victorian railroad worker housing surrounds a tiny but pretty area of grass, swamp and eucalyptus. No leash necessary.

If you follow Railroad Avenue to its end, across the line into Pinole, there's a tiny and beautifully landscaped city park behind the wastewater treatment plant (which smells fresh as a rose). You must keep your dog on-leash here.

2-7b From Interstate 80, exit at Pinole Valley Road and travel north. Pinole Valley Road becomes Tennent Avenue, then Railroad Avenue. Park somewhere around the Civic Arts Facility, a cluster of Victorian buildings in a grove of palms and eucalyptus. The Pinole city park is open from one-half hour before sunrise to one-half hour after sunset. (510) 724-9004. The San Pablo Bay Regional Park is open from 5 a.m. to 10 p.m. (510) 635-0135.

2-8

LAFAYETTE

PARKS, BEACHES & RECREATION AREAS

Briones Regional Park

From both main entrances to this park, you can walk one-quarter of a mile and be lost in sunny, rolling hills or cool oak woodlands. Unless you stick to the stream bottoms, it's not a good park for hot summer days. But with a good supply of your own water, you and your dog, blissfully leash-free, can walk gentle ups and downs all day on fire roads or foot trails.

The north entrance requires an immediate uphill climb into the hills, but you're rewarded with a quick view of Mount Diablo and the piping of ground squirrels, all of whom are long gone safely into their burrows by the time your dog realizes that they might be fun to chase. We did see a young black lab racing on his own up and down the steep hillsides, just for the joy of it. If your dog is a self-starter, this end of the park is fine for you. The **Alhambra Creek Trail**, which follows Alhambra Creek, does offer water in the rainy season. Avoid the **John Muir Nature Area** (shaded on your brochure map), where dogs aren't allowed.

We prefer the south entrance at **Bear Creek**, just east of the inaccessible (to dogs) Briones Reservoir. Here you have an immediate choice of open hills or woodsy canyon, and the land is level for a few miles. **The Homestead Valley Trail** leads gently up and down through cool, sharp-scented bay and oak woodlands. Even in the bone-dry winter of 1991, one pool was standing in Bear Creek.

Watch for deer, horses and cattle—Dabney is fond of rolling in fresh cow flop! This is a fine experience for man and beast.

2-8a From Highway 24, take the Orinda exit; go north on Camino Pablo, then right (north) on Bear Creek Road to Briones Road, to the park entrance. The park is open from 8 a.m. to 10 p.m. Parking fee is $2.50, dog fee $1. (510) 635-0135.

Lafayette Reservoir 

This park, like all run by the East Bay Municipal Utility District, is a bit rules-crazy, but it's well-maintained and clean, nestled in wooded hills. Dogs like Dabney, who love freedom and plenty of scraps on the ground, don't feel quite at home here. But since it's a multi-use park and a reservoir, too, the rules are understandable. Dogs must be leashed; pooper scooper dispensers and trash bins are everywhere; signs repeat: "Leash Laws Enforced."

Drinking fountains and restrooms are plentiful, but you must carry a dog dish or use your hands. Picnicking, fishing, biking and just strolling around the reservoir paths are popular activities on weekends. It's a quiet park, partly because motorboats are not allowed. You can rent a rowboat, but your dog can't go out with you. (The only reservoir that allows dogs in rented boats is Del Valle Regional Recreation Area; see listing under Alameda County, page 43.)

The **Shore Trail** is smooth concrete, ideal for strollers and wheelchairs. Better for a dog walk is the dirt **Rim Trail**, which circles the reservoir higher up. This path has its ups and downs, but certainly isn't tiring. From here, there are pretty views of the reservoir and surrounding suburbs.

2-8b From Highway 24, exit at Acalanes Road/Mount Diablo Boulevard. Go west on Mount Diablo Boulevard and watch for the sign for the turnoff to the reservoir. Parking is metered, or $4 for the whole day. Open dawn to 6 p.m. in winter, dawn to 8 p.m. in summer. (510) 284-9669.

RESTAURANTS

Geppetto's Cafe: Gourmet coffee, gelati and pastries may be enjoyed at sidewalk tables, and dogs are welcome. It's a good spot for a cool drink after a hot summer hike in Briones. 3563 Mount Diablo Boulevard. (510) 284-1261.

2-9

MARTINEZ

Martinez has a charming historic district right off the entrance to its regional shoreline park, so spend some time walking with your dog around the Amtrak station and antique shops. You'll see plenty of fellow strollers taking a break from the train.

PARKS, BEACHES & RECREATION AREAS

Hidden Lakes Open Space 

Although the city park called **Hidden Valley Park** doesn't allow dogs, the open space to the south of it does, and you don't need to leash. It's crossed by one of the East Bay Regional Parks' trails, the **California Riding and Hiking Trail,** on its way from the **Carquinez Strait Regional Shoreline** to where it connects with the **Contra Costa Canal Trail.** (Call (510) 531-9300 to order a map of the Contra Costa Regional Trails.)

2-9a One entrance to Hidden Lakes, with restrooms and fresh water for you and your dog, is off Morello Avenue where it intersects with Chilpancingo Parkway. Open from 5 a.m. to 10 p.m. (510) 635-0135.

Martinez Regional Shoreline 

This is another East Bay Regional Parks District shoreline designed primarily for people. Bicycling, fishing, soccer, bocce, softball fields, biking and boat rentals are available. The restoration of the shoreline's saltwater marshes means that your dog can't go into the most natural portions, and he must be leashed elsewhere, too, such as the sports and picnic areas or on the marina pier. The poor guy can't play in the pond or in Alhambra Creek, either.

2-9b From Highway 4, take the Alhambra Avenue exit and drive north to Escobar Street. Take a right on Escobar, then a left on Ferry Street, over tracks, to the park entrance and parking lots. Open sunrise to sunset. (510) 635-0135.

2-10

ORINDA

PARKS, BEACHES & RECREATION AREAS

Robert Sibley Volcanic Regional Preserve 

This park is actually closer to Oakland, but lies in Contra Costa County. From the entrance on Skyline Boulevard, you can get on the **Skyline National Trail** and walk north to **Tilden Park** or south to **Redwood.** Or, for a shorter stroll, take the road to **Round Top,** the highest peak in the Berkeley Hills.

Prettier and less steep is the road to the quarries. It's partly paved and smooth enough for a wheelchair or stroller, but becomes smooth dirt about halfway to the quarries. Both trails are labeled for geological features revealing the park's volcanic history. (Pick up a brochure at the Visitor Center.) At the quarry pits, there's a good view of Mount Diablo. This is a dry, scrubby and cattle-grazed area, but in the rainy season your dog may be lucky enough to find swimming in a pit near the quarries. No leash is necessary. In spring, look for poppies and lupines.

2-10a From Highway 24 east of the Caldecott Tunnel, exit on Fish Ranch Road and drive north to Grizzly Peak Boulevard, and take a left. Go south on Grizzly Peak to the intersection with Skyline Boulevard. Go left on Skyline. Just to the east of the intersection is the entrance. Open 5 a.m. to 10 p.m. (510) 635-0135.

San Pablo Dam Reservoir

This is East Bay Municipal Utility District (EBMUD) territory, but geographically closest to Orinda. As on all EBMUD lands, you pay dearly and are constantly reminded of the rules, but in this case, it's worth it. Local fishing expert Tom Stienstra ranks this reservoir the number one fishing spot in his list of Bay Area lakes, for both beauty and good fishing. It's stocked with more trout than any lake in California.

The park has a playground for kids and many picnic tables under cool pines. You can picnic right by the water or fish from shore with your dog. Dogs aren't allowed on the fishing docks, though. And EBMUD absolutely forbids any dog/water contact (or human/water contact, for that matter) in the reservoir, since it's a drinking water source. For this reason, you can't take a dog out even in your own boat.

On the paved and dirt trails around the reservoir, you must keep your dog leashed. But they are lovely trails and often empty once you wind into the hills. The dirt trails get rougher as you leave the popular fishing areas. You'll have to ford some creek beds or streams, and there's too much poison oak for comfort if your dog doesn't step daintily right down the middle of the trail. Maybe EBMUD regards poison oak as one of its weapons in its war against off-leash dogs. The trails are wild and woodsy, though, and we recommend them highly.

2-10b From Interstate 80, exit at San Pablo Dam Road and drive south. From Highway 24, exit Camino Del Pablo/San Pablo Dam Road and go north. Entrance fee, year-round, is $4 for parking and $1 for dogs. Park hours vary seasonally. You can buy a season ticket for $60 a car or $60 a boat. (510) 223-1661.

2-11

PINOLE

PARKS, BEACHES & RECREATION AREAS

Pinole Valley Park 

This city park is contiguous with **Sobrante Ridge Regional Preserve**, and partakes of its wildness after you pass the softball diamond, basketball court, kids' playground and sandbox at the entrance. Keep your dog on her leash. The paved bike path off to the right past the children's playground leads to **Alhambra Creek**—a good plunge for your dog, if he can negotiate the banks wearing a leash. The path then becomes fire trail and ambles through brush, oaks and nicely varied deciduous trees. This trail is quite wild and litter-free. It ends at an outlet on Alhambra Road.

2-11a The entrance is at Pinole Valley Road and Simas Avenue. Hours are from one-half hour before sunrise to one-half hour after sunset. (510) 724-9004.

2-12

PLEASANT HILL

PARKS, BEACHES & RECREATION AREAS

Paso Nogal Park 

This large park, run by the Pleasant Hill Recreation and Parks District, is natural land—gentle slopes with oak trees and smooth, wide dirt trails, except for a level lawn at the entrance that's excellent for fetching. Dogs must be on-leash in the park, but the lawn area is popularly used as a leash-free dog run by locals. Owners are expected to carry a leash and cooperate with park rangers if there's a complaint. But "no complaint, no problem" is the operable phrase here. There's a parking lot and water fountain.

2-12a At Morello Avenue and Paso Nogal Drive. Open sunrise to sunset. (510) 682-0896.

2-13

PORT COSTA

Port Costa is a sleepy, picturesque town of Victorian cottages. In the 19th century, if you remember Frank Norris' book *The Octopus*, it was a booming wheat export dock.

PARKS, BEACHES & RECREATION AREAS

Carquinez Strait Regional Shoreline 

This regional shoreline, run by the East Bay Regional Parks, lies just east of Crockett. From the **Bull Valley Staging Area**, on Carquinez Scenic Drive, you can choose one of two leash-free hillside trails. The **Carquinez Overlook Loop**, to the right, gives better views of Port Costa, the Carquinez Bridge and Benicia. We surprised a deer here sleeping in the shade of a eucalyptus clump.

The eastern portion of the park, east of **Port Costa**, is contiguous with **Martinez Regional Shoreline**. But beware: You can't get there from here. (Carquinez Scenic Drive is closed at a spot between Port Costa and Martinez. You must turn south on twisty McEwen Road to Highway 4 instead. For Martinez Regional Shoreline Park, see page 73.)

2-13a To get to the Carquinez Strait Regional Shoreline from Interstate 80, exit at Crockett and drive east on Pomona Street through town. Pomona turns into Carquinez Scenic Drive, from which you'll see the staging area. Open 5 a.m. to 10 p.m. (510) 531-9300.

2-14

RICHMOND

Point Richmond, the Richmond neighborhood tucked between the Richmond-San Rafael Bridge and Miller-Knox Regional Shoreline, is a cheerful small-town hangout for you and your dog. You might stop here for a snack on your way to the Miller-Knox Regional Shoreline or Point Pinole.

Sit on a bench in the Point Richmond Triangle, the town center. You'll be surrounded by nicely preserved Victorian buildings, the Hotel Mac and many delis and bakeries, some with outdoor tables. We were asked not to mention one by name because it welcomes cats as well as dogs! The Santa Fe rattles past periodically, blowing the first two notes of "Here Comes the Bride."

From Interstate 580, on the Richmond end of the Richmond-San Rafael Bridge, exit at Cutting Boulevard and drive west to town. Bear right on Richmond Avenue. The Triangle is at the intersection of Richmond, Washington Avenue and Park Place.

Parks, Beaches & Recreation Areas

Kennedy Grove Regional Recreation Area 

This is a large and pleasant picnic and play area for softball, volleyball and horseshoes, operated by the East Bay Regional Park District. Dogs must remain leashed. A few short trails lead toward the San Pablo Dam, but the East Bay Municipal Utility District has unaccountably closed the connection between the jurisdictions, so you can't get to the reservoir trails from here.

2-14a From Interstate 80, take the San Pablo Dam Road exit and go south; the entrance is a quarter-mile past the intersection of Castro Ranch Road. Gates are open 8 a.m. to 8 p.m. There's a $2.50 parking fee and $1 dog fee on weekends and holidays. (510) 635-0135.

Miller-Knox Regional Shoreline 

The usual East Bay Regional Park rules apply here, which means your dog must be leashed in developed areas but can run free on the hillside trails east of Dornan Drive.

West of Dornan is a generous expanse of grass, pine and eucalyptus trees with picnic tables, a lagoon with egrets (no swimming) and Keller Beach (dogs prohibited). It's breezy here, and prettier than most shoreline parks by virtue of its protecting gentle hills, whose trails offer terrific views of the Richmond-San Rafael Bridge, Mount Tamalpais, Angel Island and San Francisco. Ground squirrels stand right by their holes and pipe their alarms. Although you can't bring your dog onto Keller Beach, there's a paved path above it along riprap shoreline, where your dog can reach the water if he's so inclined. In the picnic areas, watch for discarded chicken bones!

You can also tour the **Richmond Yacht Harbor** by continuing on Dornan Drive south to Brickyard Cove Road, a left turn past the railroad tracks. Or, from Garrard Boulevard, drive south till you see the Brickyard Cove housing development. The paved paths lining the harbor offer views of yachts, San Francisco, Oakland and Bay Bridge.

2-14b From either Interstate 80 or Interstate 580, exit at Cutting Boulevard and go west to Garrard Boulevard. Go left (south), pass through a tunnel and park in one of two lots off Dornan Drive. Gates open 8 a.m. and close at 8 p.m. (510) 635-0135.

Point Isabel Regional Shoreline 

One exception to the East Bay Regional Parks' rule that dogs must be on-leash in "developed" areas is Point Isabel Regional Shoreline, a decidedly unwild but pleasant shoreline park with grass and paved paths—swarming with dogs. Unofficially, in fact, it's a dog park.

The large lawn area is designed for fetching, Frisbee and obedience training. People are often seen lobbing tennis balls for their expert retrievers, or hollering, "Hey! Run! Go!" at a dog who doesn't seem to be getting enough exercise. The dog owners police themselves and their dogs very effectively. Rules are: Owner must carry a leash, and if your dog becomes aggressive, you must leash him; the dog must be under voice control or within your sight; you must pick up after him; and you must stop your dog from digging and must fill any holes he creates! Seems fair.

And owners, as in most parks frequented by dogs, love to socialize. Even the shyest person will feel brave enough to start a conversation with another dog owner. It's one of life's mysteries that only children and animals give you an excuse to talk to strangers.

There are benches, picnic tables, restrooms, a water fountain for people and dogs, and many racks full of bags for scooping. A bulletin board posts lost-and-found dog notices, news of AARF (Area for Animals to Run Free) and its campaign for more open dog-run space, and membership information for the Point Isabel Dog Owners' Association, PIDO, which keeps the scooper dispensers full and otherwise looks out for dogs' interests in the park. If you're interested in volunteering or just want information, write to: Mildred Karler, 933 Shevlin Drive, El Cerrito, CA 94530. Annual dues are $5 per family.

Cinder paths run along the riprap waterfront, where you can watch windsurfers against a backdrop of the Golden Gate and Bay Bridges, San Francisco, the Marin headlands and Mount Tamalpais. On a brisk day, a little surf even splashes against the rocks.

2-14c From Interstate 80 in Richmond, exit at Central Avenue and go west to the park entrance, next to the U.S. Postal Service Bulk Mail Center. The park is open from 5 a.m. to 10 p.m. (510) 635-0135.

Point Pinole Regional Shoreline 

Of all the East Bay Regional Parks' shorelines, this is the farthest from civilization and its discontents, and thus the cleanest and least spoiled. It's also huge and a heavenly walk for dog or owner, with its views of Mount Tamalpais across San Pablo Bay, thistles, dock, salt marsh, beaches, eucalyptus groves and expanses of wild grassland waving in the breeze, like silk. Unfortunately, the breeze is usually more like a wind—sometimes even a hurricane. Some of the eucalyptuses are so wind-carved they could be mistaken for cypresses.

There are good bike trails here, and your dog should be leashed for safety on these, but on the unpaved trails he's free—even on the dirt paths through marshes, such as the **Marsh Trail**. Just make sure he stays on the trail and doesn't go into the marsh itself. Dogs may not go on the fishing pier or on the shuttle bus to the pier.

2-14d From Interstate 80, exit at Hilltop Drive, go west and take a right (north) on San Pablo Avenue, then left (west) on Atlas Road to the park entrance. A dog fee of $1 and a $2.50 parking fee are charged on weekends and holidays. Gates open 7 a.m. and close at 8 p.m. (510) 635-0135.

Sobrante Ridge Regional Preserve

Like many East Bay regional open spaces, this one is such a well-kept secret that we might never have found our way without advice from kind rangers at Kennedy Grove. After a brief climb up a fire trail, through grass, dwarf manzanita, oaks and coyote brush, you have a choice of several ridgetop trails that don't loop. There's a bit of poison oak, too. This is a good leash-free winter climb. It's hot and waterless in summer, so carry water for yourself and your dog. A pleasant breeze usually blows through, mitigating the heat.

2-14e From Interstate 80 in Richmond, exit at San Pablo Dam Road, drive south to Castro Ranch Road. Turn left (north) on Castro Ranch, then left at Conestoga Way, going into the Carriage Hills housing development. Take another left on Carriage Drive and a right on Coach Drive. Park at the end of Coach and walk into the preserve. Or from Pinole, exit Interstate 80 at Pinole Valley Road, south; Pinole Valley will become Alhambra Valley Road. Then bear right on Castro Ranch Road, and left on Conestoga Way. Open 5 a.m. to 10 p.m. (510) 635-0135.

Wildcat Canyon Regional Park

This is Tilden Park's northern twin, an East Bay Regional Park. Tilden has its attractive spots, but it is designed for people; Wildcat seems made for dogs, because almost nothing is happening there except growing things, sun, fog and wind. And you can leave your dog's leash in your pocket.

Large coast live oaks, madrones, bay laurels and all kinds of chaparral thrive on the east side. And since the area was ranchland from the days of Spanish land grants, and traces of house foundations remain, it isn't surprising that a lot of exotic plants flourish here alongside the expected ones. You'll find berries, nasturtiums and cardoon thistle, which looks like an artichoke allowed to grow up. All kinds of grasses—oat, rye and barley, even some native bunch grasses—and wildflowers cover the western hillsides, the mustard in soft yellow clouds. If the day is windy, the waving grasses and shifting cloud shadows will give you the eerie feeling that the hills themselves are a silky animal twitching its fur.

At the entrance parking lot is **Wildcat Creek**, which gets low but usually not entirely dry in summer. Dabney always takes a plunge. Then you might follow the **Wildcat Creek Trail**, actually an abandoned paved road—great for a bike ride—which travels gently uphill and then follows the southern ridge of the park. Or follow any of the nameless side trails, which are wonderfully wild and solitary. You can hear train whistles all the way up from Emeryville and the dull roar of civilization below, but somehow it can't get to you up here.

Other trails lead through groves of pines, or follow Wildcat Creek. The park is roughly three miles long. If you come to the boundary with Tilden, remember that dogs aren't allowed in the Nature Area across the line. You can get on the **East Bay Skyline National Recreation Trail** (Nimitz Way), running along the park's north side. Don't branch off onto the Eagle Trail, however; it belongs to the East Bay Municipal Utility District, which requires a permit and frowns on dogs. But there's plenty of room here. You and your dog could spend several blissful days in Wildcat.

2-14f From Interstate 80, southbound, take the McBryde exit and turn left (east) on McBryde to the park entrance. If you're northbound, take the Amador/Solano exit. Go three blocks left (north) on Amador and turn right (east) on McBryde to the entrance. No fees are charged. Open 5 a.m. to 10 p.m. (510) 635-0135.

RESTAURANTS

Ellie's Boarding House Reach: Home-style soup and sandwiches, dinners. People stop and talk, here and all over Point Richmond. 145 West Richmond Avenue. (510) 235-0416.

2-15

SAN RAMON

LODGINGS & CAMPGROUNDS

San Ramon Marriott at Bishop Ranch: Exit east off Interstate 680 at Bollinger Canyon Road. Go north on Sunset, west on Bishop Drive. 2600 Bishop Drive, San Ramon, CA 94583. Rates are around $110 for a double Sunday through Thursday, $60 to $80 Friday and Saturday. (510) 867-9200.

2-16

WALNUT CREEK

Walnut Creek's secret is its beautiful creeks and canals, former irrigation ditches that now beautify golf courses and housing developments. **Walnut Creek, San Ramon Creek, the Contra Costa Canal** and the **Ygnacio Canal** all pass through town. Dogs must be leashed everywhere, except in the undeveloped areas of city-owned open spaces—Acalanes Ridge, Shell Ridge and Sugarloaf.

PARKS, BEACHES & RECREATION AREAS

Acalanes Ridge Open Space Recreation Area

In 1974, the city of Walnut Creek set aside the open spaces named above for a limited-use "land bank." No official hours have been set—they are open "during daylight hours"—since the space is still undeveloped. So far, only **Shell Ridge** and **Sugarloaf** are staffed by rangers and marked at entry points with signs. Dogs must be "under voice or sight command." Hoo boy! The trails are open to hikers, dogs, horses and bicycles, however, so on a fine day, your dog may have competition.

Acalanes Ridge, close to Briones Regional Park, is crossed by the **Briones to Diablo Regional Trail**. Like the others, it lacks water.

2-16a A good entry point is from Camino Verde Circle, reached by driving south on Camino Verde from the intersection of Pleasant Hill Road and Geary Road. For information on any of the open spaces, call (510) 256-3560.

Arbolado Park

This park, just an overgrown orchard soon to be surrounded by housing developments, is nevertheless a good access point to the **Ygnacio Canal Trail**, one of the network of smoothly paved trails that make for pleasant walks in Walnut Creek. Dogs must be leashed.

2-16b On Arbolado Drive just east of Oak Grove Road. Open 24 hours. (510) 943-5858.

Diablo Foothills Regional Park 

It's heartbreaking that dogs aren't allowed on trails in Mount Diablo State Park (see listing, page 83), but you can get close at this East Bay Regional Park. A paved trail leads into the park from Castle Rock Road. You can hike south about one mile to hook up with the **Briones to Diablo Regional Trail**. (Leash on paved multi-use paths is the rule.) It's another mile to the state park border, at which point your dog becomes *canine non grata*.

2-16c From Interstate 680, exit at Ignacio Valley Road, travel east to Walnut Avenue, turn right (east) and go to Castle Rock Road; turn right (south) and stop at the turnoff to Pine Creek Road. That's the trail entrance. (Don't follow Castle Rock Road all the way to the end; that's Castle Rock Recreation Area, open to group reservations only.) Open 5 a.m. to 10 p.m. (510) 635-0135.

Heather Farms City Park 

This largest city park in Walnut Creek is well-designed for people, but not for dogs. They must be leashed; the lawns are manicured and the lake artificial; there's no swimming and not enough shade.

However, along the west side of the park is an attractive portion of the **Briones to Diablo Trail**, run by the East Bay Regional Park system. You'll find an entrance off Marchbanks Drive, next to the Diablo Hills Golf Course. This paved trail, good for bikes or strollers, winds along a tule-lined creek and among oaks and willows by the lake. (One June day, someone arriving with bread inspired a comical orchestra of honking geese, quacking ducks, redwing blackbirds' liquid cries and some fat pigeons, joining in with a low cello.) Dogs are required to be on-leash here, but Dabney has been known to cheat briefly for a plunge into the cool creek.

If you follow this Briones to Diablo Trail north a short distance, you'll run into the **Contra Costa Canal Trail**, running east and west.

2-16d The park is on Ygnacio Valley Road at Marchbanks Drive. Open during daylight hours. (510) 943-5858.

Larkey Park 

This is a small, undistinguished city park with picnic tables under pine trees, a pool and lots of gym equipment for children, but we mention it because the **Briones to Diablo Trail** (see listing at beginning of chapter) runs through it, and it's also home to the **Alexander Lindsay Junior Museum**. Your dog can't enter, but would he ever love it! The museum contains living, wriggling samples of local wildlife, most of them injured animals that have been rescued and brought there: raccoons, opossums, snakes, hawks, vultures and fish. Children may "check out" some animals to take home as temporary pets.

2-16e At Buena Vista Avenue and First Avenue. Open during daylight hours. (510) 935-1978 (museum); (510) 943-5858 (park).

Lime Ridge Open Space Recreation Area

Walnut Creek shares jurisdiction of this open space with Concord (see Concord listings for a description).

2-16f There is as yet no official entry point from Walnut Creek. (510) 256-3560.

Mount Diablo State Park

As in nearly all state parks, dogs may drive with you to the vista points, parking lots, picnic areas and campgrounds of Mount Diablo, but may not enter the trails. Day use fee is $5, plus $1 for a dog. Since dogs are so vigorously discouraged, we recommend you simply appreciate Diablo's incomparable beauty from a distance and visit Briones or Las Trampas instead.

You may, of course, take your dog along on the death-defying road to the summit of Mount Diablo, at 3,849 feet, with its views of the delta, the Santa Cruz Mountains, the Farallon Islands 25 miles out to sea, the Sierra...sometimes farther. Some claim that in the old days of clearer air, you could see Mount Shasta. It's also said that only one other high point on Earth—Mount Kilimanjaro in Africa—lets you take in more land area at once.

It's too bad dogs just don't get any kick out of views.

2-16g From Interstate 680, exit at Ignacio Valley Road. Go right on Walnut Avenue (not Walnut Boulevard), then jog slightly right onto North Gate Road. This road will lead up the mountain. The Summit Museum and Visitor Center is open only on weekends, from 11 a.m. to 4 p.m. (510) 837-2525.

Shell Ridge Open Space Recreation Area

This city-run open space, along with Lime Ridge, Acalanes Ridge and Sugarloaf, is close to Mount Diablo State Park, but a poor substitute, since it consists of hot, oak-dotted hills that lack water. It's best to visit these spaces in winter.

Dogs may run off-leash everywhere but the developed areas (parking lots, picnic grounds), but "must be under positive voice and sight command." You can enter by the **Sugarloaf-Shell Ridge Trail** at the north edge.

Within the Shell Ridge open space is the **Old Borges Ranch**, a demonstration farm staffed irregularly by rangers. The ranch house itself is sometimes open on Sundays from noon to 4 p.m. Call first to check. Last June the ranch held a Western Costume Day and Pet Parade, featuring any leashed or ridden pet, and demonstrations of blacksmithing, bread-making, butter-making, and so on. The ranch may make this into a regular event. For information or to check if the ranch is open, call (510) 934-6990.

2-16h From Interstate 680, take the Ignacio Valley Road exit, go east on Ignacio Valley to Walnut Avenue (not Boulevard), turn right (east) and right again (south) on Castle Rock Road. At the corner of Comistas Drive, you'll see the trailhead. The turnoff to Borges Ranch is one-half mile past the high school. Turn right and follow signs. Or, to get to the southern end from Interstate 680, exit at Livorna Road, follow Livorna Road east to Stonegate Court, turn left (north) and park in a public spot in the housing development. Open during daylight hours. (510) 256-3560.

Sugarloaf Open Space Recreation Area

2-16i From Interstate 680, exit at Livorna Road and turn left (north) almost immediately on Sugarloaf Drive. Go left again on Sugarloaf Terrace and park in the public area of the housing development. Open during daylight hours. (510) 256-3560.

RESTAURANTS

Walnut Creek's "downtown," your respite from mallsville, is Main Street. There, you'll find several welcoming outdoor restaurants, benches for just sitting, and good weather.

J.R. Muggs: Desserts and gourmet coffee—in your mug or in the bean. The store also sells thousands of coffee mugs for all tastes. You can get a mug picturing Betty Boop, Garfield, the 49ers, your name or your horoscope. They love dogs here. 1432 North Main Street. (510) 256-9595.

La Fogata: You can sit on comfy Mexican barrel chairs outside with your dog, under a cool awning, and consume burgers or Mexican food. If you come inside (where sangría, beer and tequila are served), your dog can lie with nose pressed against the window. 1315 North Main Street. (510) 934-8121.

Le Chocolatier and Gelateria: Italian ice cream, fancy candies, gifts and stuffed animals. Treat yourself here, not your dog, if you value his teeth. But the owner is friendly. 1397 Main Street (510) 932-7636.

Nogas Korner Restaurant: Coffee shop. Your dog must be leashed. 1394 North Main Street. (510) 934-4591.

Original Hot Dog Place: Every kind of hot dog, served in a tiny shop with a neat hot dog mural on the wall and a wooden Indian outside next to the tables. 1420 Lincoln Avenue at Main. (510) 256-7302.

Pascal French Oven: Baked goodies. Waitresses often bring buckets of water out to dogs. 1372 North Main Street. (510) 932-6969.

LODGINGS & CAMPGROUNDS

Mount Diablo State Park Campground: Mount Diablo's campgrounds welcome dogs, but remember that they can't go on the trails with you and must remain on-leash or confined to your tent. Reservations are rarely needed except on popular weekends and holidays. You can usually get a spot on a first-come, first-served basis. Campsites are $12, with $5 for an extra vehicle. Fee for dogs is $1.

For more information on the campgrounds and fees, call Mount Diablo State Park Headquarters: (510) 837-2525. For reservations between May 31 and October 1, call MISTIX, (800) 444-PARK.

Walnut Creek Motor Lodge: Two blocks east off intersection of Interstate 680 and Highway 24. Northbound, exit at Ignacio Valley Road; southbound, at North Main Street. 1960 North Main Street, Walnut Creek, CA 94596. About $50 for a double. (510) 932-2811.

MORE INFO

WHERE YOUR DOG CAN'T GO

- Brooks Island Regional Shoreline, Richmond
- Hidden Valley Park, Martinez
- Huckleberry Regional Preserve
- Keller Beach, at Miller-Knox Regional Shoreline, Richmond
- Mount Diablo State Park trails
- Walnut Festival, Walnut Creek

USEFUL PHONE NUMBERS & ADDRESSES

California State Parks: Department of Parks and Recreation, Office of Public Relations, PO Box 942896, Sacramento, CA 94296. (916) 653-6995. To call within California for MISTIX campsite reservations (you may reserve up to eight weeks in advance): (800) 444-PARK, or write to MISTIX, PO Box 85705, San Diego, CA 92138.

East Bay Municipal Utility District: 500 San Pablo Dam Road, Orinda, CA 94563. (510) 835-3000; questions about trails: (510) 254-3798. Hiking permit available for $5 for one year, $10 for three years. (No dogs are allowed on any backcountry trails.)

East Bay Regional Park District: 2950 Peralta Oaks Court, Oakland, CA 94605. (510) 635-0135; camping reservations: (510) 562-CAMP.

Point Isabel Dog Owners (and Friends): write to Mildred Karler, 933 Shevlin Drive, El Cerrito, CA 94530.

Walnut Creek Department of Open Space: PO Box 8039, Walnut Creek, CA 94596. (510) 256-3560.

•Marin County•

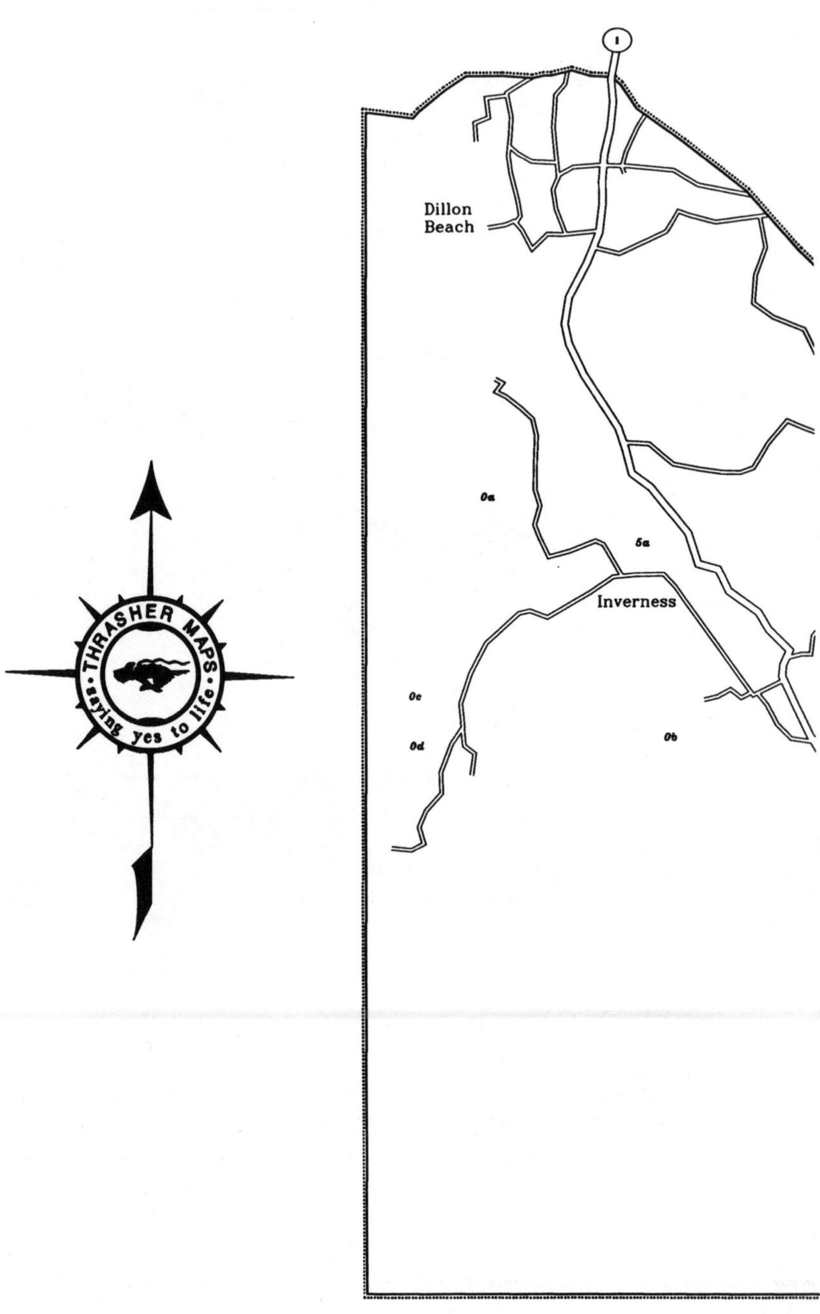
1
Dillon
Beach
0a
5a
Inverness
0c
0d
0b
THRASHER MAPS
saying yes to life

3. MARIN COUNTY (map page 88-89)

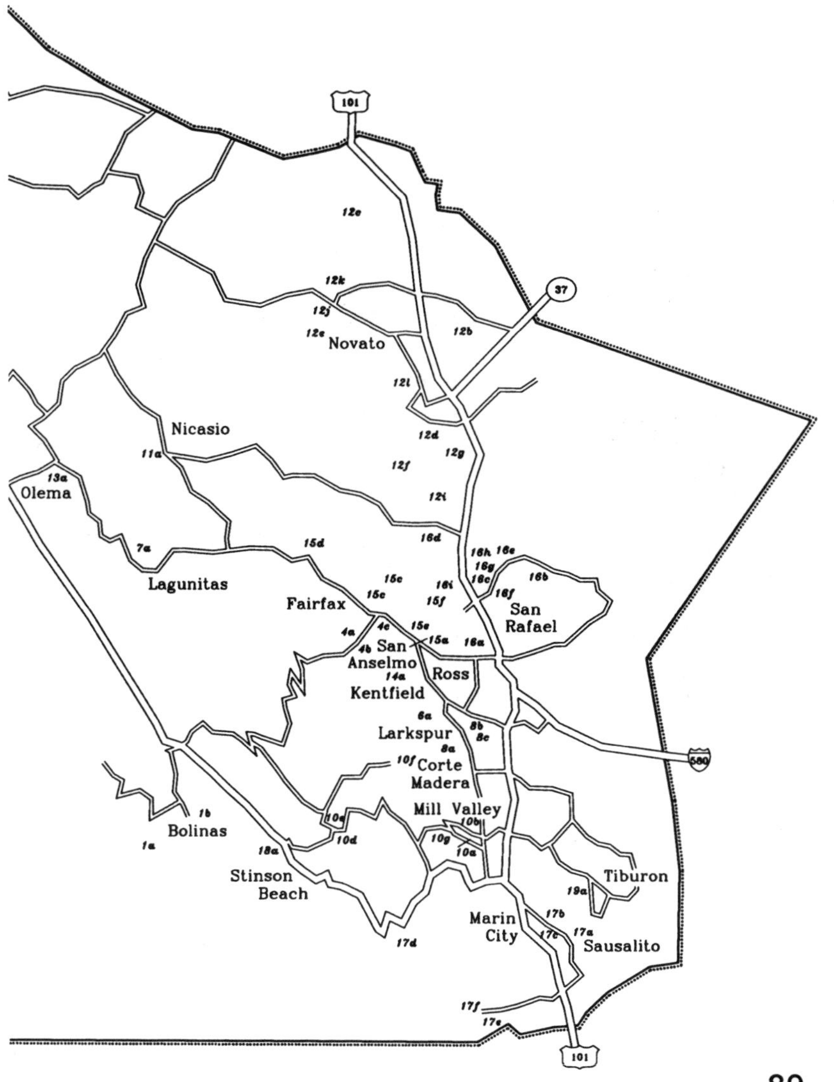

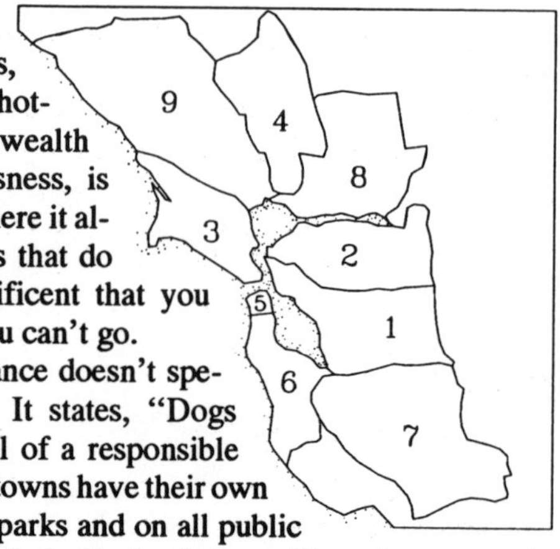

3 **Marin County**, a paradise for humans, birds and deer and a hotbed of environmentalism, wealth and general cantankerousness, is pretty restrictive about where it allows dogs. But the places that do allow dogs are so magnificent that you won't regret the places you can't go.

And the county ordinance doesn't specifically require a leash. It states, "Dogs must be under the control of a responsible person at all times." Most towns have their own leash laws, though. In all parks and on all public paths, even within the technically leash-free cities, dogs must be leashed. Nowhere should dogs run at-large. The towns that function under the county ordinance—that is, don't impose a town leash law—are Bolinas and the other unincorporated towns of West Marin, Belvedere, Greenbrae, Kentfield, Novato and San Anselmo.

In Marin, as in all formerly rural counties rapidly becoming suburban, we advise you to be courteous and thus not call attention to any need for stricter rules. And make your dog be as good an environmental citizen as you are.

STATE PARKS

- California State Parks in Marin County
- Angel Island State Park
- China Camp State Park
- Mount Tamalpais State Park
- Samuel P. Taylor State Park
- Tomales Bay State Park

Dogs may come into state park picnic and camping areas, and they're allowed on paved roads, too. But they can't go on any beaches, fire roads or trails. There are exceptions at the discretion of local park officials. One is that dogs are allowed on Village Beach on-leash in China Camp. Another is the blessed Samuel P. Taylor State Park, which allows dogs on its wide dirt fire roads, though not on foot trails. And Mount Tamalpais State Park allows dogs on some short trails leading to Marin Municipal Water District trails, which do allow dogs.

In the state parks, dogs must always be on a six-foot leash. You can't leave your dog unattended anywhere. Even if he's in your car, if rangers fear he has insufficient air on a hot day, they may break a window and take him out. (More power to them!)

The usual vehicle fee in these parklands, if you park in main lots, is $5; the dog fee is $1. Altogether, in most of the state parks, you and your dog don't get much for your money. For information, call (415) 456-1286.

GOLDEN GATE NATIONAL RECREATION AREA (GGNRA)

The GGNRA, under the National Park Service, manages a huge amount of San Francisco and Marin County real estate, and it is not stingy in the areas it permits dogs to enjoy.

The GGNRA even publishes a "Pet Trail Map," available from **Rodeo Beach Visitor Center** off Bunker Road. (Or from Golden Gate National Recreation Area, Fort Mason, Building 201, San Francisco, CA 94123. (415) 556-0560.)

Dogs may run off-leash (under voice control) on **Rodeo Beach** and around **Rodeo Lagoon**; they're permitted on-leash at **Muir Beach**. They may go off-leash on a loop formed by a portion of the **Miwok Trail, Wolf Ridge Trail** and a portion of the **Coastal Trail**, branching off from Rodeo Lagoon. And they may go on-leash on the Coastal Trail portion going off from Muir Beach. They also can go on certain backcountry portions of the Miwok Trail and on the **Oakwood Valley Trail**, off Tennessee Valley Road.

Only seeing-eye dogs are allowed in the GGNRA's campgrounds.

The trails are always open, but you may be questioned if your car remains parked anywhere in the headlands after 10 p.m. without a camping permit in the windshield. (Dogs aren't permitted in GGNRA campgrounds, but if you like midnight hikes with your dog in the headlands, you might want to get a permit just for your car.)

Detailed descriptions of these headlands beaches and trails are listed under their nearest city; for instance, headland spots are listed under Sausalito.

MARIN COUNTY PARKS

Dogs are allowed in three county parks: **John F. McInnis Park** and **Civic Center Lagoon** (on-leash), in San Rafael, and **Deer Park** in Fairfax. The rest exclude dogs:

- McNears Beach Park
- Paradise Beach Park
- Stafford Lake Park

MARIN COUNTY OPEN SPACE DISTRICT

The county manages 25 open-space preserves—grasslands, wooded trails, redwood groves, marshes and steep mountainsides. The idea is to set bits of land aside so that Marin never ends up looking like the Santa Clara Valley. The lands are also there to be enjoyed by people, including dog owners. Some camping is allowed by permit, available from the district.

Dogs may go into all of the Marin County Open Space District lands, except designated wildlife protection areas, which are clearly marked on maps obtainable from the district. These maps show you exactly where the open spaces are, but they're very hard to use, unless you also have detailed street maps to go with them.

In addition, the district plans to publish maps of its multi-use bicycle trails in the future.

Dogs must always be accompanied by an owner. Another rule—that mountain bikes are allowed only on fire trails—is good news for dogs. Best of all, dogs needn't be leashed as long as they're "under owner's voice control." Hallelujah. At trailheads, you'll see the universal "dog on-leash" symbol, but in the open space districts that means "dog on-leash or under control."

The district recommends, though, that you carry a leash in case of "wildlife encounters," especially where deer are plentiful, or near wetlands and other sensitive areas. Also watch out for other dogs, bicycles and horses. Several of the lands are co-managed by the Open Space District and the Marin Municipal Water District. On those, you must leash.

The lands are undeveloped—there are no toilets, trash cans, drinkable water sources or parking lots. You can usually find parking at or near entrances, but not always. Take care not to block driveways or fire roads when you park. Many of the lands border residential areas, so remember that you're essentially passing through people's back yards.

In this chapter, we'll give descriptions and directions to some of the many access points to the 25 preserves. Each is listed under its nearest city. We've omitted ones that offer no parking at all or must be entered from busy highways, and those that largely exclude dogs because of protected nature areas (see list at end of chapter: WHERE

YOUR DOG CAN'T GO). All the open spaces are free and open 24 hours. To order your own free maps, and for further information, call (415) 499-6387.

MARIN MUNICIPAL WATER DISTRICT

Dogs are welcome on-leash in much of the Marin Municipal Water District's magnificent watershed, including the trails and reservoirs on the slopes of Mount Tamalpais above Mill Valley. All trails are open from sunrise to sunset. There's no dog fee, but a $3 vehicle entrance fee is charged on some roads. Unfortunately, body contact—both human and canine—with the water supply is prohibited. (415) 924-4600.

POINT REYES NATIONAL SEASHORE

The National Seashore is a delicate ecosystem and a national treasure, so its strict and exclusive rules for dogs are understandable. They aren't allowed on any backcountry trails, with the exception of the **Bolinas Ridge Trail**, part of the Golden Gate National Recreation Area but managed by the Seashore.

And dogs may go only on designated beaches, and then only on-leash: the left (south) end of **Limantour Beach, Santa Maria Beach, Point Reyes Beach South, Point Reyes Beach North**, and **Kehoe Beach**.

Dogs aren't allowed in the Seashore's campgrounds.

Don't miss those designated beaches, though! They are more than worth the drive. They're free, and they're open sunrise to sunset. Before you go, it's a good idea to check the weather and tide tables. A high tide can trap you and your dog against a cliff. The entire 11-mile northwestern shore of Point Reyes bristles with dangers: icy cold water, rough surf, loose footing, rip tides, sharks and sneaker waves. It's not considered safe for human wading, so don't let your dog enter the water, either.

That said, enjoy these forbiddingly gorgeous, awe-inspiring beaches. You won't be tempted to do anything really stupid, such as swim in such freezing water. Just don't turn your back on the surf, and stay away from cliff edges.

Weather information for the Seashore beaches, which can vary from gale force winds to fog to rare but heavenly sun, is recorded daily at this number: (415) 663-9029. For general park information, call (415) 663-1092.

Bear Valley Visitor Center and park headquarters, on Bear Valley Road just west of Olema, is definitely the first place you should stop. It has an elegant and informative natural history museum, helpful rangers, trail maps to the Seashore and a printed list of lodgings.

Kehoe Beach

This is our favorite of the Seashore beaches that allow dogs, since it's both the most beautiful and the least accessible. The only parking is at roadside. You take a half-mile cinder path through wildflowers and thistles, with marsh on one side and hill on the other. In the morning, you may see some mule deer. Then, you come out on medium-brown sand that stretches forever. Since the water is shallow, the surf repeats its crests in multiple white rows, as in Hawaii. Behind you are limestone cliffs. Scattered rocks offer tidepools filled with mussels, crabs, anemones, barnacles, snails and sea flora.

In such a paradise of shore life, the leash rule makes sense. The chief reasons for leashing dogs at the Point Reyes National Seashore beaches—or for banning them altogether—are the harbor seals that haul out onto the beaches and are in no position to get away fast from a charging dog, and snowy plovers, a threatened shorebird that nests on the ground.

3-0a From Inverness, follow Sir Francis Drake Boulevard to the fork; bear right on Pierce Point Road; park beside the road where you see the sign and walk about one-half mile to beach. Open sunrise to sunset. (415) 663-1092.

Limantour Beach

This bountiful beach is most people's favorite, so it's often crowded. From the main parking lot, walk one quarter-mile through tule marsh, grasses and brush and scattered pines, past Limantour Estero. (Dogs are prohibited on the side trails.)

Rules for dogs are clearly marked at the Seashore—a refreshing exception to the obscure and contradictory rules in so many parks. For example, approaching Limantour Beach on the path, you'll see a sign that says dogs are prohibited to your right, allowed to your left. This beach is plenty big, so it's an excellent arrangement that keeps dog owners and dog-avoiders equally happy. You may walk with your dog to **Santa Maria Beach.**

3-0b Look for the turnoff to Bear Valley Road, which runs between Olema and Inverness Park. Take Bear Valley from either direction to Limantour Road; turn south on Limantour all the way to the beach. Open sunrise to sunset. (415) 663-1092.

Point Reyes Beach North

Point Reyes Beach North is a generous, functional beach. There's no long trail from the parking lot, no special tidepools or rocks, just a long, clean, beautiful running beach for the two of you. Officially, however, the dog must be leashed.

3-0c From Inverness, take Highway 1 west to intersection of Sir Frances Drake Highway. Turn south and watch for the turnoff. Open sunrise to sunset. (415) 663-1092.

Point Reyes Beach South

Point Reyes Beach South is a little narrower and steeper than Point Reyes Beach North, and it has a few interesting sandstone outcroppings with wind-carved holes. It has a bit less of that wide-open feeling. Leash the dog.

3-0d Follow the directions for Point Reyes Beach North; it's the next beach southward. Open sunrise to sunset. (415) 663-1092.

3-1

BOLINAS

Bolinas is famous for hiding from curious visitors—thereby drawing hordes of them. Town citizens regularly take down the turnoff sign on Highway 1. So if you're coming from the east (San Francisco area), turn left at the unmarked road where Bolinas Lagoon ends. If you're coming from the west, turn right where the lagoon begins.

Sometimes it seems as if half the inhabitants of Bolinas are dogs, most of them black. They stand guard outside bars, curl at shop owners' feet, snooze in the middle of the road. There's no city hall in Bolinas, an unincorporated area, and no Chamber of Commerce. Dogs are always welcome here, but cars, horses, bicycles and too many unleashed dogs compete for space. Be thoughtful and keep your pooch leashed in town.

Parks, Beaches & Recreation Areas

Agate Beach

The county ordinance applies here: dogs on-leash or under control. There are lots of dogs on this narrow beach flanked by rock cliffs.

Kelp bulbs pop satisfyingly underfoot. Watch that the high tide doesn't sneak up on you. There are portable toilets at the parking lot.

3-1a From the Olema-Bolinas Road (the Bolinas turnoff from Highway 1), turn west on Mesa Road, left (south) on Overlook Drive, right (west) on Elm Road, all the way to the end. Open sunrise to sunset. (415) 499-6387.

Bolinas Beach 

At the end of the main street, Wharf Road, is a sand and pebble beach at the foot of a bluff. Dogs are free to run, of course. But watch for horses—with riders and without—thundering past without warning. It's animal anarchy here, and not the cleanest beach in Marin. We give it points for fun, though.

3-1b Open 24 hours. (415) 499-6387.

RESTAURANTS

Bolinas Bay Bakery & Cafe: Pizza, entrees, salads, desserts, brunch, espresso coffee, teas and a variety of baked goodies. The ramp up to the deck tables renders them wheelchair and dog-accessible. 20 Wharf Road. (415) 868-0211.

The Shop: A very friendly spot for breakfast, lunch and dinner, beer, wine and ice cream. Across the street from Smiley's bar, only one of the establishments where dogs run around naked. 46 Wharf Road. (415) 868-9984.

FAIRS & FESTIVALS

Fourth of July: Fourth of July in Bolinas is like nowhere else. The town holds a tug-of-war with Stinson Beach; teams of men and women compete with ropes across the 100 feet of Bolinas Lagoon separating the towns, and the losers go into the drink! For information call the West Marin Chamber of Commerce, (415) 663-9232.

3-2 CORTE MADERA

PARKS, BEACHES & RECREATION AREAS

No dogs are allowed in any park in Corte Madera.

3-3 DILLON BEACH

Tiny, unincorporated Dillon Beach doesn't allow dogs on the magnificent beach that is its *raison d'etre*, but a private campground there does.

Lodgings & Campgrounds

Lawson's Landing Campground: A large site at the mouth of Tomales Bay for "open camping." That is, sites are where you find them, and unreservable. There's room for about 35 or 40 vehicles and their occupants. Camping is first-come, first-served; it's $10 per car, and there's no extra fee for dogs. Best of all, the campground doesn't insist that you leash, as long as your pup is well-behaved. The campground is closed in December and January. It's not on the beach, but you can walk there. (You can't bring your dog to the beach, though.) PO Box 67, Dillon Beach, CA 94929. (707) 878-2443.

3-4

FAIRFAX

Parks, Beaches & Recreation Areas

Cascade Canyon Open Space Preserve

As on all of Marin's open space lands, dogs can be leashless in this undeveloped area. The trail sticks close to **San Anselmo Creek**, which is reduced to a dry creekbed in summer. A no-bicycles trail branches off to the right and disappears into the creek; the left branch fords the creek. When the water's high, you may be stopped right here. But in summer, you can walk a long way.

Side trails lead you into shady glens of laurel and other deciduous trees, but there's lots of poison oak, too. Stay on the trail, and if your dog isn't the staying-on-trail type, it might pay to leash her!

The fire road (left fork) is the same as Cascade Canyon Road, vehicle-free except for rangers, that leads all the way into the Marin Municipal Water District lands of Mount Tamalpais. (Once you enter these, you must leash.)

3-4a The park is at the end of Cascade Drive. Park on the street at the very end of Cascade. There's a Town of Fairfax sign saying "Elliott Nature Preserve," but it's official open space. Open 24 hours. (415) 499-6387.

Deer Park

This is one of only three county parks to which you may bring a dog, but she must be leashed, and a sign says "Leash Law Enforced."

A level dirt trail bordered with bay laurels, redwoods and oaks follows a creek, which is dry in summer. Later, the trail grows twisted and rougher—not good for casual strollers—and heads into the deeper woodlands. Watch toddlers carefully; there are some unprotected drop-offs by the creek. Even on weekends, you may be alone here. The delicious smell of bay is thick. There are picnic tables and portable toilets.

3-4b Park in the lot at the end of Porteous Avenue. Open from sunrise to sunset. (415) 499-6387.

Fairfax Park 

Just a small, cool spot downtown under some redwoods. There's a creek, but your dog can't get to it. Leash is required.

3-4c Open sunrise to sunset. (415) 453-1584. At Cascade Drive and Park Road.

3-5

INVERNESS

Parks, Beaches & Recreation Areas

Tomales Bay State Park 

Think three times before bringing a dog here. It's one of the most restrictive of the state parks, consisting mostly of delicate beach and marshland. Dogs may go only to the picnic area by the second parking lot, only on-leash, and restricted to your picnic table! Except for a quick stop, we suggest going to one of the recommended Point Reyes National Seashore beaches instead. (See listing at beginning of chapter.)

3-5a Tomales Bay State Park is four miles north of Inverness on Sir Francis Drake Boulevard. Open 8 a.m. to sunset. (415) 669-1140.

Lodgings & Campgrounds

Manka's Inverness Lodge: Often, humans and their dogs spend the night here, eat breakfast and decide never to return home. It's an old hunting lodge, surrounded by woods and the beaches and mudflats of Tomales Bay—and the owners love dogs. You should reserve well ahead, though, since Manka's has only one dog-habitable cabin (about $130). Two-night minimum, and it's $10 extra for the dog. Don't miss the elegant weekend brunch.

In the town of Inverness, look for the uphill turn off Sir Frances Drake Boulevard, corner of Argyle and Callender. PO Box 1110, Inverness, CA 94937. (415) 669-1034.

Motel Inverness: The friendly owners allow dogs and serve you coffee in the morning. A double room is around $70. 12718 Sir Francis Drake Boulevard, Inverness, CA 94937. (415) 669-1081.

3-6

KENTFIELD

PARKS, BEACHES & RECREATION AREAS

Northridge/Baltimore Canyon Open Space Preserve

From this spot, access is good for a lot of fire trails through the ridges connecting with Mount Tamalpais and water district lands. Leash isn't required, but bikes are also allowed on these trails, so be careful. You'll be starting out fairly high on the slope.

3-6a Two access points are from the ends of Crown Road and Evergreen Drive. Open 24 hours. (415) 499-6387.

3-7

LAGUNITAS

PARKS, BEACHES & RECREATION AREAS

Samuel P. Taylor State Park

An exception among the state parks: Dog access is generous! You can take a dog into the picnic areas, and here that's worth doing. The main picnic area right off Sir Francis Drake Boulevard is cool and often lively with the grinding call of jays. It's an easy place to bring out-of-state visitors who may just want to eat a sandwich, hug a redwood and go home. There are hollow trees stretching 20 feet across that you can actually stand inside.

But best of all, you and your dog may spend a whole day here on the wide fire trails—roughly 20 miles of them—clearly differentiated on the map you get at the entrance. Dogs may not go on the foot trails, but the fire trails are delightful enough. You can take the bicycle/horse trail from near the entrance along **Papermill Creek**, rising for four miles to **Barnabe Peak**, at 1,466 feet. Unfortunately, your dog must stay leashed, but you may actually appreciate that when you see the excellent artist's drawing of a poison oak cluster on the park's map—it's everywhere.

3-7a The entrance is right on Sir Francis Drake Boulevard about two miles west of Lagunitas. Fees are $5 for parking, $1 for dog. The park is open from 8 a.m. to 8 p.m. (415) 488-9897.

LODGINGS & CAMPGROUNDS

Samuel P. Taylor State Park Campground: Dogs are allowed in these campsites, always leashed. The park has 60 sites with drinking water, restrooms and hot showers; some spaces can take small trailers, but no hookups are available. Sites are $14 for one car; $5 is charged for an extra vehicle, and $1 for a dog. You can reserve a site through MISTIX: (800) 444-PARK.

3-8

LARKSPUR

PARKS, BEACHES & RECREATION AREAS

Blithedale Summit 

Open Space Preserve

The access point at the end of Madrone Avenue—the north end of this open space—is a delightful walk in hot weather, through cool redwoods that let some light filter through. This isn't one of those really dark, drippy canyons; you're at a medium-high altitude on the slopes of Mount Tamalpais. The trail follows **Larkspur Creek,** which retains some pools in summer. Cross the footbridge and follow the slightly rough foot trail, where strollers aren't a good idea.

The drive up narrow Madrone Avenue is an adventure in itself; redwoods grow right in the street. According to a sign at the entrance, the part of this space belonging to the city of Larkspur is closed from sunset to sunrise, and dogs should be leashed.

3-8a The county open space is open 24 hours. (415) 499-6387.

Bon Air Path 

The Marin County Parks Department, the Open Space District, various cities and the County Flood Control District combine to maintain a series of "multi-use" paved trails for hikers, runners, cyclists and dog walkers willing to share space. (Horses are excluded.)

Bon Air Path goes 1.8 miles from Bon Air Road, following **Corte Madera Creek,** westward to the town of Ross and eastward to the Larkspur Landing shopping center, near the ferry terminal. "Pick up after your pet," as the signs repeat, and keep your dog on-leash, if only for his own safety. Dabney, for instance, is deaf and blind when it comes to bikes and refuses to stay out of their way.

3-8b From Sir Francis Drake Boulevard, turn south on Bon Air Road; from Magnolia Drive, turn north. The path entrance is at

Creekside Park, across from Marin General Hospital. There's roadside parking and toilets. The path is open 24 hours. (415) 499-6387. You can get more information on the county's bike trails from the Bicycle Trails Council of Marin: (415) 456-7512. The Marin County Open Space District has new bike maps in the works, too: (415) 499-6387.

Creekside Park

This is the small, attractive county park where the multi-purpose **Bon Air Path** starts. There are lots of paths by Corte Madera Creek and a kids' gym. You must leash your dog, and be sure to keep him out of marshy areas. A bulletin board displays excellent bike trail maps and descriptions of local flora and fauna. (415) 499-6387.

Piper Park

Here's an ordinary people-style city park—athletic facilities, playground, picnic tables, community garden—that has also included what your dog needs! A small fenced area next to the community garden, Canine Commons, is just the ticket if your dog is a fetcher or an escape artist, or hates the leash, or loves to meet other dogs. The drawback is its small size. There's one striving little tree. Still, it's better than nothing.

Rules: Owner must be there; dog must be licensed; owner must clean up; no unruly dogs; and no females in heat. A water dish and metal scoopers are supplied.

An informative bulletin board posts useful information on where dogs are allowed, and the rules for them throughout the county, published by the Marin County Humane Society. Send for it: 171 Bel Marin Keys Boulevard, Novato, CA 94949. (415) 883-4621.

The Larkspur City Recreation Department runs Piper Park. You can play or watch softball, volleyball, tennis and even cricket. Outside the Canine Commons, dogs must be leashed—and they really mean it.

3-8c Between Doherty Drive and Corte Madera Creek. Hours are dawn to dusk. (415) 927-5031.

RESTAURANTS

Firehouse Bar-B-Que: The barbecue is elegant but not cheap, and the view from the sidewalk tables is of Larkspur Landing's parking lot, but your dog's nose will quiver at the scent of ribs. 2401 Larkspur Landing Circle. (415) 461-7427.

DIVERSIONS

Brunch and munch: Only in Marin? Could be: Brunch with your dog at the For Paws pet store at the Larkspur Landing mall. On the first Sunday of every summer month at noon, champagne for you and kibble quiche for your dog are served at outside chairs with umbrellas. It's free, unless you wish to donate to the Marin Humane Society. Brunches are served from June through September. For Paws is at 1017 Larkspur Landing Circle. (415) 461-2820.

Have your dog blessed: For Paws pet store also holds a Blessing of the Animals ceremony on the first Sunday in May. In past years, blessings have been bestowed by ordained Episcopal priests; a woman once brought a bottle of water from the River Jordan.

Dress for trick-or-treating: Dogs certainly take naturally to the treating part of Halloween. For Paws presents an annual Doggy Costume Contest on the Sunday before Halloween. The competition is fierce for four costume awards; some 400 dogs attended last year, and owners work all year on their canine costumes. If your dog thinks dressing up is beneath her, there's a special Nude Beach area for water dogs and sophisticates—inflatable pools supplied with balls. In 1991, one of the judges was Grace Slick. So long as your dog likes crowds of other dogs looking silly, you shouldn't miss this. A $5 donation is requested for the Marin Humane Society.

3-9

MARIN CITY

DIVERSIONS

Shop for scraps: You and your dog can have hours of cheap fun at the Marin City Flea Market, the best outdoor market in the area for real people's real stuff, and interesting antiques. If your dog is a scrap-shopper, though, you may wish you had left him at home. There are too many tempting discarded morsels here. Dabney tends to pull the leash one way while Lyle strains in the other, each looking for a bargain. You and your dog are both sure to make new friends. Leash is mandatory.

Exit Highway 101 at Sausalito/Marin City. Bear right and park in one of several lots, which charge from $2 to $5. The market is held each Saturday from 6 a.m. to 4 p.m., Sunday from 5 a.m. to 4 p.m. (415) 332-1441.

3-10 MILL VALLEY

PARKS, BEACHES & RECREATION AREAS

Bayfront Park

This park is good-looking and well-designed for every kind of family activity *and* for dogs. It gets an A in planning from us. There's an exercise course; lawns are green and silky, picnic areas clean and attractive. The multi-use trails for bicycles, strollers and what-not may be used only by leashed dogs. (There are bikes galore.) But here's the canine payoff: a special dog run next to an estuary, where dogs are free to bathe.

The dog-use area starts where the brown grass begins. Beware, owners of escape artists: The area is huge, but not fenced. No scoops or water are furnished, but the **Richardson Bay Estuary** is right there to jump into. There aren't many trash cans, either, but the city does a very good job of cleaning up regularly.

At the end of the run there's even a marsh that dogs can explore, if you're willing to put a very mucky friend back into the car with you. Luckily, this marsh is all organic muck, free from the dangerous trash that fills many unprotected bay marshes.

For a dog park, this one offers an unparalleled view—Mount Tam, with horses and bikes trotting and whizzing by harmlessly on their own separate trail in the foreground, mockingbirds singing in the bushes.

There is only one fountain for humans and dogs, and it's located at the park entrance, nowhere near the dog run.

3-10a The parking lot is on Sycamore Avenue, just after you cross Camino Alto, next to the wastewater treatment plant. Keep your dog leashed near the steep-sided sewage ponds; dogs have drowned in them. Also, be sure to keep your dog leashed until you've left the parking lot and crossed the bike path. Some riders really whiz through here. (415) 383-1370. Open during daylight hours.

Camino Alto Open Space Preserve 

In this accessible open space, your dog may run free on a wide fire trail along a ridge connecting with Mount Tamalpais. You'll walk through bay laurels, madrones and chaparral, looking down on soaring vultures and the bay, Highway 1, the hills and the headlands. A small imperfection is that you can hear the *whoosh* of traffic. You should carry water.

3-10b Park at the end of Escalon Drive, just west of Camino Alto. Open 24 hours. (415) 499-6387.

Cascade Park 

Just driving to this verdant place on the slopes of Mount Tamalpais is a treat in itself—along park-like, redwood-filtered Cascade Drive. Because it borders Marin Municipal Water District land, which allows dogs on-leash, you can walk forever into its redwood and mixed-deciduous forest on wild, but well-kept, dirt paths. Cascade Creek is accessible and wet even in summer.

3-10c Open during daylight hours. The fairly informal parking area is off Cascade Drive near its western end. (415) 383-1370.

Mount Tamalpais State Park 

Generally, dogs are restricted to paved roads here. But dogs may stay in one of the campgrounds—**Pantoll Station** (see listing, page 107)—and there are a few spots to which you can take your dog, near the summit. The views from there are something you, if not your dog, will certainly appreciate on a clear day.

Stop for lunch and water for all at the **Bootjack Picnic Area**, west of Mountain Home Inn on Panoramic Highway and about a half mile east of the turnoff to the summit, Pantoll Road. The tables are attractively sited on the hillside under oak trees. This picnic ground is an access point for the **Bootjack Trail** and **Matt Davis Trail.** The Matt Davis Trail is off-limits, but you and your dog may—hallelujah!—use the 100 feet of Bootjack Trail that leads you into Marin Municipal Water District land, where leashed dogs are allowed. (You must travel north on the Bootjack Trail, though, not south; it's all state park in that direction.) Heading northward, you can hook up with the **Old Stage Fire Road** and the **Old Railroad Grade Fire Road**, which are water district roads going almost the whole distance to the summit.

3-10d The Bootjack Picnic Area parking lot charges $5 to park. (Once you pay in any one state park lot, your receipt is good for any other spot that you hit that day.)

3-10e You can also enter the Old Stage Fire Road right across from the Pantoll Ranger Station, at the intersection of Panoramic Highway and Pantoll Road. Your dog has special permission to cross the 100-feet or so of state park trail approaching water district trail.

Mount Tamalpais Summit 

The summit of Mount Tam is worth the $5 fee that you're charged merely to drive there. But in addition to the magnificent views, you may also take your dog on one trail up there ($1 dog fee).

You'll find a small refreshment stand, restrooms, visitor center and viewing platforms. On clear days, you can see nine counties. In summer, white fingers of fog obscure a good part of your view as they creep between the "knuckles" of Marin's ridges.

It's too bad your dog doesn't care about views. But he will take eagerly on-leash to the smoothly paved **Verna Dunshee Trail**, about one-mile long, running almost level around the summit. About three-quarters of this trail is also wheelchair-accessible.

3-10f From Highway 101, take the Stinson Beach/Highway 1 exit. Follow Highway 1 to Panoramic Highway, which will be a right turn. Continue on Panoramic to the right turn off to Pantoll Road; Pantoll soon becomes East Ridgecrest Road and goes to the summit, then loops back for your trip down. (415) 388-2070.

Mount Tamalpais—Marin Municipal Water District Lands 

Your very best bet for a dog walk high on the mountain is to find one of the water district fire roads near the summit. Your dog must be leashed, but at least she can go on the trails with you, and you both can experience the greenness of this wonderful mountain. At this elevation, the green comes from chaparral, pine and madrone.

Just below the summit on East Ridgecrest Boulevard, watch for the water district's gate and sign. This is the **Old Railroad Grade Fire Road**, which descends to 1,785-feet from the entry point just west of the summit. Farther down it intersects with Old Stage Fire Road. It emerges at the **Bootjack Picnic Area**. En route, you'll cross three creeks. For obvious reasons, you'll be happier in warm weather taking this road down, not up; get someone to meet you in a car at the Bootjack picnic site.

Another spot to pick up a water district trail is off Panoramic Highway just west of Mountain Home Inn. Look for the Marin Municipal Water District sign by the fire station. Park at the state park parking lot west of Mountain Home Inn and walk down this fire road, called **Gravity Car Road** (though it's unmarked), through mixed pines, redwoods, fir, madrone and scrub. Keep your eyes open for fast-moving mountain bikes.

Mountain Theatre 

For a very short but lovely walk that's legal for dogs—on-leash—turn right off East Ridgecrest Boulevard just after Pantoll Road becomes East Ridgecrest, at the Rock Springs Picnic Area. Park in the lot beside the road and take the paved trail to the Mountain Theatre (officially the Sydney B. Cushing Memorial Theatre). It's an attractive 10-minute walk through madrone, oak and redwoods to the theater, with its stone "bleachers." Dogs are even allowed to attend performances with you, so long as they're leashed. (415) 388-2070.

Old Mill Park 

Refresh your dog under cool redwoods right in the town of Mill Valley. The old mill, built in 1834, was recently restored. There are benches, restrooms and fountain, kids' swings and a slide, and a wooden bridge over Old Mill Creek. Well-maintained paths run along the creek, which is dog-accessible, though she is supposed to be leashed. One picnic table sits within the hugest "fairy ring" we've ever seen—40 feet across. Imagine the size of the mother tree whose stump engendered this ring of saplings!

3-10g On Throckmorton Avenue at Olive Street, near the public library. Open during daylight hours. (415) 383-1370.

Restaurants

The Depot Cafe and Bookstore: Serves sandwiches, salads, soups, desserts, gourmet coffee. This place is Mill Valley's town square and everybody's back yard. You and your dog may sit at cafe tables, benches or picnic tables and snack or just bask in the sun—if you don't mind skateboarders, bikes, chess players, crying kids, telephones, Frisbees, hacky-sack and guitar music happening right next to you. These are Marin kids, the kind who will reach out to your dog's face without a moment's hesitation. Mellow is the watchword here! Both sun and shade available, at least after midafternoon. On the Plaza. (415) 383-2665.

Lodgings & Campgrounds

Howard Johnson Motor Lodge: Off Highway 101 at the Stinson Beach exit, by the Richardson Bay Bridge. 160 Shoreline Highway,

Mill Valley, CA 94941. About $80 for a double; $10 extra for dog. (415) 332-5700.

Pantoll Station Campground, Mount Tamalpais State Park: There are 16 developed walk-in sites in the park that allow dogs (the rest are environmental campgrounds). Toilets but no showers; $14 per night plus $1 for dog. (415) 388-2070, or reserve through MISTIX: (800) 444-PARK.

3-11

NICASIO

Nicasio is only a picturesque jog in Nicasio Valley Road, but if you're touring the western Marin hills, stop by the reservoir for a quick stroll. Unfortunately, it's against Marin Municipal Water District regulations to let your puppy swim.

PARKS, BEACHES & RECREATION AREAS

Nicasio Reservoir 

If you're driving west from Nicasio, turn left where the road crosses the Petaluma-Point Reyes Road. You'll see some small parking turnouts, from which you can take narrow foot trails down to the water. Dogs must be leashed, there are no trees, and in summer it's hot, and the grass is bristling with foxtails. The reservoir is good for fishing only; no dog or human dipping allowed.

3-11a Open sunrise to sunset. (415) 924-4600.

3-12

NOVATO

Novato is one of the Marin cities whose dog ordinance is the county's: Dog must be on-leash or under verbal command. Its city parks require leash, though.

PARKS, BEACHES & RECREATION AREAS

Deer Island Open Space Preserve 

This preserve is called an island because it's a high point in the flood plain of the **Petaluma River**, an oak-crowned hill surrounded by miles of dock and tules. You can easily imagine it surrounded by shallow water, Miwok canoes slipping through rafts of ducks. The trail is a 1.8-mile loop of gentle ups and downs above ponds and marshy fields. There are some sturdy old oaks among the mixed deciduous groves, and lots of laurels. The trail is partly shaded. There is no water accessible to your dog; carry some. No bikes are allowed on the trail.

3-12a From Highway 101, exit at San Marin Drive/Atherton; take a right on Olive Avenue, a left on Deer Island Lane. Park in a small lot at the trailhead, by a small engineering company building. Open 24 hours. (415) 499-6387.

Miwok Park

This is one of the best city parks we've visited. Dogs must be on-leash, but it offers a great combination of dog pleasures and human amenities. Paved paths, good for strollers, wind through pine trees. There are bocce ball courts, horseshoes, a kids' gym and a lovely shaded picnic area with grills.

Outside the **Museum of the American Indian**, located in this park, is an intriguing display of California native plants that the coastal Miwok used for food, clothing and shelter.

Best of all for canines, **Novato Creek** flows deep and 30 to 40 feet wide—even in summer. Dabney loves it. A woman we encountered with a golden retriever told us that the muddy bottom can sometimes be soft and treacherous, so keep a close eye on your dog if he goes swimming.

3-12b At Novato Boulevard and Oliva Drive. Open from 6 a.m. to 10 p.m. (415) 897-4323.

Mount Burdell Open Space Preserve

Mount Burdell is the largest of Marin's open space preserves. You'll share it with cattle, but there's plenty of room. There are eight or 10 miles of cinder and dirt paths through its grasslands dotted with oaks, including part of the **Bay Area Ridge Trail.**

About one-eighth of a mile up the trail starting at San Andreas Drive there's a creek, but it's dry in summer. In winter, you might find the preserve's **Hidden Lake**. Dogs may run "under voice control" here, but as in all these open spaces, it's a good idea to carry a leash in case you meet a herd of cattle or mountain bikes. In summer, there are lots of foxtails, and fire danger is high. No fires are ever allowed. Camping is allowed by permit, but of course there are no facilities.

3-12c From San Marin Avenue, turn north on San Andreas Drive. Park on the street and carry plenty of water. Open 24 hours. (415) 499-6387.

Ignacio Valley Open Space Preserve 

3-12d To get to this open space, exit Highway 101 at Ignacio Boulevard and drive west. Turn left (south) on Country Club Drive, then right on Eagle Drive. The trailhead is at the end of Eagle. Open 24 hours. (415) 499-6387.

Indian Tree Open Space Preserve 

This open space and **Verissimo Hills Open Space Preserve** (see below) are good to know about because they're just east of Stafford Lake County Park. Watch for horses here, but you needn't leash.

3-12e From Highway 101, exit at San Marin Drive/Atherton Avenue; drive west on San Marin. After San Marin turns into Sutro Avenue, take a right onto Vineyard Road. Park along the dirt county road that begins at the trailhead. Open 24 hours. (415) 499-6387.

Indian Valley Open Space Preserve 

A grand open space that, combined with **Ignacio Valley Open Space** and **Lucas Valley Open Space**, covers a huge area of the north side of **Big Rock Ridge**. There are lots of dogs here, in leashless ecstasy. The trail is partly sunny, partly shaded by laurels.

3-12f From Highway 101, exit at DeLong Avenue and go west on DeLong, which becomes Diablo Avenue. Take a left on Hill Road and a right on Indian Valley Road. Drive to the first stop sign. A yellow fire hydrant will be on your left; park on this road before you walk left at the spur road marked "Not a Through Street," just south of Old Ranch Road. Cross Arroyo Avichi Creek right at the entrance (dry in summer). Open 24 hours. (415) 499-6387.

Loma Verde Open Space Preserve 

3-12g There are two access points to this open space. One, south of the Marin Country Club, is a waterless, tree-covered hillside with a fire trail. Bikes are allowed. It's good if you like easily reachable high spots; there are good views of San Pablo Bay. Exit Highway 101 at Ignacio Boulevard. Go west to Fairway Drive and turn left (south), then left on Alameda de la Loma, then right on Pebble Beach Drive. Access is at the end of Pebble Beach.

3-12h The second access point is through the Posada West housing development. From Alameda del Prado, turn south on Posada del Sol. At the end of this street is the trail opening. Open 24 hours. (415) 499-6387.

Lucas Valley Open Space Preserve

This space of rolling, oak-dotted hills, which shares **Big Rock Ridge** with **Ignacio Valley Open Space Preserve**, affords great views of Novato and Lucas Valley developments. There are a dozen access points, most from Lucas Valley and Marinwood.

3-12i One access point is reached by turning left (north) off Lucas Valley Road on Mount Shasta Drive, then a brief right turn on Vogelsang Drive. Park near this dead end and walk in. Open 24 hours. (415) 499-6387.

Neil O'Hair Park

This city-owned open space is on the map, but it's undeveloped and unmarked as a park. You can enter, though, from the point on Sutro Avenue, where it crosses Novato Creek. A sign labels the spot the **Kiwanis Fishing Hole.** The smell of horses from the ranch next door is delicious to dogs, and the creek is nice and deep, even in summer. You can follow a dirt fire trail up into the dry hills, curving around to the right through thick oaks and laurels.

3-12j At the corner of Sutro Avenue (where it becomes San Marin Drive) and Novato Boulevard. The only parking is on the street. Since it's an unofficial park, it doesn't seem to have official hours or an official leash rule, but leash in the Kiwanis Fishing Hole area if your dog could disturb anyone's peace. (415) 897-4323.

Verissimo Hills Open Space Preserve

The usual east Marin open space of golden hills with clumps of oak. It has narrow foot trails only; bikes are prohibited. As you enter the area, you'll see a fork; take the trail uphill to the left. This path features fine views of the hills as well as nearby residential areas. Note that this open space preserve is co-managed by the Marin Municipal Water District, which means that if you're in doubt, leash. Be sure to close the gate to keep cattle inside.

3-12k From Highway 101, exit at San Marin Drive/Atherton Avenue; drive west on San Marin. Turn right (west) on Center Road. Go all the way to the end, where you can park. Open 24 hours. (415) 499-6387.

Scottsdale Pond 

This is county land lacking shade and located right off the freeway, too, but it's a really good dog swimming hole. Carry a leash. Some waterfowl nest nearby, so make sure your dog stays in the water itself and doesn't disturb them.

3-12I Exit Highway 101 at Rowland Boulevard and drive west on Rowland. Park on the street, right by the water's edge. Open 24 hours. (415) 897-4323.

DIVERSIONS

Start singing lessons now: If your dog is a howler, or you think he has it in him, the Novato Human Needs Center sponsors an annual **Crooning Canine Contest** as part of Novato's Fourth of July Heritage Days. Prizes are awarded for solos and ensembles, to both dogs and owners. Judges look for tonal quality, enthusiasm, stage presence, originality and showmanship.

The Crooning Canine Contest is held at Pioneer Park, on Simmons Lane one block north of Novato Boulevard. (415) 897-4147.

3-13

OLEMA

PARKS, BEACHES & RECREATION AREAS

Bolinas Ridge Trail 

This **Golden Gate National Recreation Area** trail, part of the **Bay Area Ridge Trail**, is not for sissies—canine or human. It climbs steadily up for 11 miles from the Olema end, giving you gorgeous views of Tomales Bay, Bolinas and the ocean, ending up at the Bolinas-Fairfax Road below Alpine Lake.

You must keep your dog leashed. One good reason for this is that there are cattle roaming unfenced along the trail. And the trail is very popular with non-sissy mountain bicyclists. (The trail is wide, but of dirt and rock.) From the western end, you'll walk through rolling grassland with cypress clumps. It's dry in summer, so carry plenty of water! Rock outcrops sport crowns of poison oak, too, so beware.

You may be able to cope with 11 miles of this, but remember your dog's bare pads and don't overdo it. Also, it isn't much fun to walk 11 miles with him on a leash—for either of you.

Unfortunately, only the **Bolinas Ridge Trail** is open to dogs; you can't take any of the spur trails going south.

3-13a The western end begins about one mile north of Olema on Sir Francis Drake Boulevard. There's roadside parking only. Open 24 hours. (415) 556-0560 or (415) 663-1092.

LODGINGS & CAMPGROUNDS

Olema Ranch Camps: These are sites for tents or trailers, some with barbecues. All sites have open fire facilities, water and hot showers. Full trailer hookup is $23; basic tent site for two people is $16. Dog, $1. 10155 Highway 1, Olema, CA 94950. To reserve: (800) 479-CAMP or (415) 663-8001.

3-14

ROSS

PARKS, BEACHES & RECREATION AREAS

Natalie Coffin Greene Park 

Dogs are welcome but must be leashed in this Ross city park. It's an enchanted mixed forest of redwood and deciduous trees, typical of the lush Mount Tamalpais watershed. The picnic area has an old-fashioned shelter and barbecue built of logs and stone.

The park borders generic Marin Municipal Water District land, and from the park, you can pick up the wide cinder fire road leading to **Phoenix Lake**, a five-minute walk. Bikes, hikers and leashed dogs are all welcome on this road, but the lake is a reservoir, so no body contact is allowed—for man or beast.

The road continues, depending how far you want to walk, to **Lagunitas Lake**, **Bon Tempe Lake**, **Alpine Lake** and **Kent Lake**. (No body contact in any of them: sorry, doggies!) Combined, the water district offers 94 miles of road and 44 miles of trail in this area, meandering through hillsides, densely forested with pine, oak, madrone and a variety of other trees. For a trail map, send a SASE to: Sky Oaks Ranger Station, PO Box 865, Fairfax, CA 94978, Attention: Trail Map.

3-14a At the corner of Sir Francis Drake Boulevard and Lagunitas Road, go west on Lagunitas all the way to the end, past the country club. You'll find a parking lot and some portable toilets. Natalie Coffin Greene Park is open sunrise to sunset. (415) 453-6020.

3-15 SAN ANSELMO

San Anselmo is blessed with six parks within its limits. It also has no leash law of its own. Under the county ordinance, dogs must be on-leash "or under control." San Anselmo Avenue is a laid-back stroll with a dog, and you can both cool your paws in San Anselmo Creek, which runs through town.

PARKS, BEACHES & RECREATION AREAS

Creek Park

San Anselmo Creek runs between Sir Frances Drake Boulevard—which has a wide variety of antique shops—and San Anselmo Avenue, the main shopping street. A bridge connects the two streets.

Creek Park, small but handy and clean, is next to a free public lot with some shady spaces. Along the creek banks on the Sir Francis Drake side are picnic tables on a lawn with beautiful willows and maples. Lots of people lounge on the grass. Wooden steps lead down to the water. Dabney loves to jump in on a hot summer day. He plunged in once next to some children catching minnows, helping herd the fish into their hands. There's plenty of shade in which to picnic, or lie on the grass, while resting between shopping binges for antiques. "No unleashed dogs except at heel," reads the polite sign.

3-15a Turn into parking lot from Sir Frances Drake Boulevard, near "The Hub" (intersection of Sir Frances Drake and Red Hill Avenue). Open from one-half hour before sunrise to one-half hour after sunset. (415) 258-4645.

Faude Open Space Preserve 

You get a view of the hills and Mount Tamalpais from here, but in summer, the hills are dry and barren. Carry water. No leash is necessary.

3-15b From Sir Frances Drake Boulevard, go right on Broadmoor Avenue. At the end, take a right on Indian Rock Road. You may park on the street. The city owns this open space, open 24 hours. (415) 499-6387.

Faude Park 

This is a city park and quite a steep climb up from the playing fields. With your dog, it's better to enter from the hill end, where there's a fire trail through scrub oak, bay laurel and madrone, with a view of Mount Tam and San Anselmo. No leash necessary, but watch for broken bottles where teens carouse.

3-15c Park at Elkhorn Way and Alice Way. Open sunrise to sunset. (415) 258-4645.

Loma Alta Open Space Preserve 

An exceptional open space—a little canyon amid bare hills, lined with oaks, bay laurel and buckeye. There's plenty of shade. The trail follows **White Hill Creek**, which is dry in the summer. No leash required.

3-15d You can park at the trailhead at the end of Glen Avenue, a turn north off Sir Francis Drake Boulevard. Open 24 hours. (415) 499-6387.

Memorial Park 

This pleasant and popular city park has tennis courts, three baseball diamonds and a children's play area. A volunteer group, Memorial Park Dog Owners Association, publishes a newsletter and keeps an eye out for scooper-scofflaws. Its focus now, though, is to keep the park open to dogs. Some people just don't like dogs in this park and are fighting to ban them. But as of this printing, dogs are still allowed.

3-15e Off Sunnyhills Drive. Open sunrise to sunset. (415) 258-4645.

Sorich Ranch Park 

The biggest and by far the wildest city park in San Anselmo is Sorich Ranch Park, an undeveloped open space soaring up to a ridgetop from which you can see a distant make-believe San Francisco skyline across the bay. From the very top of the ridge, you also can see Mount Tamalpais and most of San Rafael, including the one-of-a-kind turquoise and salmon Marin County Civic Center designed by Frank Lloyd Wright. (Some Marinites are glad there's only one.)

The entrance from the San Anselmo side is at the end of San Francisco Boulevard, and the path is pretty much straight up. But if you aren't up to a 10-minute puffing ascent, you can just stroll in the meadows at the bottom. No leash is required, and the park is uncrowded and often pleasantly breezy. There's no water available, and it can be scorching in summer. Good news, though: The Memorial

Park Dog Owners Association (see Memorial Park listing, page 114) is planning to install water fountains.

3-15f The open space is open 24 hours. (415) 258-4645.

RESTAURANTS

The Arbor: An inviting all-around cafe with many umbrella-shaded tables on a wooden deck. They're friendly toward dogs here, but prefer that you chain them outside the fence next to your table. 636 San Anselmo Avenue. (415) 459-5708.

3-16

SAN RAFAEL

PARKS, BEACHES & RECREATION AREAS

Boyd Park

This is not a very doggy park, until you drive past the Dollar mansion (now the Falkirk Cultural Center) into the hills on Robert Dollar Scenic Drive to the undeveloped portion. The only parking is at a turnout off the drive, but at that spot, the drive becomes a dirt fire trail, closed to autos, that mounts the ridgecrest in a steady uphill climb through brush, oak and madrone. Leash your pup and start walking. No water is available, so carry some. You'll get a breathtaking view of the Richmond-San Rafael Bridge, the Bay Bridge, the Oakland skyline and Mount Tam.

3-16a Robert Dollar Scenic Drive begins at the end of Laurel Place. Open 7 a.m. to 7 p.m. (415) 485-3333.

China Camp State Park 

You shouldn't miss a drive through this lovely park, but it's inhospitable to dogs except at **Village Beach**, the site of the 1890s Chinese fishing village for which the park is named. As you drive in, you'll see a rare piece of bay, marsh and oak-covered hills as the Miwoks saw it. The hills, like islands, rise from saltmarsh seas of pickleweed and cordgrass. You'll see the "No Dogs" symbol at every trailhead, in case you're tempted. However, with your dog, you *may* visit any of three picnic grounds on the way in via North San Pedro Road: **Buckeye Point** and **Weber Point** both have tables in shade or sun overlooking San Pablo Bay, mudflats at low tide, and the hills beyond the bay. **Bullhead Flat** lets you get right next to the water, but there's no shade at the tables. All these spots are open from 8 a.m. to sunset.

Watch for the sign to China Camp Village, a left turn into a lot, where there's some shade. You'll see the rickety old pier and the wood-and-tin village. Park, leash your dog and walk down to the village and beach. On weekdays, this park is a lot less crowded. There are more picnic tables overlooking the water by the parking lot, an interpretive exhibit (open from 10 a.m. to 5 p.m., and open to the air so that your dog can casually stroll in with you if it isn't crowded), and a refreshment stand serving shrimp, crab and beer. You can eat at picnic tables right on the beach—small, but pleasantly sheltered by hillsides, with gentle surf.

Swimming is encouraged here, and it's often warm enough. Derelict fishing boats and shacks are preserved on the beach. You can walk all the way to a rocky point at the south end, but watch out for the luxuriant poison oak in the brush along the beach. You may also find occasional broken glass.

3-16b From Highway 101, take the North San Pedro Road exit and follow it all the way into the park and China Camp. (Don't go near McNears Beach County Park just south of China Camp. Dogs are strictly forbidden.) The park gates are open from 8 a.m. to 5 p.m., 8 a.m. to 7 p.m. during Daylight Savings Time. (415) 456-0766.

Civic Center Lagoon County Park 

Dogs are allowed on-leash in this well-tended greensward surrounding the lagoon, complete with fountain and ducks. Picnic tables are sited by the water under willows. You could lunch wearing white gloves here. The Civic Center buildings, Frank Lloyd Wright's fantasy, are by far the most interesting government structures in the Bay Area and worth the trip by themselves.

3-16c From Highway 101, exit at North San Pedro Road and follow signs to the Civic Center. (415) 499-6387.

Jerry Russom Memorial Park 

Finding this undeveloped piece of land run by the city isn't easy. It's on the map, off Lucas Valley Road, but there are no signs. You enter by parking at a roadside turnout and walking around a locked gate designed to keep vehicles out. This is the paved **Old Lucas Valley Road**, now a foot trail. Blackberries to your left at the start of the road are an unexpected treat in season. This is a good running track, if you don't mind asphalt, and good for strollers, too. But stay on the road, because there's poison oak aplenty. In some spots, the creek paralleling the road is dog-accessible and full, even in summer. A dirt path winds off into the hills, too. Carry water if you try it. One small drawback: You can hear traffic noise from the highway.

3-16d Drive west on Lucas Valley Road to where Lassen Street goes off to the right. Take a left there into the unmarked turnout and park. Leash isn't mandatory, but if your dog is the type to crash recklessly through clumps of poison oak, you'd be wise to leash up. Open 24 hours. (415) 485-3333.

John F. McInnis County Park

This is an all-round, got-everything park: two softball fields, two soccer fields, tennis courts, picnic area, a scale-model car track, a golf driving range and a dirt creekside nature trail. In one parking lot is a big hot dog stand. Best of all for trustworthy dogs, they can be off-leash, so long as they're under verbal command. This park isn't particularly pretty, but it's very utilitarian.

3-16e From Highway 101, exit at Smith Ranch Road. Hours are 8 a.m. to 10 p.m. (415) 499-6387.

San Pedro Mountain Open Space Preserve

A narrow footpath rises through a madrone forest, moderately but inexorably upwards. But if you make it up far enough, your reward is terrific views of the bay and Marin's peaks. It's often dry, so carry water. Deer are plentiful, so it's kind to leash your dog if you don't trust him completely to stay by your side.

3-16f Park at the entrance at the end of Woodoaks Drive, a short street off San Pedro Road just north of the Jewish Community Center of Marin. Open 24 hours. (415) 499-6387.

Santa Margarita Island Open Space Preserve

What a wonderful, secret place this is! **Gallinas Creek**, fortified by levees, is lined with rickety piers and small boats, like a bit of the Delta. You can cross to a tiny island via a footbridge and climb the hill you'll find there, covered with oaks and boulders, or walk around the edge on a dirt path. Watch for poison oak on the hill. Though of course it isn't true, you can feel as if no one has been here before you except Coast Miwoks.

3-16g From North San Pedro Road, turn west on Meadow Drive. Where it ends, at the western end of Vendola Drive, is the footbridge. You can park on the street. Carry water if you plan to stay long. Open 24 hours. (415) 499-6387.

Santa Venetia Marsh Open Space Preserve

This is one of only a few saltwater marshes where dogs may go unleashed, but they must stay on the trails. Unless you have a real water dog, that won't be a problem; it's a good spot for an escape artist to be off-leash, since he can't get far on solid ground. It's cool and breezy here, but gentler than any San Francisco Bay shore park. The grasses and pickleweed make a pretty mixture of colors, and swallows dart above the ground hunting insects.

3-16h Vendola Drive has two distinct parts, and you can get to the marsh from the end of either. At the western end of the creekside segment of Vendola, at the corner of Meadow Drive, is a footbridge leading to Santa Margarita Island (described above). Open 24 hours. (415) 499-6387.

Terra Linda—Sleepy Hollow Divide Open Space Preserve

There are many entrances to this ridgeline preserve, but generally the best are the highest on the ridge. We'll describe the one that starts you at a good high point, so that you don't have to climb. From the entrance at the end of Ridgewood Drive, you can walk into **Sorich Ranch Park** (maintained in an undeveloped state by San Anselmo). From that ridge, you can see—expending no sweat whatsoever—the city of San Rafael, Highway 101, the wonderful turquoise-roofed Marin Civic Center, the bay, and the hills of Solano County on the other side.

Carry water. No leash is necessary, unless you're worried about your dog tangling with deer.

3-16i Park near the very end of Ridgewood Drive. The entrance is unmarked, and you have to step over a low locked gate. Open 24 hours. (415) 499-6387.

RESTAURANTS

Le Chalet Basque: On your way to China Camp, stop for lunch here. European-style cooking, both fancy and *ordinaire*; wine and beer is served at a large number of umbrella-shaded tables behind an iron gate. The proprietor welcomes well-behaved, quiet dogs, but they must be tied up behind the gate. He'll still be close enough to smell the boeuf bourgignon—from outside the eating area. 405 North San Pedro Road. (415) 479-1070.

Lodgings & Campgrounds

China Camp State Park Campgrounds: There are 31 primitive walk-in sites. As in all state parks, dogs must always be leashed or confined to your tent. $14 for a tent site, $1 for dog. Reserve through MISTIX: (800) 444-PARK.

Holiday Inn: Take the Terra Linda exit from Highway 101. 1010 Northgate Drive, San Rafael, CA 94903. (415) 479-8800. Around $100 for a double; $10 extra for dog plus a refundable $50 deposit.

Villa Inn: From Highway 101 northbound, exit at Central San Rafael. Travel three blocks north, then three blocks west on Fourth Street. From the southbound 101 direction, exit at Lincoln Avenue. 1600 Lincoln Avenue, San Rafael, CA 94901. About $70 for a double. Well-mannered dogs allowed with a $20 deposit; however, no pit bulls, no dobermans and no puppies! (415) 456-4975.

3-17

SAUSALITO

Even if you live here, you should play tourist and stroll around Sausalito's harbor in the brilliant sea light (or luminous sea fog). On weekends, it's especially pleasant early in the day, before the ferries disgorge their passengers. You can visit bookstores and cafes with your dog tied up outside; we didn't find any with outdoor tables, probably because the weather is often too cool. But the city's attitude toward dogs is relaxed. And if you're on your way to the blustery Marin Headlands, fortify yourself with a big breakfast.

Parks, Beaches & Recreation Areas

Dunphy Park 🐾🐾🐾

A small but accessible park by the bay with grass, willows, picnic tables and a volleyball court. Best of all, there's a small beach, and canine swimming is fine. You can watch sailing and windsurfing from there, too. Dogs officially must be on-leash, but a good number of them swim and romp unfettered.

3-17a At Bridgeway and Bee Streets, there's a parking lot. The park is closed between 11 p.m. and 5 a.m. (415) 289-4125.

Marinship Park

This park isn't much, but it's worth a sniff to your dog if you're visiting the nearby **Army Corps of Engineers' Bay Model**—a fascinating working hydraulic model of the bay that you can stare at for hours. (It's indoors; no dogs there.) Follow signs to the Bay Model. Marinship Park is a big green square with tennis courts and bathrooms. A sign says the leash law is enforced.

3-17b On Marinship Way between Bridgeway and the bay. Closes at sunset. (415) 289-4125.

Remington Dog Park

Sausalito's new **Remington Dog Park** is named after the dog whose owner, Dianne Chute, raised the money to put the park together. It's more than an acre, all fenced, on a grassy slope with trees. An informative bulletin board, leash rack, benches, scoopers and water are furnished. Future plans include a three-tiered fountain—to suit any size dog—and a training area.

From the day it was finished, Remington and his dog friends have made terrific use of this place. "It's the social hub of Sausalito," says cartoonist Phil Frank, "where the elite with four feet meet."

What a boon to freedom-loving Sausalito dogs, who otherwise must be leashed everywhere in town. Rules are: Be there with your dog, pick up after her, and take her away if she gets aggressive.

3-17c D.O.G. (Dog Owners Group) of Sausalito maintains the park and publishes a newsletter. Write to: D.O.G., 690 Butte Street, Sausalito, CA 94965, or call Dianne Chute at (415) 332-6086. The dog park is on the grounds of **Martin Luther King Park**, on Bridgeway at Ebbtide Avenue. Park in the large lot at the end of Ebbtide. Open 24 hours.

Muir Beach

This beach is actually at the tiny town of Muir Beach, but since it's within the Marin Headlands area of the Golden Gate National Recreation Area, we're listing it under Sausalito, the gateway to the headlands.

Muir Beach allows dogs on-leash only. It's small, but a real gem, with rugged sand dunes spotted with plants, a parking lot and large picnic area, a small lagoon with tules, and its share of wind. **Redwood Creek** empties into the ocean here.

3-17d You can reach Muir Beach the long way, hiking about five miles from the Marin Headlands Visitor Center (see Rodeo Beach listing below), or the easy way, via Highway 1. From Highway 1, watch for the turnoff for the beach. The beach closes at 10 p.m. (415) 331-1540.

Rodeo Beach & Lagoon 

Rodeo Lagoon is lined with tules and pickleweed. Here, ocean water splashes into the lagoon in winter and rainfall swells it until it overflows, continually mixing salt and fresh water. Birds love this fecund lagoon.

It's one of the few marshes to allow dogs, who delight in the sheltered swimming. They needn't be leashed. Be courteous if you see birders, though. Birdwatching and dogs don't mix. An attractive wooden walkway leads across the lagoon to the beach.

Rodeo Beach is small but pretty, made of the dark sand common in Marin. Large rocks on shore are covered with "whitewash," birders' polite name for guano. Letting your dog swim in Marin County surf is always risky—currents are strong, and trying to rescue a dog who is being swept away is to risk your own life. Not only that: While on the beach, watch your dog like a hawk and don't turn your own back on the surf. Especially in winter, a "sneaker" wave can sweep you and your dog away.

3-17e From the Marin Headlands Visitor Center, follow the sign west. Open from sunrise to 10 p.m. (415) 331-1540.

Marin Headlands Trails 

From Rodeo Beach, you can circle the lagoon or head up into the hills. You're in for a gorgeous walk—or a gorgeous and challenging walk, depending on the weather. Look at a map of the Bay Area, and it will be obvious why the headlands' trees all grow at an eastward slant. In summer, especially, cold ocean air funnels through the Golden Gate, sucked in by the Central Valley's heat—chilling the headlands and the inhabitants of western San Francisco with fog and wind. The Bay Area may be "air-conditioned by God," but the headlands sit right at the air inflow, and it's set on "high." Never come here without at least one jacket.

Your dog will love the wind. The combination of fishy breeze and aromatic brush from the hillsides sends ours into olfactory ecstasy. What looks from a distance like green fuzz on these headlands is a profusion of wildflowers and low brush. Indian paintbrush, hemlock, sticky monkeyflower, ferns, dock, morning glory, blackberry, sage and thousands more species grow here—even some stunted but effective poison oak on the windward sides. (On the lee of the hills, it's not stunted.) Groves of eucalyptus grow on the crests. You hear a lovely low rustle and roar of wind, surf, birds and insects— and the squeak and groan of eucalyptus rubbing against each other. Pinch some sage between your fingers and sniff; if you can ever leave California again after that, you're a stronger person than we are.

From the beach and lagoon, you can hike the circle formed by the **Miwok Trail** starting at the eastern end of the lagoon, meeting the **Wolf Ridge Trail**, then meeting the **Coastal Trail** (ala the Pacific Coast Trail), back to where you started. Or you can pick up the Coastal Trail behind the youth hostel, which is behind the Visitor Center, and hike east to where the trail hits McCullough Road, then double back.

Sights along these trails include World War II gun emplacements, the Golden Gate Bridge and San Francisco. As the trail rises and falls, you will discover a blessing: You'll be intermittently sheltered from the wind, and in these pockets, if the sun warms your back, you'll think you've died and gone to heaven. Your dog can run off-leash on all these trails.

If you want to hike from Rodeo to Muir Beach, you must put her on-leash at the point where the Coastal Trail branches off westward. But the great thing is that you can travel nearly the whole width of the headlands with your dog.

No natural water is available in the headlands. Be sure to carry plenty for both of you. And it's tick country, so search carefully when you get home.

3-17f Open 24 hours, but after 10 p.m. your car may need a camping permit. (415) 331-1540.

3-18

STINSON BEACH

It's fun to poke around Stinson, which is swarming with surfers and tourists on beautiful days. There's a relaxed attitude toward dogs at the outdoor snack shop tables. Bolinas Lagoon, stretching along Highway 1 between Stinson Beach and Bolinas, is tempting but environmentally fragile, so you should picnic along the water only if your dog is controllable. You'll also be taking a chance with muddy paws in your car. Don't go near Audubon Canyon Ranch, where herons and egrets nest.

PARKS, BEACHES & RECREATION AREAS

Stinson Beach

Highway 1 to Stinson and Bolinas is worth the curves you'll negotiate. Don't be in a hurry. On sunny weekends, traffic will be heavy. Try it on a foggy day—it's otherworldly. Dogs don't care whether or not the sun is shining, anyway.

Before setting out, we asked around. "Go to Stinson," said a friend. "There are dogs everywhere." "Dogs aren't allowed on Stinson Beach," said a Golden Gate National Recreation Area ranger. "Stinson is *swarming* with dogs," said another friend.

A kind woman in the Muir Woods bookstore solved the mystery. "No dogs on Stinson," she said sternly, "but there's this little part at the north end that isn't Stinson. We call it Dog Beach."

Indeed, the county-managed stretch where private houses are built at the north end does allow dogs on-leash. Which is itself a bit of a contradiction, because as you walk along with your obediently leashed dog, dogs who live in the houses lining the county stretch, and who don't have to wear leashes, come prancing out like the local law enforcement to check out the new kid. Leashed and leashless, dogs are indeed everywhere at Stinson. It's merry, and there's plenty of room for them.

You and your dog will be equally happy on Stinson Beach, with its backdrop of low hills and lining of dunes. Keep the dog off the dunes where they're roped off, being "repaired" by the forces of nature. Dogs are allowed in Stinson Beach's picnic area by **Eskoot Creek,** a pretty setting redolent with tantalizing smells.

3-18a Take the beach turnoff from Highway 1. Turn right at the parking lot and park at the far north end. Walk right by the sign that says "No Pets on Beach"—you can't avoid it—and turn right. Where the houses start is the county beach. You'll see a sign dividing the two jurisdictions saying "End of Guarded Beach." Beach hours are 9 a.m. to 10 p.m. (415) 868-0942.

3-19

TIBURON

The town of Tiburon is almost too Disneyland-perfect, with its green lawns and fountains, brick sidewalks and lack of smells. On a sunny day you can't beat the clean, safe street atmosphere for eating and strolling. Dogs, of course, must be as polite and well-behaved as their owners. Tiburon did a good job of planning for parking: There's almost none except for one large lot costing $2 for the first hour and up, which means that cars aren't driving around searching for a spot. Just give up and park there.

The town has also arranged for fogbanks to lie harmlessly to the west—usually over Sausalito. You and your dog can walk onto the ferry dock and watch boats of the Red & White Fleet come in and out, destination San Francisco or Angel Island. Dogs aren't allowed on Angel Island, but they can take pleasure with you sniffing the exciting scent of boat motor oil on the dock.

If you get a sudden impulse to take off for San Francisco, do it! One recreational secret of the Bay Area is that you may take your dog with you on the Red & White Fleet ferries, except to Angel Island or Alcatraz. (See Miscellaneous Dog Adventures, on page 295.)

Parks, Beaches & Recreation Areas

Richardson Bay Park

Generally known as the **Tiburon Bike Path,** this is a terrific multi-use park, unusual because it can be safely enjoyed by both bicyclists and dogs. It stretches two-thirds the length of Tiburon's peninsula and has parking at both ends. The larger lot is at the northern end. A dirt road, Brunini Way (no vehicles), leads into the park at the north end. You'll find a quiet, natural bay shoreline with a bit of marsh. There's some flotsam and jetsam, but only the highest quality, of course.

Keep walking and you'll enter **McKegney Green,** the name of the wide bike path that runs for two miles along Tiburon Boulevard toward downtown. (It doesn't go all the way, though.) Your dog must be leashed. The path, marked for running trainers, swings past benches overlooking the bay and a kids' jungle gym.

Soon the path splits and goes past both sides of a stretch of soccer fields, fenced wildlife ponds (no dogs!) and a parcourse. You can take your dog on either side, but be aware that bicyclists use both. You'll also share this path, on a fair weekend day, with roller skaters and parents pushing strollers. On the green are sunbathers and kite fliers.

The view is of Mount Tamalpais and Belvedere, with the Bay Bridge, San Francisco and the Golden Gate Bridge peeking out from behind it. Bring a jacket—it can be breezy here—and carry water for your dog if you're walking far. The only fountains are for people.

3-19a The park parallels Tiburon Boulevard. Hours are from one hour before sunrise to one hour after sunset. (415) 435-4355.

Shoreline Park 

A genteel greensward bordering the harbor. Impeccable behavior required of your dog, and on-leash, too.

3-19b Off Paradise Drive, in town. Open 24 hours. (415) 435-0956.

RESTAURANTS

Paradise Hamburgers and Ice Cream: This place furnishes bike racks and lots of tables, and they'll gladly water dogs as well as people. 1694 Tiburon Boulevard. (415) 435-8823.

FAIRS & FESTIVALS

Fourth of July Festival at Shoreline Park: The usual philosophy applies: If your dog can't stand firecrackers, leave her at home. (415) 435-5633.

MORE INFO

WHERE YOUR DOG CAN'T GO

- Olompali State Historic Park
- Tomales Bay State Park
- Corte Madera: All city parks
- Renaissance Pleasure Faire, Novato
- San Anselmo Art & Wine Festival
- Bothin Marsh Open Space Preserve (dogs must stay on the multi-use path that runs through the marsh)
- Roy's Redwoods Open Space Preserve
- Rush Creek Open Space Preserve
- Dillon Beach
- McNears Beach County Park
- Muir Woods National Monument (Dogs shouldn't even get out of your car at the parking lot. Only guide dogs are admitted. Instead, take your dog to Mill Valley's Cascade Park, or Natalie Coffin Greene Park in Ross)
- Paradise Beach County Park, Tiburon

- Point Reyes National Seashore: All backcountry trails and all beaches except those described in this chapter; all campgrounds

USEFUL PHONE NUMBERS & ADDRESSES

Bicycle Trails Council of Marin: PO Box 13842, San Rafael, CA 94913. (415) 456-7512.

California State Parks: Department of Parks and Recreation, Office of Public Relations, PO Box 942896, Sacramento, CA 94296. (916) 653-6995. Information on Marin County state parks: (415) 456-1286. To call within California for MISTIX campsite reservations (you may reserve up to eight weeks in advance): (800) 444-PARK, or write to MISTIX, PO Box 85705, San Diego, CA 92138.

Golden Gate National Recreation Area: Fort Mason, Building 201, San Francisco, CA 94123. (415) 556-0560.

Golden Gate National Recreation Area, Marin Headquarters: Fort Cronkhite, CA 94965. (415) 331-1540.

Marin County Humane Society: 171 Bel Marin Keys Boulevard, Novato, CA 94949. (415) 883-4621. Ask for the society's one-page guide to dog rules in the county.

Marin County Department of Parks, Open Space and Cultural Services: Marin County Civic Center, Room 417, San Rafael, CA 94903. (415) 499-6387.

Marin Municipal Water District: 220 Nellen Avenue, Corte Madera, CA 94925. (415) 924-4600. For a trail map, send an SASE to: Sky Oaks Ranger Station, Attention Trail Map, PO Box 865, Fairfax, CA 94978.

Muir and Stinson Beaches Information: (415) 868-0942. Weather: (415) 868-1922.

Point Reyes National Seashore: Point Reyes, CA 94956. (415) 663-1092. Weather information: (415) 663-9029.

West Marin Chamber of Commerce: PO Box 1045, Point Reyes Station, CA 94956. (415) 663-9232.

·Napa County·

128
2a
Lake Berryessa
5c
5d
St. Helena
1a
Calistoga
29
128

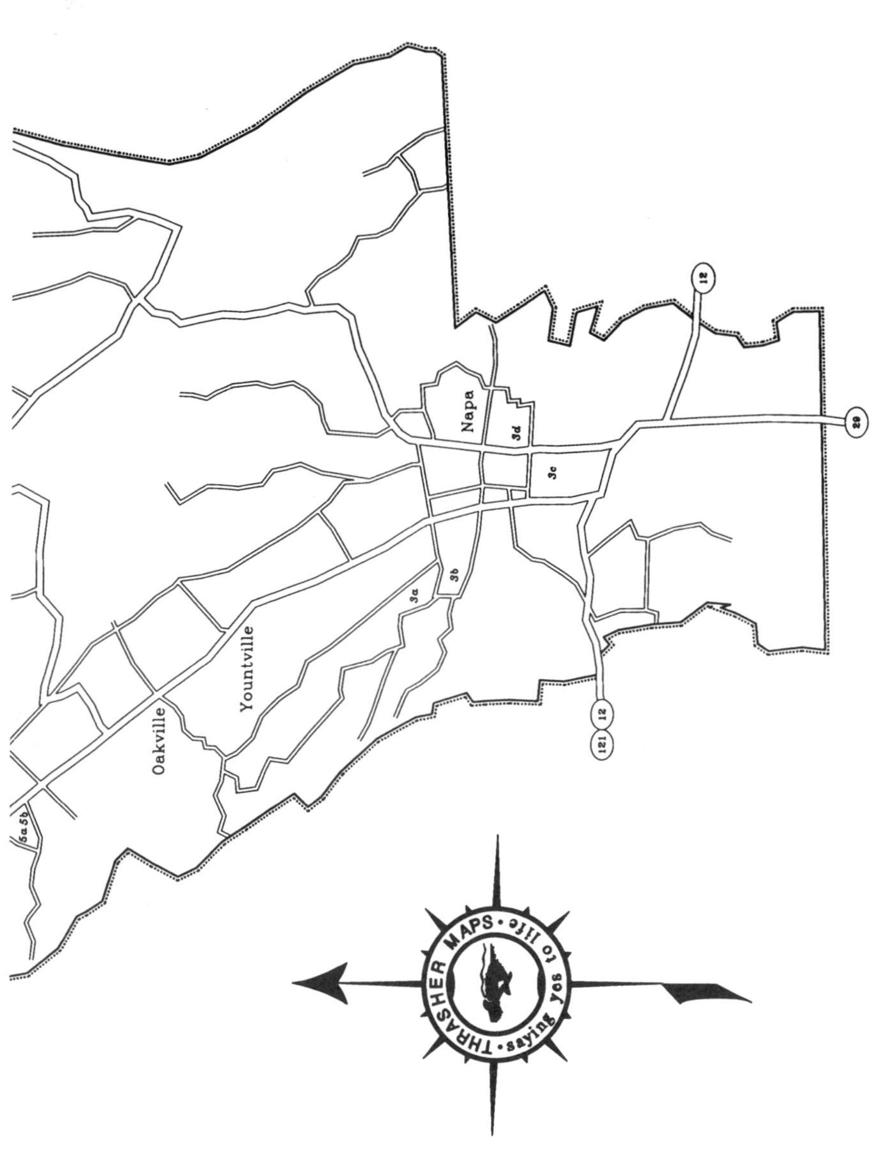
Napa
3d
3c
3b
3a
Yountville
Oakville
5a 5b
12
29
12
121
THRASHER MAPS • saying yes to life •

4

With its lush, fertile and inviting vineyards, farms and parks, **Napa County** has so much rural land you automatically assume it's dog heaven. Not true. It can be dog hell if you're looking for a place to pull over for a relief session in the heart of wine country.

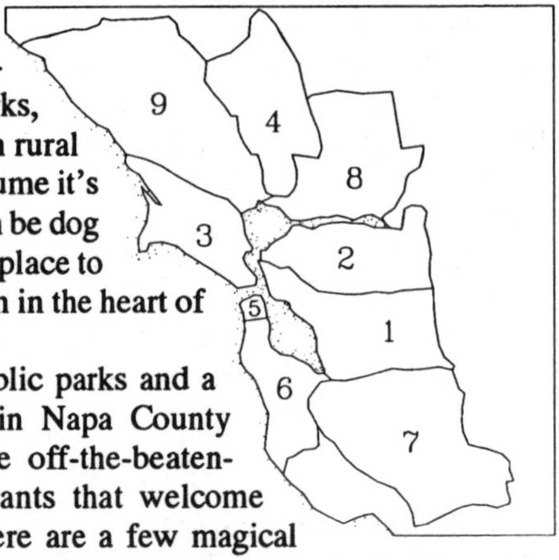

Actually, only nine public parks and a few miscellaneous sites in Napa County allow dogs, and most are off-the-beaten-path. Fortunately, restaurants that welcome dogs are plentiful, and there are a few magical places for them to spend the night. Some wineries even allow dogs to visit, but rules are always changing. It's best to call your favorite wineries ahead of time so you and your dog don't incur the grapes of a vintner's wrath.

STATE PARKS

- California State Parks in Napa County
- Henry Coe State Park, halfway between St. Helena and Calistoga

---

4-1

CALISTOGA

Dogs aren't allowed in either of Calistoga's municipal parks, but if you're camping, or visiting one of two private roadside attractions (see Lodgings and Campgrounds, and Diversions), your dog will feel at home here. One campground actually has a lake where your dog is welcome to take a dip. The only public park that allows dogs is in the nearby Bothe-Napa State Park, and the rules there are so strict it's barely worth a sniff.

Bothe-Napa State Park

Dogs are relegated to the paved roads, and it's a crime because of all the alluring trails. Hiking the highways can be fun, though: Joe seemed especially captivated by a man who was burning bacon over the campfire, his wife yelling that this was *some* vacation.

A wilderness haven this park is not, at least for you and your dog. Dogs must be leashed at all times. One of the two roads they're allowed on parallels Highway 29 and is so close you can see the drivers' eyes, bloodshot from too much wine-tasting.

On the positive end, the roads are stunning in autumn when the leaves change color. And dogs are allowed to camp with you, on-leash. Dogs are also allowed in some of the picnic areas just off the roads.

4-1a The park is on Highway 29, halfway between St. Helena and Calistoga, just north of Bale Lane. The entrance is on the west side of the road, and the address is 3801 North St. Helena Highway (Highway 29). Day use fee is $5; the park is open from 8 a.m. to sunset. (707) 942-4575.

RESTAURANTS

Calistoga Drive Inn: Plenty of outdoor tables for dining on good drive-in style food. 1207 Foothill Boulevard (Highway 128). (707) 942-0543.

Home Plate: Far from the tourist parking woes in town, this inexpensive, unassuming short-order restaurant makes some of the best grilled cheese sandwiches that ever melted in a mouth. Dine at one of three big outdoor tables. 2448 Foothill Boulevard (Highway 128). (707) 942-5646.

Lord Derby Arms English Pub & Restaurant: You drink one of 11 import beers offered on draft here, and your dog can drink a fine bowl of water supplied by the staff. The outside deck, also known as the beer garden, has 13 shaded tables and is comfortable on all but the hottest of afternoons. Food is served until late at night, and you can choose from typical English pub grub like fish and chips or bangers and mash. 1923 Lake Street. (707) 942-9155.

LODGINGS & CAMPGROUNDS

Bothe-Napa State Park: Campsites are $14, plus $1 extra for the dog. Call (800) 444-PARK for reservations.

Calistoga Ranch Campground RV Resort: There's a lake here where dogs love to swim, but otherwise you're asked to keep them on-leash on the hiking trails and in the camping areas. The owners keep guinea hens to keep the rattlesnakes away, and you don't want your puppy to tangle with either creature. Tent camping is $16. RV sites are $16 to $18. It's $1 extra for a dog. 580 Lommel Road. (707) 942-6565.

Napa County Fairgrounds: A far cry from the great outdoors, this flat landscape with few trees is at least a good, inexpensive campground if all the motels are booked. Dogs must be on-leash, and you're allowed to bring one dog in free of charge. Tent sites are $10, RV sites $12. 1435 Oak Street. (707) 942-5111.

Pink Mansion: An 1875 Victorian, very picturesque and very pink. The owners love dogs—they have a huge one themselves. But if you have a bird dog or a cat dog, think twice about staying here: Also in residence are chickens, doves and felines. Double rooms cost right around $95. 1415 Foothill Boulevard (Highway 128). (707) 942-0558.

Washington Street Lodging: Relax in any of several cabins, each with its own little kitchen. You're just a couple of blocks from Calistoga's main drag here. The owner has a cat, but she says if the cat doesn't like your dog, he'll make himself scarce. Average price for a double is $80. 1605 Washington Street. (707) 942-6968.

FAIRS & FESTIVALS

Calistoga Community Christmas Bazaar: Go Christmas shopping with your leashed dog at this big sale with dozens of booths. Every December at the Napa County Fairgrounds. (707) 942-5111.

DIVERSIONS

The two places dogs can actually roam among the trees in this town happen to be at two private roadside attractions. Call them kitschy, call them tacky—they're more fun to explore than most public parks in this county.

Sniff out a petrified forest: You and your leashed dog can roam among trees entombed by a volcanic explosions 3.4 million years ago. **The Petrified Forest** is at 4100 Petrified Forest Road, off Highway 128. It's actually in the outskirts of Sonoma County, but its address is in Calistoga. The trail is a quarter-mile loop, partly paved. Admission is $3 for adults. There are dozens of tables around the gift shop, so pack a picnic. Open from 10 a.m. to 6 p.m. in summer, 10 a.m. to 5 p.m. in winter. (707) 942-6667.

During a summertime visit, Joe found out why they call it the Petrified Forest. For him, it had nothing to do with the fact that we were surrounded by trees of stone. The sign announced in big bold letters, "Once Towering Redwoods—Now the Rock of Ages." But Joe didn't know the true meaning of petrified until we encountered—the elves.

They were the Elves of Ages, the ceramic kind you find on suburban lawns and know beyond a doubt they'll be discovered by archaelogists a million years from now. The ones with the leering grins and bewitching eyes that children find enchanting by day and have nightmares about at night. They appeared everywhere Joe looked—sitting beside giant ceramic storybooks, standing beside stony trees.

The elves were at eye level for an airedale, and they were all staring at him. Every time he saw a new one, he backed away with his tail between his legs and twisted his head around to make sure it wasn't following him. We couldn't help wondering how airedales have been so popular for front-line duty during wars.

But then came the petrifying elf. He didn't look any different from the others. But as soon as Joe laid eyes on him and his donkey companion, his tail went down and he turned 90 degrees. For at least two minutes, he was too frightened to look at the elf, growling instead at a manzanita tree. When he peeked and the elf was still staring at him, he decided enough was enough and bolted—leash and all.

He was waiting by the wishing well when we finally caught up to him. He would have left the park if he could have negotiated the turnstile by himself.—M.G.

See Old Faithful in your own back yard: You know you're in for a treat when a big sign greets you at the entry to Old Faithful Geyser: "Many Notable People Have Come to SEE HEAR AND LEARN the mysteries of this WONDER OF NATURE which captures the imagination. IT'S AMAZING."

And indeed, when dogs see the 350-degree plume of water gushing 60 feet into the air, they generally stare for a few seconds with their mouths agape. But the sight of tourists jumping in front of the geyser for a quick photo before the eruption subsides quickly bores them. Dogs then try to wander to the snack bar and persuade the person on the other end of the leash to buy a couple of hot dogs. But even more fascinating is the scent of goat and pig in nearby pens.

If your dog is the brave sort, don't hesitate to bring him to visit Clow, the fainting goat, or Valentino, the Vietnamese pot-bellied pig. Clow butts her head against her fence at first, but she's only playing. After a few minutes, she was calming Joe's fears by licking him on the nose. Soon he was in love. But he never quite got used to the big black pig. When Valentino grunted a swinish hello, Joe trembled and slunk away.

Old Faithful erupts every 40 minutes, and the eruptions last about five. Picnic tables are plentiful, so bring a snack or buy one here between eruptions. A sign at the site warns that dogs aren't allowed in the geyser viewing area, but you can bring your dog—securely leashed—within a safe distance of the geyser and not get scolded or scalded.

The geyser and its menagerie are between Highways 128 and 29, on Tubbs Lane. Open 9 a.m. to 6 p.m. in summer, 9 a.m. to 5 p.m. in winter. Admission is $3.50 for adults. (707) 942-6463.

4-2

LAKE BERRYESSA

PARKS, BEACHES & RECREATION AREAS

Lake Berryessa 

Lake Berryessa, the largest manmade lake in California, offers 165 miles of shoreline for human and canine enjoyment. All seven resort areas on the lake allow leashed dogs. Better yet, they allow them off-leash to swim. The summer heat is stifling here, so your dog will want to take advantage of that.

Most resorts rent fishing boats and allow dogs to go along on your angling adventure. The fishing is fantastic, especially for fall trout. It's cooler then, too, so you won't have to contend with so many water skiers, and your dog won't roast.

One resort, **Markley Cove**, offers houseboat rentals. At $1,100 for four days, it's expensive. But these houseboats can sleep 10, so when you split the price, it's reasonable, and your dog will feel right at home.

If you just want to hike and swim for an afternoon, explore the **Smittle Creek Trail**. The entrance is just north of the lake's Visitor

Center, on Knoxville Road. The trail takes you up and down the fingers of the lake. Dogs must be leashed, except when swimming.

4-2a To get to Lake Berryessa from the Rutherford area, take Highway 128 and turn left at the Lake Berryessa/Spanish Flat sign. It's a very curvy route, so take it easy if you or your dog tend toward carsickness. Hours for Smittle Creek Trail are sunrise to sunset. For more information about the lake, call the Bureau of Reclamation Visitor Information Center at (707) 966-2111. For questions about lakeside businesses, call the Lake Berryessa Chamber of Commerce at (800) 726-1256.

LODGINGS & CAMPGROUNDS

Here is a list of Lake Berryessa resorts. Prices and amenities vary depending on the season and the extent of the drought, so call the individual resorts for information.

Berryessa Marina Resort: $1 extra per day for a dog. (707) 966-2161.

Markley Cove: (800) 242-6287.

Pleasure Cove Resort: Dogs are $2 extra a day. (800) 640-4334.

Putah Creek Resort: Dogs are allowed in the lodgings here. Average cost is $43 a night. (707) 966-2116.

Rancho Monticello Resort: (707) 966-2188.

Spanish Flat Resort: Dogs aren't allowed on rental boats here. (707) 966-7700.

Steele Park: Dogs are allowed in the campground here, but not in the motel. Dog swimming is allowed. (800) 522-2123.

4-3

NAPA

The city of Napa has some 40 parks. Dogs are allowed in four, each of which has an off-leash section. You'll see dogs in some of the bigger parks, such as the Lake Hennessey Recreation Area, but they're not officially sanctioned, so we can't officially mention them.

PARKS, BEACHES & RECREATION AREAS

Alston Park

With 157 acres of rolling hills surrounded by vineyards, Alston Park seems to stretch out forever. The lower part of the land used to be a prune orchard, and these prunes are just about the only trees you'll find here.

From there on up, the park is wide-open land with a lone tree here and there. Without shade, dogs and people can fry on hot summer days. But the park is magical during early morning in the summer, or any cooler time of year.

Miles of trails take you and your dog to places far from the road and the sound of traffic. Dogs are supposed to be off-leash only in the lower, flat section of the park. Signs mark the area. It's better than nothing, and it's reasonably safe from traffic. A water fountain and a water closet also grace the entrance.

4-3a From Highway 29, take Trower Avenue southwest to the end, at Dry Creek Road. The parking lot for the park is a short jog to your right on Dry Creek Road, and across the street. Open from dawn to dusk. (707) 257-9529.

Century Oaks Park

This park is a cruel hoax on canines. Dogs are restricted to a dangerous dog run—a tiny postage stamp of an area without fences, just off a busy street. And as for the park's name, which promises granddaddy oak trees, we're talking saplings here—maybe a dozen in the whole dog run area. We don't know how many are in the rest of the park, because dogs aren't allowed there even on-leash.

4-3b The dog run area (we suggest keeping all but the most highly trained dogs on-leash here) is on Brown's Valley Road, just off Westview Drive. Park on Westview Drive and walk around the corner to the dog run. The short walk to the park, with its shade and shrubs, is more enjoyable than the park itself. Open dawn to dusk. (707) 257-9529.

John F. Kennedy Memorial Park 

Throw your dog's leash to the wind here and ramble along the **Napa River**. Dogs are allowed in the undeveloped areas near the park's boat marina. The only spot to avoid is a marshland that's more land than marsh during dry times.

Dogs enjoy chasing each other around the flat, grassy area beside the parking lot. There's also a dirt trail that runs along the river. You can take it from either side of the marina, although as of this writing, the signs designate only the south side as a dog exercise area. The scenery isn't terrific—radio towers and construction cranes dot the horizon—but dogs without a sense of decor don't seem to mind.

Dogs like to amble by the river, which is down a fair incline from the trail. But be careful if you've got a water dog, because jet-skiers and motor boaters have been known to mow over anything in their path. There's no drinking water in the dog area, and it gets mighty hot in the summer, so bring your own.

4-3c Take Highway 221 to Streblow Drive, and follow the signs past the Napa Municipal Golf Course and Napa Valley College to the boat marina/launch area. Park in the lot, and look for the trail by the river. Open from dawn to dusk. (707) 257-9529.

Shurtleff Park 

The farther away from the road you go, the better in this long, narrow park. It gets shadier and thicker with large firs and eucalyptus trees. Dogs are allowed off-leash as soon as you feel they're safe from the road.

The park is almost entirely fenced, but there are a few escape hatches. Two are at the entrance, and two others along the side that lead you into the schoolyard of Phillips Elementary School. This isn't normally a problem, unless your dog runs into the day care center at lunch time, as Joe once did. A teacher escorted him out by the scruff of his neck before he could steal someone's peanut butter sandwich.

4-3d On Shelter Street at Shurtleff, beside Phillips Elementary School. Open dawn to dusk. (707) 257-9529.

RESTAURANTS

Brown's Valley Yogurt & Espresso Bar: Cool off with a cold frozen one at the outside tables shaded by a wooden awning. 3265 Brown's Valley Road. (707) 252-4977.

Dawg Patch: If your dog likes hot dogs, then these dogs are your dog's. Eat them at the bench outside, on the way to John F. Kennedy Memorial Park. 1453 West Imola Avenue. (707) 255-8656.

Honey Treat Yogurt Shop: The non-fat frozen yogurt here will make you feel 10 pounds lighter and 10 degrees cooler after a long walk with the dog. 1080 Coombs Street. (707) 255-6633.

Rio Poco: Great burritos and easy take-out packages make eating on the outside bench a pleasure. Veteran's Park may beckon from across the street, but unfortunately you're not allowed with your dog. 807 Main Street. (707) 253-8203.

Stone and Vine: There's a new menu here every day, and the food is so delicious you won't know it's good for you. Try the triple stack garden sandwich. They've got several tables on the side that's closed to traffic. 1202 1st Street. (707) 226-1202.

Witter's Tea & Coffee Company: Two ornate old benches under the shade of two trees and an awning make this a pleasant place to sip some cappuccino. 1202 Main Street. (707) 226-2044.

LODGINGS & CAMPGROUNDS

Best Western Inn: Small dogs are welcome here. 100 Soscol Avenue, Napa, CA 94558. Average price for a double: $80. (707) 257-1930.

Clarion Inn Napa Valley: 3425 Solano Avenue, Napa, CA 94402. Average room price: $75. Dogs are $10 extra per day. (707) 253-7433.

FAIRS & FESTIVALS

Napa has several street fairs throughout the year, but most are so crowded that we recommend dogs stay home. The only exception:

Christmas Kickoff Parade: Santa visits the wine country and winds through downtown Napa in late November. (707) 257-0322.

4-4

OAKVILLE

While there aren't any parks in this town of 300 people, there are a few good places to dine with your dog while resting between wine country destinations.

RESTAURANTS

Ambrose Heath: As if an elegant, shady back patio with a fountain and a garden view weren't enough, the gourmet-style California food is delicious, too. The staff will also give your dog a bowl of water, making this a favorite of ours. 7848 St. Helena Highway (Highway 29). (707) 944-0766.

Oakville Grocery: Buy some eats inside and consume them on the antique benches out front. 7856 St. Helena Highway (Highway 29). (707) 944-8802.

Pometta's Delicatessen: Barbecued chicken is the specialty, so watch out for bones if you bring your dog to the outdoor tables here. The owners have some friendly dogs of their own. 7787 St. Helena Highway (Highway 29). (707) 944-2365.

4-5

ST. HELENA

PARKS, BEACHES & RECREATION AREAS

Baldwin Park 

Baldwin Park has everything you could want in a park, except size. But what it lacks in acreage, it makes up for in dog appeal. Set off a small road, it's almost entirely fenced in and full of flowering trees, oaks and big pines. A dirt path winds through green grass from one end of the park to the other, passing by a water fountain and a conveniently placed garbage can.

Unfortunately, dogs must be leashed, but it's still a pleasant place to stretch all your legs after a tour through wine country. Open dawn to dusk.

4-5a On Spring Street between Stockton Street and North Crane Avenue. (707) 963-5706.

Crane Park 

If you bring your dog here on a sunny weekend, you'll be bombarded with softballs, volleyballs, soccer balls, baseballs, tennis balls and a horseshoe or two. Not to mention evil glares from the people whose games you've interrupted. Best to visit during the week, when this sports-oriented park is a little less busy.

The shady, wooded area in the rear of the park is the best place for dogs. Although they must be leashed, there's plenty of romping room. It's in the middle of a picnic area where dogs love to scour the ground with their snouts.

4-5b The park is on South Crane Avenue at Vallejo Street. Open dawn to dusk. (707) 963-5706.

Lyman Park 

You'll think you're on a movie set for some old-time village scene when you and your dog wander into this small, cozy park on historic Main Street. Leash is mandatory, but the park has a gazebo, lots of trees and benches, a flower garden and—best of all for dogs—an antique horse/dog water fountain. The top part is for horses, the lower bowl for dogs. Horses aren't allowed here anymore, so if your dog is huge, he might as well sip from the equine bowl.

4-5c The park is nestled snugly between the police station and a funeral home, at 1400 Main Street. Open from dawn to dusk. (707) 963-5706.

Stonebridge Park 

This park is so tiny that if you jog for five seconds you'll have run its entire length. It's OK for leashed dogs who have an aesthetic appreciation of landscaping, or who are desperate to relieve themselves. The spot is lush, with big oaks perched high above the Napa River. The only benches are natural ones—a stone slab at one end of the park, two logs on the other. No garbage cans litter this park, so when your dog does her thing, you must do yours and drive it to the nearest trash barrel.

4-5d On Pope Street, just south of the river. Open dawn to dusk. (707) 963-5706.

Restaurants

Showley's at Miramonte: "West Coast fresh" is how this place describes the sumptuous food. At 1327 Railroad Avenue. (707) 963-1200.

Taylor's Refresher: Ice cream, burgers and lots of outdoor tables. 933 Main Street. (707) 963-3486.

Valley Deli: Good deli food, and a couple of sidewalk tables. 1138 Main Street. (707) 963-7710.

Vintner's Village: This extensive wine country center just north of town has an outdoor deck at a deli and a huge, shady picnic area, where dogs love to join their owners as they sample wine. 3111 North St. Helena Highway (Highway 29). Call (707) 963-4082 for information on the deli, picnicking and wine tasting.

Lodgings & Campgrounds

Harvest Inn: Leashed dogs who stay in this tudor-style lodging can wander the inn's 21 acres of gardens, vineyards, fields and ponds. They prefer small dogs here, and there's a $5 per night charge for them. Average price for a double is $170. At One Main Street, St. Helena, CA 94574. (707) 963-WINE.

Hyphen Inn: Stay in one of two country cottages, each with a patio, in the middle of this large, lush country estate. Dog-friendly owners serve up a fresh European breakfast. Cottages are approximately $135. Since this is a private residence, the owners don't give their address unless you stay there. The mailing address is PO Box 190, St. Helena, CA 94574. (707) 942-0434.

4-6

YOUNTVILLE

Unlike the Yountville town government, which bans dogs from its parks, restaurateurs here have the right idea. Several exquisite restaurants welcome dogs to their patios, which are generally shaded and very accommodating to people and their canines. The only word of warning is to avoid these restaurants when they're packed with people from the tour buses that occasionally descend on the town. It's just too crowded for dogs, who usually get tripped on and later photographed as tourist souvenirs.

RESTAURANTS

California Cafe Bar & Grill: California cuisine reigns here, with fresh seafood as the focal point. Several outdoor tables with oversized umbrellas keep you and your dog cool. 6795 Washington Street. (707) 944-2330.

Compadres Mexican Bar & Grill: Tropical landscaping, intoxicating jasmine and honeysuckle, and umbrellas over tables make this one of the most pleasant restaurants for spending a few hours with your dog. Try the pollo borracho, a whole chicken cooked with white wine and tequila. 6539 Washington Street, at the Vintage 1870 complex. (707) 944-2406.

Java Express: This place sells espresso drinks, bakery goods, sandwiches, granola, fresh lemonade—anything you and your dog would want after being kicked out of local parks. Eat and drink and relax at the outdoor tables. 6795 Washington Street. (707) 944-9700.

Red Rock Vintage Cafe: A great place for people who love burgers or omelets. Eat with your dog at the deck in back of the cheery, ivy-covered brick building. 6535 Washington Street, at the Vintage 1870 complex. (707) 944-2614.

Yountville Market: This Old West-style building houses a general store where you can grab some edibles and snack at the benches out front. 6770 Washington Street. (707) 944-1393.

Yountville Pastry Shop: Eat pastries, sandwiches or pizza at the wooden outdoor patio. 6525 Washington Street, at the Vintage 1870 complex. (707) 944-2138.

LODGINGS & CAMPGROUNDS

Vintage Inn: This contemporary country-style hotel allows dogs for an extra cleanup fee of $35 for your entire stay. You're located right next door to some of the Bay Area's best restaurants that take dogs. Average price for a double is $135. It's at 6541 Washington Street, Yountville, CA 94599. (707) 944-1112.

MORE INFO

WHERE YOUR DOG CAN'T GO

- Heather Oaks Park, Calistoga
- Las Posadas State Forest: You'll see dogs there, but forestry people say they don't allow them in order to protect the park's flora and fauna. If you value deer, you'll take your dog to another park.
- Napa: The city of Napa has 40 parks. Dogs are allowed in only four of them. See listings under Napa.
- Napa Town and Country Fairgrounds, Napa
- Pioneer Park, Calistoga
- Robert Louis Stevenson Memorial Park
- Skyline Park
- Veteran's Park, Yountville
- Yountville Park, Yountville

USEFUL PHONE NUMBERS & ADDRESSES

Bothe-Napa State Park: 3801 North St. Helena Highway (Highway 29), Calistoga, CA 94515. (707) 942-4575. Camping reservations: Call (800) 444-7275.

Lake Berryessa Chamber of Commerce: PO Box 9164, Napa, CA 94558. (800) 726-1256.

Napa (city) Department of Parks and Recreation: PO Box 660, Napa, CA 94559. (707) 257-9529.

·San Francisco County·

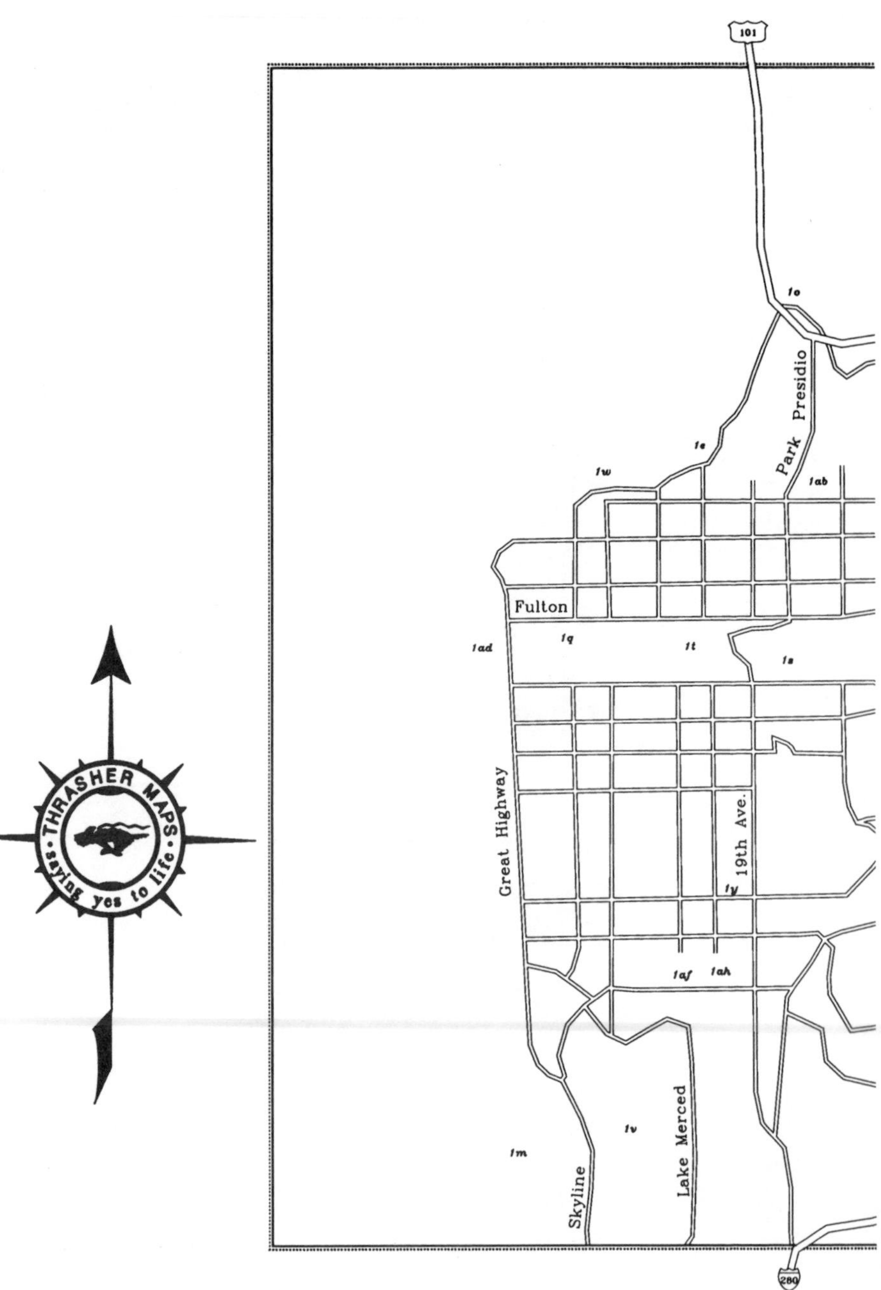
101
1o
Park Presidio
1e
1w
1ab
Fulton
1ad
1q
1t
1s
Great Highway
19th Ave.
1y
THRASHER MAPS
saying yes to life
1af
1ah
1v
1m
Skyline
Lake Merced
280

5. SAN FRANCISCO COUNTY (map page 144-145)

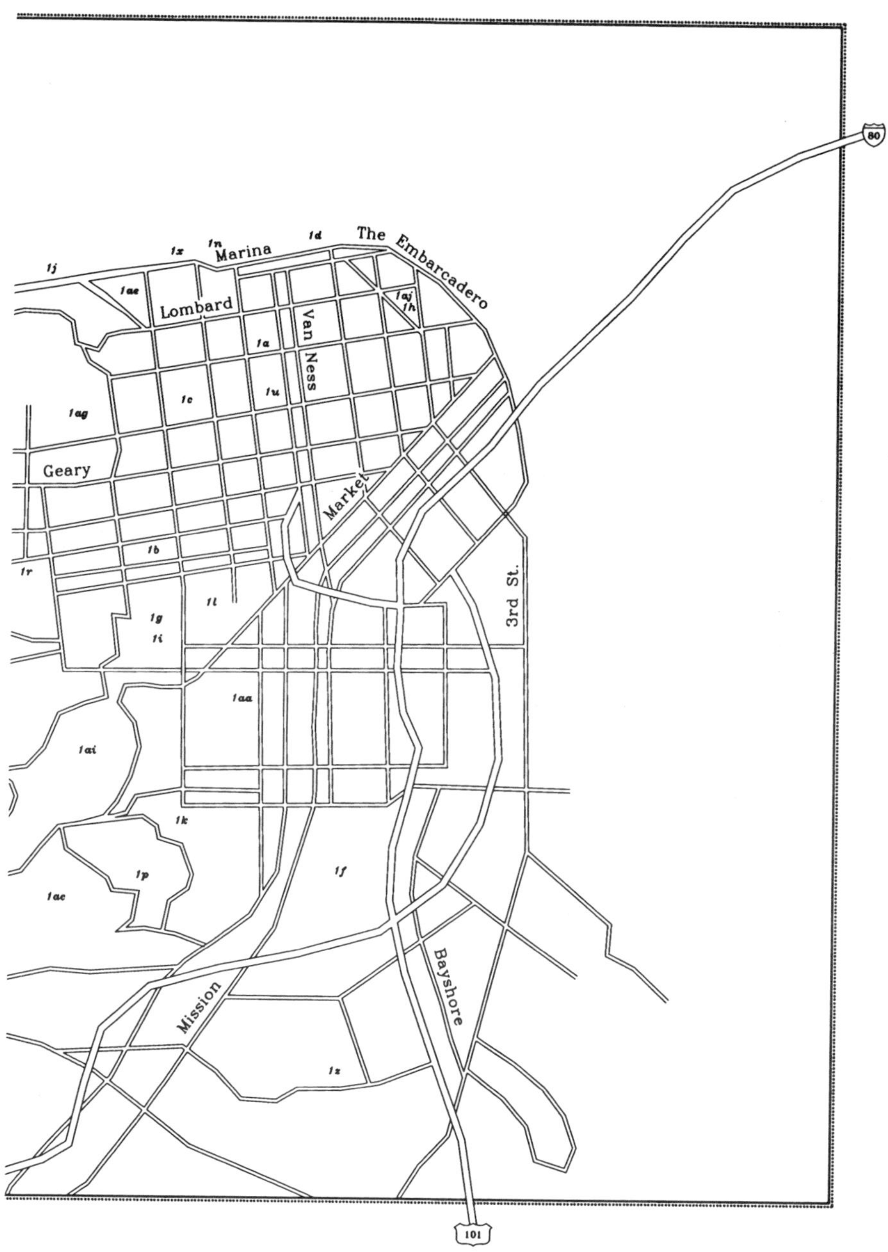

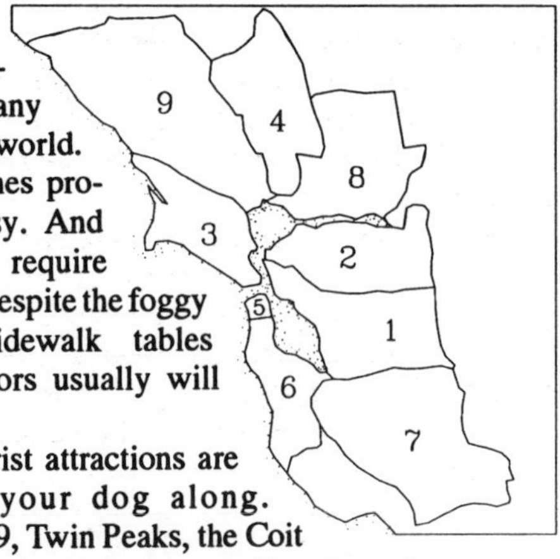

5

San Francisco probably offers a better life for dogs than any other major city in the world. Some 25 parks and beaches provide off-leash dog ecstasy. And most of those that do require leashes are also first rate. Despite the foggy weather, cafes with sidewalk tables abound, and the proprietors usually will welcome your hound.

The city's biggest tourist attractions are perfect for bringing your dog along. Fisherman's Wharf, Pier 39, Twin Peaks, the Coit Tower grounds—you name it, dogs are probably allowed.

Many of the city's parks are so woodsy that there's no way to tell you're only a few miles from the center of a bustling metropolis. That's what makes San Francisco a paradise on Earth for dogs, as well as for dog-loving people.

5-1

SAN FRANCISCO

PARKS, BEACHES & RECREATION AREAS

Allyne Park 🐾🐾

This one's known as one of the most romantic little parks in the city; your dog may get into trouble here if she doesn't watch her step. On sunny days or moonlit nights, you're almost sure to find friends and lovers lazing around on the grass, gazing into each other's eyes, blissfully unaware that your dog is about to swipe the French bread from their picnic basket.

We like this park because it's enclosed by a tall wooden fence. But watch out if you have small dogs; they can escape underneath certain sections of the fence and gate. Because of the cultivated gardens, and because people frequently leave the park's two gates open, dogs must be on-leash.

5-1a At the corner of Green and Gough streets. Open 6 a.m. to 10 p.m. (415) 666-7200.

Alamo Square Park 

A postcard comes to life here for you and your dog. This is where the famed Painted Ladies hold court over the city. These six brightly colored Victorian homes are even better in person than they are on a postcard.

Walk up the east side of the park, near Steiner Street, to enjoy the view of the old houses with the modern city skyline in the background. If your dog doesn't care about architecture, she'll love the fields and hills that make up this park. There's plenty of room to roam on-leash. There's also a playground and a tennis court.

5-1b The park is bordered by Fulton, Hayes, Scott and Steiner streets. Open 6 a.m. to 10 p.m. (415) 666-7200.

Alta Plaza Park 

Smack in the middle of Pacific Heights, this park is where all the best breeds and most magnificent mutts gather daily. They flock to the hill on the north side of the park and conduct their dog business in the most discriminating fashion. It's not uncommon to see 25 dogs trotting around the park. Owners often address each other by their dogs' names—"Shane's mom! How are you?"

Make sure to visit the **Dog Park Walk of Fame** while you're up there—two long cement gutters with dozens of dog names carved into them. For two days after the cement was poured alongside the paved path in 1991, dog owners with sticks or keys got down on hands and knees and engraved their dogs into immortality.

The park's off-leash run is actually on the other side of the playground and tennis courts, on the second level up from Clay Street. You can distinguish it by the two cement trash cans that warn non-dog owners, "Dog Litter Only." Bushes line the paved walkway, and it's far enough from traffic that you don't have to worry about cars.

5-1c The park is bordered by Jackson, Clay, Steiner and Scott streets. Open 6 a.m. to 10 p.m. (415) 666-7200.

Aquatic Park 

You've got tourist friends in town and don't feel like taking them for the usual amble through Fisherman's Wharf? Here's a great plan that lets you be semi-sporting about the whole thing while you take your dog for a jaunt. Drop them off at Aquatic Park, point them toward the tourist attractions and walk your dog right there.

Aquatic Park is just a few minutes from Ghirardelli Square, Fisherman's Wharf, a cable car line and the Hyde Street Pier. It's also a decent place for a leashed dog to romp, with its large grassy field and plenty of pine trees, benches and flowers. But stay away from the little beach—no dogs allowed. If you feel like shopping for T-shirts, jewelry or arts and crafts, you can take your dog along **Beach Street**, where dozens of sidewalk vendors sell their wares (see DIVERSIONS, page 171).

5-1d The park is on Beach Street between Hyde and Polk streets. Open 24 hours. (415) 556-2904.

Baker Beach 

This beach brings your dog as close as she can get off-leash to the ocean side of the Golden Gate Bridge. And what a sight it is. Though in summer you shouldn't hold out much hope for a sunny day here, this sandy shoreline is ideal for a romp in the misty air. And dogs really appreciate Baker Beach in the summer. It's almost always cool and breezy.

If you like to sunbathe without a bathing suit and want to take your dog along, the very north end of the beach (closest to the bridge) is perfect. It's the only official nude beach in Northern California where dogs are welcome. Make sure he doesn't get too up-close and personal with your exposed co-bathers.

The south end is also intriguing, but dogs must be on-leash. There are trails to explore and lots of picnic tables behind both ends of the beach. Leashes are required here, too. Also behind the beach is **Battery Chamberlain**, with its 95,000-pound cannon aimed toward the sea.

5-1e From either direction take Lincoln Boulevard to Bowley Street, then make the first turn onto Gibson Road. You'll find two parking lots. The first one will put you closer to the off-leash area, which starts at the north end of the lot, closest to the Golden Gate Bridge. The beach is open 24 hours, but parking lots are open only from 6 a.m. to 10 p.m. in the summer and 6 a.m. to 7 p.m. in winter. (415) 556-8371.

Bernal Heights Park 

The last time we visited this park, a dozen wolf-shepherds were the only dogs atop the amber hill. They ran and played in such pure wolf fashion it was hard to believe they weren't the genuine item. The icy wind hit the powerlines overhead and made a low, Arctic whistle.

The scene left an indelible impression that even in the middle of a city like San Francisco, the wild is just beneath the surface.

The rugged hills here are fairly rigorous for bipeds, but dogs have a magnificent time bolting up and down. Humans can enjoy the view of the Golden Gate and Bay Bridges. The vista makes up for the austere look of the treeless park. Dogs are allowed off-leash on the hills bordered by Bernal Heights Boulevard. It can be very windy and cold, so bundle up.

5-1f Enter at Carver Street and Bernal Heights Boulevard, or keep going on Bernal Heights Boulevard until just past Anderson Street. Open 6 a.m. to 10 p.m. (415) 666-7200.

Buena Vista Park 

The presence of vagrants who sometimes congregate at the front of the park has scared off lots of would-be park users, but it shouldn't. They're generally a friendly lot, posing no threat to folks exploring the park's upper limits with a dog.

This park is a real find for anyone living near the Haight-Ashbury district. Hike along the myriad dirt and paved trails winding through the hills, enveloped by eucalyptus and redwood trees. Some of the gutters are lined with pieces of tombstone from a nearby cemetery. Its occupants, who died in the 1800s, were moved to Colma earlier this century. The gutters give the park a historical, haunted feeling.

From the top of the park, you can see the ocean, the bay, the Marin headlands and both the Golden Gate and Bay Bridges. Birds sing everywhere. And there are lots of benches to rest on. Dogs are allowed off-leash at the woodsy west side of the park, near Central Street.

A note: Sometimes people meet for assignations at the top of the park. If this bothers you or your dog, avoid this lovers' lane.

5-1g Enter at Buena Vista Avenue West and Central Street, or from Haight Street. Open 6 a.m. to 10 p.m. (415) 666-7200.

Coit Tower 

Dogs enjoy a nocturnal romp here as much as people do. And since they aren't allowed inside the tower, you're not missing anything but a traffic jam if you visit here after dark.

The giant lighted column must look like a huge fire hydrant to dogs; when they see it, their noses go wild. It was erected with the funds of Lillie Hitchcock Coit, a woman who had a penchant for firefighters, so maybe our pooches are onto something.

But don't let your leashed dog use the building as a source of relief. There are plenty of trees and bushes he can try to extinguish instead, while you gaze at the sparkling city lights in every direction.

5-1h We like to park at the bottom of Telegraph Hill, at Lombard Street, and walk up the winding inner path to the top. You can also continue up Lombard as it becomes the winding Telegraph Hill Boulevard and leads you to the tower. The tower itself is open from 10 a.m. to 5 p.m., but the grounds are open from 6 a.m. to 10 p.m. (415) 666-7200.

Corona Heights Park

The rust-colored boulders atop this park cast long, surreal shadows at dawn. If you and your dog are early risers, it's worth the hike to the summit to witness this. And there's a fine view any time of day of downtown and the Castro district.

Unfortunately, dogs aren't allowed off-leash on hikes up the hill. Their off-leash area is a roomy square of grass at the foot. Your best bet is to park at Museum Way and Roosevelt Avenue, and let your dog run with other dogs in the leash-free section there. Then you can go together up the hill. Fences keep dogs and people from falling down the steep cliffs. Keep in mind that there's virtually no shade, so if you have a black rug of a dog, think twice about climbing the hill on hot, sunny days.

5-1i At Museum Way and Roosevelt Avenue. Open 6 a.m. to 10 p.m. (415) 666-7200.

Crissy Field

There's nothing quite like Crissy Field at sunset: As the orange sun disappears behind the Golden Gate Bridge, you'll be viewing one of the most stunning blends of natural and manmade wonders in the world.

Crissy Field is a jewel of a park any time of day. Dogs can chase and cavort up and down the beach, and jump into the bay whenever they feel like it. It's one of very few spots in the Bay Area where they are allowed to swim in the bay. This is a particularly good place to bring a dog who has no desire to brave the waves of the Pacific. The surf here doesn't pound, it merely laps.

As you walk westward, the Golden Gate Bridge is before you, Alcatraz and bits of the city skyline behind you. Sailboats sometimes glide so close you can hear the sails flagging in the wind. There's a stretch of trees and picnic tables a few minutes into your walk, a good place to relax while your dog investigates the scents. There's also a heavily used jogging/biking path parallel to the beach, but we don't advise you to take your unleashed dog there. He's likely to get underfoot.

If the tide is low, you can walk to the end of the beach, put your dog on the leash and continue to **Fort Point** (see Fort Point listing, page 153).

5-1j Enter on Mason Street, driving past the warehouses. Go right on Mitchell Street and through a big, rough parking lot. If you go too far to the east, you'll run into a sea of windsurfers, so try starting your walk close to the western edge of the parking lot. The beach is bordered by delicate dunes undergoing restoration in many places, including the entrance, so keep canines off. Open 24 hours. (415) 556-0560.

Douglass Playground 

At first glance, this park seems to hold a lot of promise. It's fairly large, and dogs are allowed off-leash in one section. Unfortunately, that off-leash area is a skinny little path high above a baseball field. You're separated from the field by a chain link fence, but nothing of any consequence comes between you and the road. And dogs are just plain banned from most of the rest of the park. This is not a dog's idea of a good time.

5-1k Enter the dog run area at the end of 27th Street, off Douglass Street. Open 6 a.m. to 10 p.m. (415) 666-7200.

Duboce Park 

If peering into people's windows is your dog's idea of fun, this urban park is his kind of place. A couple of large buildings have ground-floor windows that seem to fascinate dogs. Perhaps there's a cat colony inside.

Your dog will probably find other dogs here to play with. They're supposed to be leashed, since they're never more than a few fast steps from the nearest street. The park is grassy and has pines and a variety of smaller trees around some of its borders. There's also a children's playground at the west end.

5-1l At Duboce Avenue between Steiner and Scott streets. Open 6 a.m. to 10 p.m. (415) 666-7200.

Fort Funston 

If there were a heaven on Earth for dogs, this would be it. This scenic ocean park lives up to its nickname—Fort Fun. It combines trails through wooded and dune areas, an eerie walk through an old military battery, and miles of ocean and sand. The best part is that even on gloomy days, you're sure to find other dogs cruising the park for a good time. It's the perfect mingling of environment and companionship, and it's all *sans* leash.

Starting from the main parking lot, next to the take-off cliff for hang gliders, you can bring your dog to the watering hole—actually a bowl underneath a drinking fountain—and fill her up. From the take-off cliff you can follow a steep trail down to the beach, but we recommend exploring above first.

Take the first trail to the north of the parking lot, and you'll meander through dunes and ice plant, encountering every kind of dog imaginable. You'll soon come to the main entrance to **Battery Davis**, which was built in 1939 to protect San Francisco from enemy ship bombardment. It's now very dark and empty, and you can still enter the chambers hidden within. Bring your flashlight, a friend, your dog and some bravery. Local kids can do some great ghost imitations. Your dog is good for warding off bogeymen, unless she won't go in at all.

Or you can skip the battery and continue along on trails on either side. Both eventually end up in the same place. If you take the trail at the rear of the battery, you'll quickly be able to see the Golden Gate Bridge and the Cliff House. At that point, you'll also see a trail that takes you back into a mini-forest. Don't go all the way down, though, or you'll end up on Highway 35.

Back on the main trails, continue past a little grove of redwoods, near the merging of the two trails. If you keep going north, there's actually a way to walk all the way to the **Golden Gate Bridge**. But be forewarned: It's a long haul—almost eight miles to **Baker Beach** alone, and more than another mile after that to the bridge.

You can get to the beach at Fort Funston by following the thin trails through the dunes shortly after the cypress groves. You'll notice that one takes you between two cliffs. Take it all the way down to the beach. Depending on the tide, you can walk for miles or just a few feet.

You can go back the way you came, or walk along the ocean and take the steep trail back up to the main parking lot. By this time, you and your dog will both be thirsting for that water fountain.

5-1m To get to Fort Funston, follow the brown signs on the Great Highway. It's about one-half mile south of the turnoff to John Muir Drive. Once on the main drive, bear right, past a little building painted with hang gliders, and drive into the main parking lot. The beach and trails are open 24 hours, but the parking lot is open only from 6 a.m. to dusk. (415) 556-8371.

Fort Mason

This park, perched high above the bay, is full of surprises. Depending on the disposition of your dog, some of the surprises are great fun. One can be downright frightening.

The best stands right in the middle of the wide open field that constitutes the main part of the park. It's a fire hydrant, and it sticks out like a sore yellow thumb from its flat green surroundings. Joyous male dogs bound up and pay it homage time and time again.

The object that seems to take dogs aback, although people find it riveting, is a gigantic bronze statue of Phillip Burton. Several feet taller and broader than life, with outstretched hand, it can send a dog fleeing as far as his mandatory leash will allow.

Lower Fort Mason is also interesting to investigate. You can walk alongside the piers and sniff the bay, or peer at the liberty ship *Jeremiah O'Brien.*

5-1n Enter the lower Fort Mason parking lot at Buchanan Street and take the stairs all the way up to upper Fort Mason. Or park along Bay Street or Laguna Street and walk in. Open 24 hours. (415) 556-0560.

Fort Point National Historical Site 

Beneath the Golden Gate Bridge, this mid-19th century brick fortification stands as a reminder of the strategic military significance San Francisco once had. Now it serves as a tourist attraction and one of the best places to view the skyline, Alcatraz and the bridge. It's also a magnificent spot for your dog to stand mesmerized by the crashing surf.

By itself, Fort Point doesn't offer much for dogs. They must be leashed, and there's only a small patch of grass. We recommend Fort Point as the goal of a long hike that starts at **Crissy Field** (see the Crissy Field listing, page 150). After walking to the west end of Crissy

Field, leash your dog and follow the **Golden Gate Promenade** toward the bridge.

Along the way, you'll come to an old pier. There are actually two piers, but the one you're allowed on is closer to the bridge. Stroll to the end for a close-up view of sailboats being tossed about on the bay. When you finally reach Fort Point, it's a tradition among dog people to continue to the westernmost point and touch the fence. There's no telling why, but you may as well try it.

5-1o To get to Fort Point without a long hike, follow the signs from Lincoln Avenue as you approach the Golden Gate Bridge. The trails and grassy areas are open 24 hours, but parking is available only from 10 a.m. to 5 p.m. (415) 556-1693.

Glen Canyon Park

From the redwood forests to the streams and grassy hills, this park was made for you and your dog. If you want to forget you've ever been in a city, this is the place to come.

The nature trail in the middle of the park follows a muddy creek and is so overgrown with brush and bramble that at times you nearly have to crawl. It's as though the trail were blazed for dogs. There are so many dragonflies of all colors and sizes near the creek, and so much lush vegetation, that you may wonder if you've stepped back to the age of the dinosaurs.

Park at Bosworth Street and O'Shaughnessy Boulevard and walk down a dirt trail past a recreation center, through the redwoods and loud birds. Stay away from the paved road—it can look deserted for hours on end, then a car whizzes by. Your dog is supposed to be leashed, but you should still be aware of the road. In a few minutes, you'll come to a long, low building. At this point, you can go left and up a hill for some secluded picnic spots, or keep going and take the nature trail. When you finally emerge from the dragonflies and dense greenery, take any of several trails up the open, rolling hills and enjoy a panorama of the park.

5-1p At Bosworth Street and O'Shaughnessy Boulevard. Open 6 a.m. to 10 p.m. (415) 666-7200.

Golden Gate Park

This famed city park provides much dog bliss, but only in the places where dogs are supposed to be leashed. Four areas are set aside for leashless dogs, but dogs-in-the-know try not to go to *those* places, for good reason.

There's a dog-run over by the buffalo, for example. It's a grassless, dusty, chain-linked pen designed for owners who'd rather go for a talk than a walk. Dogs tend to sniff each other and sit, sniff each other and take a drink from the water bowls.

We've found more amorous dogs here than in any other park, so if your dog isn't in the mood (or you don't want her to be), this isn't the place to take her.

5-1q But just in case, it's at 38th Avenue and Fulton Street. Park on Fulton Street and walk in, or take 36th Avenue into the park and go right at the first paved road. Drive all the way to the end, and there it is.

Golden Gate Park (northeast corner) 

Then there are the narrow fields at the northeast corner of the park, up by the horseshoe courts. It's a strange little area with hills and dales and dirt paths. Homeless people live here, and some don't keep good house. You'll see the campfire remains, old sleeping bags, and trash of every type. It's best to avoid this place, except in the middle of the day.

5-1r Enter at Stanyan and Fulton streets.

Golden Gate Park (south side) 

The two other areas set aside for dogs are slivers along the south end of the park. One is between Second and Seventh Avenues, and bounded on the north and south by Lincoln Way and Martin Luther King Jr. Drive. The other is on the south side of the polo field, between 34th and 38th Avenues, and Middle Drive and Martin Luther King Jr. Drive. Bring your dog to these sections if he's very good off-leash. They're too close to busy traffic for less disciplined dogs.

Golden Gate Park (Stow Lake) 

One of the *in* places in Golden Gate Park is the summit of the manmade mountain at **Stow Lake**. It's truly a sniffer's paradise. Dogs who like to look at ducks will also enjoy it. The path winds up Strawberry Hill to a breathtaking 360-degree view of the city. Unfortunately, dogs are not supposed to be off-leash. It's best to avoid this walk on weekends, when bikers and hikers are everywhere.

5-1s Stow Lake is between 15th and 19th avenues. From John F. Kennedy Drive or Martin Luther King Jr. Drive, follow the Stow Lake signs.

Golden Gate Park (by the Polo Field) 

Dogs who prefer playing Frisbee (on leash) go to the meadow just east of the polo field. It's known for wide-open dells, good bushes and plenty of gopher holes for old sports. Your best bet here is to go early in the morning.

Golden Gate Park (horse paths) 

Dogs who like to promenade—to see and be seen—take to the horse paths that radiate out from the stables. Or you can simply walk along the track that circles the field. One word of caution: The stables are rife with cats. Dogs need to know this. Leashes are mandatory, and remember—the mounted police station is uncomfortably close by.

Golden Gate Park (The Panhandle) 

That long, thin strip of park that extends eight blocks from the east end of the park to Baker Street, is a great hangout for cool dogs. It's got a real Haight-Ashbury influence in parts, and although dogs must be leashed, they love to saunter around visiting other dogs wearing bandannas.

Golden Gate Park (other spots) 

Other lesser known areas include the paths in back of **Beach Chalet**—the soccer fields between the windmills near the ocean. The paths, which run along the edge of the fields, can be a little unsavory—but to leashed dogs, they're full of nothing but good smells. There's also the hilly, piney area up behind the archery field. We haven't heard of any accidental impalements up there, but be careful.

5-1t All of Golden Gate Park is open from 6 a.m. to 10 p.m. (415) 666-7200.

Lafayette Park 

This four-square-block park gets lots of dog traffic. For some reason, even though they have a legal grassy, off-leash section, dogs prefer to play on the paved paths in front of the playground here. At least it's good for their nails.

The park is hilly and green and studded with palm trees, redwoods and well-trimmed bushes. The official dog run area is near Sacramento Street, between Octavia and Gough streets. As you enter the park from the main Sacramento Street entrance, it's on your right.

But most dogs gather atop the hill to the left, around two huge, smelly garbage cans.

5-1u The park is bounded by Laguna, Gough, Sacramento and Washington streets. Open from 10 a.m. to 6 p.m. (415) 666-7200.

Lake Merced 

As the city's largest body of water, Lake Merced is favored by Labrador retrievers, Irish setters and the like. An ideal spot to explore is the footbridge area near the south end of the lake. There are a couple of sandy beaches there that are safe from traffic, but dogs are supposed to be leashed anyway. Once you cross the bridge, you'll come to an inviting area with lots of little trees.

You'll enter a small grassy section and come to a narrow dirt trail overlooking the lake's northeast bowl. We don't recommend letting dogs off the leash until you're at least a couple of hundred feet into the park, because menacing traffic is so close by. There are birds galore and purple wildflowers in spring. The park is a tease, though, because there's no way to get to the lake—it's down a very formidable slope covered with impenetrable brush.

5-1v The off-leash section of Lake Merced is at the north end, at Lake Merced Boulevard and Middlefield Drive. Park at Middlefield Drive and Gellert Drive, and cross Lake Merced Boulevard—very carefully. At times it's like a race car track. Open 6 a.m. to 10 p.m. (415) 666-7200.

Land's End 

This is probably the most spectacular park in San Francisco. You won't believe your eyes and your dog won't believe his nose. And neither of you will believe your ears—it's so far removed from traffic that all you hear are foghorns, the calls of birds and the wind whistling through the redwoods and eucalptus. The best part: No leashes.

The towering cliffs, high above the crashing tide below, overlook virtually no civilization. For miles, all you can see is ocean, cliffs, trees, wildflowers and boats. It looks more like Mendocino did 100 years ago—at least until you round one final bend and the Golden Gate Bridge jars your senses back to semi-urban reality.

If you want to venture the entire length of the dirt trail, keep two things in mind: Don't wear tight pants—you'll have to do some high stepping in some spots, and you don't want your legs packed into your Levi's—and don't bring a young puppy or out-of-control dog.

The cliffs here can be dangerous, especially where the trail becomes narrow.

There are many entrance points, but we like to start from the parking lot at the end of Camino del Mar. Go down the wooden steps to the wide dirt trail and turn right. As you hike, you'll come to occasional wood benches overlooking wildly beautiful seascapes. Take a moment to sit down. Your dog will appreciate the chance to contemplate the wondrous odors coming through her bulbous olfactory sensor.

As you continue, you'll pass a sign that makes its point efficiently and effectively: "Caution! Cliff and surf are extremely dangerous. People have been swept from the rocks and drowned." You'll have no problem if you proceed on the main trail and ignore the temptation to follow the dozens of tiny paths down the cliff face.

In a little while, you'll come to the second such sign. This time, instead of continuing on the main path (it gets extremely precarious, even for the most sure-footed), take the trail to your right. It's a fairly hard slope, but it's safe and gets you where you want to go.

Rest at the bench halfway up, if you feel the need. The trail will soon bring you down and around to an incredible view. Keep going, and turn around when you're ready to go home. Try not to end up on the golf course, though. Golfers don't appreciate canines at tee-off time.

5-1w At the end of Camino del Mar. Open 24 hours. (415) 556-8371.

Marina Green 

The clang of halyards against masts creates a magical symphony from the nearby marinas here on windy days. Your dog's first reaction may be a puzzled 30-degree head tilt.

Most of us know the Marina Green for its high-flying kites and hard-running joggers. But it's also a decent place to take your dog, as long as he's leashed. It's too close to the rush of cars on Marina Boulevard to be comfortable off-leash, anyway.

The grass is always green here, as the park's name indicates. It's a treat for eyes overdosed on dry yellow grass and paws laden with foxtails. There's also an attractive heart parcourse, and a great view of Alcatraz.

5-1x Enter on Marina Boulevard, anywhere between Scott and Buchanan streets. Open 24 hours. (415) 556-0560.

McCoppin Square 

Bordered by trees and dotted with shrubs, this two-block-long park is a convenient area for your leashed dog at times when you can't take her to a better spot. But if there's a softball game going on, you may as well stay clear—there's barely room for outfielders here.

5-1y Enter on Santiago Street, between 22nd and 24th Avenues. Open 6 a.m. to 10 p.m. (415) 666-7200.

McLaren Park 

You and your dog can enter this park anywhere and find a trail within seconds. The surprise is that most of the trails run through remote wooded areas and windswept hills with sweeping views.

It's an ideal place to visit if you're taking someone to play soccer at the **Crocker-Amazon Playground**. They play, you walk up a hill behind the soccer fields and roam with your leashed dog. Better yet, drive to the northern part of the park, to the section bounded by John F. Shelley Drive. Dogs are allowed off-leash here, where they're far enough from traffic. Certain parts can be crowded with schoolchildren or company picnickers, so watch where you wander.

5-1z There are many entry points, but we prefer Brazil Avenue, which turns into Mansell Street in the park. Open from 6 a.m. to 10 p.m. (415) 666-7200.

Mission Dolores Park 

You can get a little history lesson while walking your dog here. A statue of Miguel Hidalgo overlooks the park, and Mexico's liberty bell hangs at the Dolores Street entrance.

History may not impress your dog, but a wide-open space for running off-leash will. It's behind the tennis courts.

There are two problems with this area, though. One: It's easy for your dog to run into the road. Even if she's the voice control type, she could find herself in Church Street traffic just by running a little too far to catch a ball.

And two: You have to be on the lookout that your dog doesn't run over people who live in the park. Joe once slid into a sleeping homeless woman and scared her so badly she screamed and ran away.

5-1aa Enter anywhere on Dolores or Church streets, between 18th and 20th Streets. Open 6 a.m. to 10 p.m. (415) 666-7200.

Mountain Lake Park 

In this sociable park, your dog can cavort with other dogs while you shoot the breeze with other dog people. The off-leash area is between two signs on the east side of the park. There's a bench for humans, and a pretty good safety net between dogs and the outside world.

The favorite game among dogs here involves a big green bush. One dog usually starts running around it for no apparent reason. Circle after circle, he'll attract more and more dogs into chasing him until almost every dog is swirling around in a dizzying loop. Watch too closely and you can get seasick.

Dogs find the rest of the park mildly entertaining, although they have to be leashed. The lake that's the park's namesake is little more than a pond. Ducks and a couple of swans live here, and the temptation may be too much for your dog. We've seen dogs drag their owners ankle-deep into the muddy pond in pursuit of a duck dinner. The park is also home to an attractive playground and a decent heart parcourse.

5-1ab For the dog run area, enter on 8th Avenue at Lake Street. Open 6 a.m. to 10 p.m. (415) 666-7200.

Mount Davidson 

Hiking to the peak of this park can be a religious experience—literally. As you emerge from the tall pine and eucalyptus trees leading to the 927-foot summit, a concrete structure looms in the distance. As you get closer you'll see that it's a gigantic cross, 103 feet tall. It's so huge, and in such a prominent spot—at the end of a long, wide path surrounded by trees—that it can be a startling sight. On his first vision, Joe backed out of his collar and collided with a tree. Since leashes are the law here, we had to quickly put him back together.

In 1934, President Roosevelt became the first to flick the switch and light the cross. It's visible for miles, especially vivid under its nighttime floodlighting. On a night hike up Mount Davidson, you can follow the glow to the top.

Since you enter the park at such a high altitude, it's only about a 10-minute pilgrimage to the peak. But you can make it a much longer walk by experimenting with different trails.

5-1ac Enter at Dalewood Way and Lansdale Avenue. Open 6 a.m. to 10 p.m. (415) 666-7200.

Ocean Beach

This broad, four-mile-long beach with a crashing surf isn't exactly Palm Beach. It's usually cold and windy, and full of seaweed, jellyfish, jagged bits of shells and less savory deposits from the Pacific. In other words, it's a dog's dream come true.

There are usually very few bathers here, so let your dog run off-leash and have the time of his life. If you walk for an hour, you'll probably run into at least two dozen other dogs. They seem especially inspired to frolic here, so it's possible to give your dog all the exercise he needs while you sit on the sand and read a book. By the end of Chapter 2, you'll have a thoroughly pooped pooch. Bring water for him, though. We've seen too many dogs try to drink from the ocean, thirsty after playing so hard.

5-1ad You can park along the ocean, between the Cliff House and Balboa Street. Walk south on the sidewalk until you hit the beach. Or park in the spaces between Fulton Street and Lincoln Way. There's also a parking lot at Sloat Boulevard. Open 24 hours. (415) 556-8371.

Palace of Fine Arts

The glory of ancient Rome embraces you even as you approach this relic of the 1915 Panama-Pacific Exposition. From the huge colonnaded rotunda to the serene reflecting pool, the place drips with Romanesque splendor.

The Palace is especially grand under its night lighting. It's also an ideal place to take your dog while the kids go to the **Exploratorium**, located inside. Walk around the paved path that winds through the grand columns and around the pond. But keep your eyes peeled for people feeding the multitudes of pigeons, ducks and geese. Dogs like Joe love to break up the feeding frenzy with an abrupt tug on the mandatory leash. Feathers fly, dried bread scatters everywhere.

5-1ae The best place to enter for the full Roman effect is on Baker Street, between North Point and Jefferson Streets. The grounds are open from 6 a.m. to 10 p.m. (415) 666-7200.

Pine Lake Park

Adjacent to **Stern Grove**, its more famous cousin, Pine Lake Park can be even more fun for dogs because it has **Laguna Puerca**, a small lake at the west end of the park. Swimming isn't allowed, but there's always the muddy shore for wallowing.

The lake is in a valley at the bottom of steep slopes, so there's not much need to worry about traffic. Leashes are supposed to be on at all times, in any case. At the lake's east end, there's a big field where dogs can really cut loose—as far as leashes allow.

5-1af Enter at Crestlake Drive and Wawona Street and follow the paved path, which quickly turns into a dirt trail. Open 6 a.m. to 10 p.m. (415) 666-7200.

Presidio of San Francisco 

Dogs and their people like to pretend that the Presidio is their very own country estate, acre after rolling acre of secret pathways, open meadows and dense groves of eucalyptus and redwoods.

In fact, after 1994 the park *will* belong to you—when the Army turns it over to the Golden Gate National Recreation Area. Now *there's* a good use of your tax money!

Dogs are supposed to be leashed at all times, but despite the Presidio military police's reputation as overzealous traffic enforcers, we've never seen anyone busted for walking a leashless dog. But there's always a first, so be warned.

Our favorite tour is to park just north of the Arguello Boulevard entrance, at a roadside parking area on the west side of Arguello. Follow the path in and go down the hill as it gets wider. It will loop past wildflowers and seasonal sweetpeas. Bear left at the first major fork and hike through a thick forest area, then bear right when that path gives you a choice. You'll hike up and down a gentle sequence of hills. Pull over and enjoy the larger hills to the west. Dogs thrill at speeding up and down them for no apparent reason. You'll run into a few more side trails along the way. Explore them as you wish, watching out for traffic on nearby roads.

In these hills, in the spring, you'll come across patches of bright yellow jonquils, many of them in formations resembling letters of the alphabet. An elderly British fellow who keeps a good rapport with other dog owners plants them as a memorial to dogs who have died. There's a "G" for George at the foot of the first large hill. The man likes to plant the flowers in the spots favored by the deceased dogs, whose spirits still live on their very own 1,500-acre country estate. (See also "Explore a Military Pet Cemetery," under DIVERSIONS, page 172.)

5-1ag The Presidio is open 24 hours. (415) 561-2211.

Stern Grove 

Until the 1991 concert season, dogs were welcome at all Stern Grove music festivals. Unfortunately, complaints about hygiene and noise changed this policy. Though dogs aren't allowed at the concert meadow, as of this printing, they are still tolerated around the peripheral hills, on-leash. Bring a picnic, a bottle of wine, a rawhide bone and, of course, a pooper scooper.

Stern Grove is a treasure of trees, hills, meadows and birds. There's even a spot where dogs are allowed off-leash. Unfortunately, it's one of the least attractive areas in the park—very close to the street—although trees act as an effective barrier. And if you perch on the inner edge, the dog run area isn't a bad place to listen to a concert. The violins get a little tinny at that distance, but your dog won't care.

5-1ah For the dog run area, enter on Wawona Street between 21st and 23rd Avenues. Open 6 a.m. to 10 p.m. (415) 666-7200.

Twin Peaks 

So dogs aren't allowed at the Top of the Mark. So what. The view from up here will put all those No Dogs Allowed establishments to shame, and it's cheaper to entertain guests up here—free, in fact.

The summits of the twin peaks are higher than 900-feet. It's usually *cold* up there, so bundle up. You can drive to the northern peak and park in the lot. It's very touristy, but on this peak, signs tell you what you're looking at—Tiburon, Nob Hill, Mount Diablo, Japantown and Mount Tamalpais. Your dog won't get much exercise, though, since all he can do is walk around the paved viewing area on-leash. And frankly, ours are bored by the marvelous vistas.

For your dog's sake, try exploring the other peak. It's a bare hill with wooden stairs up one side. While dogs must be on-leash, it's not bad exercise. And the view—at almost 20-feet higher than the other peak—is magnificent. From here you can see other potential walks for you and your dog on the lower hills, where the views are almost as dynamic and the air is a little warmer. Be sure to keep your dog on-leash, because the road is never far away.

5-1ai On Twin Peaks Boulevard, just north of Portola Drive. Open 6 a.m. to 10 p.m. (415) 666-7200.

Washington Square 

Grab a gelato, leash your dog and relax in this park in the middle of North Beach. There are plenty of benches, and enough trees to make your dog comfortable with his surroundings. The park is only about one block square, but it's great for a stroll when you're hitting the cafes of our Little Italy. And if you have a child with you, so much the better. There's a small playground that's popular with local parents.

Washington Square is right across from the ornate Saints Peter and Paul Catholic Church, and the Transamerica pyramid looks close enough to reach out and touch.

5-1aj Enter the park at any of its four borders: Stockton, Post, Powell or Geary Streets. Try not to drive to North Beach. Even during the day, parking's a bear. Open 6 a.m. to 10 p.m. (415) 666-7200.

RESTAURANTS

Angelina's Caffe: Conveniently located one-half block from Cal's Discount Pet Supply, Angelina's is a good place for you and your dog to take a break from shopping. It's got everything from soup to pine nuts, and a large variety of coffee. Enjoy them at one of six sidewalk tables. You can also stock on up on Italian souvenirs here, but watch out for the red, white and green hats. 6000 California Street. (415) 221-7801.

Bakers of Paris: Eat French on a bench here. The croissants are out of this world. 3989 24th Street. (415) 863-8725.

Beach Street Cafe: Only one sidewalk table, but it's a good place to break for a gourmet sandwich or pastry while strolling around Fisherman's Wharf. 777 Beach Street. (415) 885-1912.

Bepples Pie Shop: Joe thinks their cherry pie is tops. So do we. Eat a piece at the bench outside after a window-shopping spree on Union Street. 1934 Union Street. (415) 931-6225.

Blue Danube Coffee House: Have your cake and eat soup and sandwiches, too, at five tables outside this charming cafe. You can even indulge in a wide selection of beer or wine, but you'll have to drink alone if your dog is under 21. On sunny days, it may be hard to find an empty spot. 306 Clement Street. (415) 221-9041.

Boudin Sourdough Bakery & Cafe: Boudin sourdough bread has few rivals in San Francisco. This bakery is smack in the middle of all the Fisherman's Wharf activity and has plenty of outdoor tables. 156 Jefferson Street. (415) 928-1849.

Bugatti's Espresso Cafe: A popular spot with neighborhood dogs, Bugatti's has some of the best espresso and light food in town. 3001 Webster Street. (415) 922-4888.

Cafe Espresso: Sip a cappuccino while you and your dog enjoy the Anchorage Shopping Center's afternoon entertainment. Every day from noon to 5 p.m., you can hear jazz, blues, folk or a special surprise musical guest. Anchorage Shopping Center, 2800 Leavenworth Street. (415) 776-3420.

Caffe Freddy's: A real find in North Beach, especially if you want a touch of California influence to your Italian food. Pizzettas are the specialty here. A favorite has goat cheese and smoked salmon, but there are eight different kinds. 901 Columbus Avenue. (415) 922-0151.

The Cannery: This old Del Monte packing plant is home to several restaurants with courtyard tables for you and your dog, and there's often entertainment here. Some of the restaurants don't have courtyard service after dark because it's too cold, so call first to find out. The Cannery is at 2801 Leavenworth Street.

Le Garden Caffe: German, American, Italian—just about any kind of food you feel like. And there are plenty of tables, right next door to the courtyard's stage. (415) 928-4340.

Jackson Beach: Delicious Italian food here, with a multitude of pastas. (415) 771-5225.

Las Margaritas Restaurant: Seven kinds of margaritas, mesquite-grilled shark and a great view of the courtyard below make this one of the more popular Mexican restaurants this side of the Mission district. (415) 776-6996.

Cleo's: Two sidewalk tables provide you with a front-row view of the lower Haight. The food is good, and mostly vegetarian, and outdoors the atmosphere's...er...funky. 698 Haight Street. (415) 252-7912.

Coffee Merchant: Lots of people come here to wake up with their dogs. We see them downing caffeine at the outside benches at any hour. 1248 9th Avenue. (415) 665-1915.

Coffee Roastery: They roast their own coffee here, and you can drink it at the benches outside. 2191 Union Street. (415) 922-9559.

Colonial Deli: Great Mideast food, and you can enjoy it at one of four sidewalk tables—so long as your dog isn't dangerous, says one of owners. 624 Irving Street. (415) 681-5858.

Curbside Cafe: The servers here are very dog friendly, and the continental cuisine is top-notch. Try not to let your dog block the sidewalk. It's a tight squeeze here. 2417 California Street. (415) 929-9030.

Embarcadero Center: This is the biggest collection of outdoor cafes in the city. If you take your dog when you go to work in the financial district, you can brown-bag it at the dozens of tables and chairs and decks in the huge concrete courtyard, or choose from any of several restaurants with outdoor tables. Be aware, though, that some eateries aren't open on weekends. Embarcadero Center is at the foot of Market Street, between Clay and Sacramento Streets. A sampling of outdoor cafes:

Carriage House Grill: Seafood is the specialty here, but you can get chicken and chops, too. Unfortunately, there's outdoor service only when it's sunny, so your dog may not be able to eat with you on a typical foggy San Francisco day. 3 Embarcadero Center. (415) 433-7444.

Harbor Village Restaurant: If you've never had dim sum with your dog, this is the place to try it. 4 Embarcadero Center. (415) 781-8833.

The Holding Company: The selection here changes with the seasons, but you and your dog can always be guaranteed a good hamburger. 2 Embarcadero Center. (415) 986-0797.

Marcello's Pizza: The calzones here are among the best we've ever tasted, and the gourmet pizzas are *deliciozo*. 5 Embarcadero Center. (415) 781-1300.

Salmagundi: The perfect place if salads and homemade soups are your preferred lunchtime fare. 2 Embarcadero Center. (415) 982-5603.

Scott's Seafood Grill & Bar: Just as the name says, and fresh. 3 Embarcadero Center. (415) 981-0622.

Ghirardelli Square: What was once a chocolate factory is now one of the classiest tourist shopping centers in the country. More important than that, it's got a lot to offer residents and their dogs. Ghirardelli Square is at 900 North Point Street. Here are some restaurants with outdoor cafes:

Boudin Sourdough Bakery & Cafe: Dine on pastries, croissants, cheesecake or huge sandwiches as you gaze across Beach Street at the bay. (415) 928-7404.

Compadres Mexican Bar & Grill: The terrace outside this second-floor restaurant provides you and your dog with a first-rate view of the bay, the boats at Hyde Street Pier and Alcatraz. The food is as good as the scenery, and if it's too sunny, you can dine at tables with umbrellas. (415) 885-2266.

Ghirardelli Fountain & Candy: Here's where you can get some of that famous rich Ghirardelli ice cream with all the fixings. Just remember: The more of it your dog gets, the fewer sit-ups you have to do. (415) 771-4903.

Ghirardelli's Too!: A healthier alternative to the above, Ghirardelli's Too offers non-fat yogurt desserts. (415) 474-1414.

Vicolo Pizzeria: We love this place for its gourmet pizzas with light and flaky cornmeal crusts, and for all the room for dogs at the tables outside. (415) 776-1331.

Gino Gelateria: This cafe, with its own gelato factory and some of the best tartufo and tiramisu in the region, is a must for anyone doing the North Beach scene with a dog. An older woman visits every day with her little white dog to eat gelato at one of the sidewalk tables. She brings a plastic bowl with ice, and the owners fill it with water. Both dog and woman down their refreshments in bliss. The owners say they'll do the same for anyone else with a dog. 601 Columbus Avenue. (415) 981-4664.

Horse Shoe Cafe: Good coffee and pastries at a down-to-earth cafe with two sidewalk tables. 566 Haight Street. (415) 626-8852.

Hyde Street Bistro: This is one of only a few fancy Bay Area restaurants where dogs are allowed. Two outdoor tables, covered with white tablecloths, and a superb selection of Austrian and northern Italian dishes make dining here— even with the most unkempt mutt—a delight. 1521 Hyde Street. (415) 441-7778.

Josie's Cabaret & Juice Joint: They love dogs here. They've even got one, and he'll come out to greet you when he feels like it. The food is tasty and vegetarian. When it's sunny out, there are three tables on the sidewalk. 3583 16th Street. (415) 861-7933.

La Canasta: This Mexican take-out restaurant is where we get our favorite burritos. When Joe is with us, we like to sit on the bench outside while we wait—and often while we eat. 2219 Filbert Street. (415) 921-3003.

La Mediterranee: Dog owners are lucky— there are two of these top Mideast/Greek restaurants in the city, and both put tables outside in decent weather. We highly recommend the vegetarian plate, even for meat eaters. At 2210 Fillmore Street, (415) 921-2956; and at 288 Noe Street, 431-7210.

La Patisserie: The croissants are often a little too dark and crunchy, but it's a good place to grab a bite after a hike in the Presidio. 397 Arguello Boulevard. (415) 386-6633.

La Trattoria: You must tie your dog on the other side of the railing that separates the patio from the sidewalk, but you can still be just inches apart if you get a table at the railing. The Italian food is so good that it's worth the extra trouble. 1507 Polk Street. (415) 771-6363.

Market Place Restaurant: In an unlikely location on the ground floor of the Hyatt Embarcadero is this magnificent restaurant with a 130-seat patio, where Larry the owner welcomes each and every well-behaved dog. The patio makes a dog feel right at home, too, with flowering shrubs and weeping willow trees. Make sure your dog realizes this is a restaurant, not a park. The seafood dishes, with a Cajun flair, are unusual. And there's a hopping afternoon happy hour, too. To enter with a dog, *don't* go through the Hyatt. At the bottom of the Hyatt, directly across from One Market Plaza, is a blue awning with the restaurant's name. Go in the door and immediately head for the patio. Someone will probably be there to guide you to the right part of the restaurant. At 5 Embarcadero Center. (415) 788-1234.

Nob Hill Noshery: Eat hearty deli food at the tables outside, or dine just inside the entrance and do what the owners of a Saint Bernard do. They tie him up at a pole right outside the door, and they're still only a few feet away as they dine inside. The Saint Bernard, a regular here, likes to stretch across the width of the doorway as people try to come and go. 1400 Pacific Avenue. (415) 928-6674.

Pier 39: If your dog doesn't mind flocks of tourists, there's a wide selection of decent eateries with outdoor tables for the two of you here. Your dog gets to smell the bay and sniff at the sea lions below, and for you there's often entertainment. Pier 39 is off the Embarcadero, near Jefferson Street. Some of the restaurants where you and your dog are allowed:

Burger Cafe: Every burger imaginable is waiting for your dog to drool over. The mushroom cheeseburger is a big hit. (415) 986-5966.

Chowder's: Fried seafood and several types of chowder make Pier 39 really feel like a pier. (415) 391-4737.

Eagle Cafe: Eggs, potatoes, burgers, cheese—good heavy food for a cold day is yours for the asking. Management asks that the number of dogs at the outdoor tables be limited to one at a time, so if you see another dog begging for scraps, move on to another restaurant. (415) 433-3689.

Le Carousel: The next best thing to being on the carousel at the end of the pier (no dogs allowed) is this restaurant with a carousel theme, with painted ponies everywhere. It also has a large deli with a selection of cakes and pastries. (415) 433-4160.

Sal's Pizzeria: You and your dog can get a real taste of San Francisco by biting into any of Sal's special pizzas. There's the 49er special, with sausage, pepperoni, onions and mushrooms. The Earthquake, with sausage, salami, mushrooms and tomatoes, was a hit with Joe. (415) 398-1198.

Polly Ann Ice Cream: Here, dogs are treated like people, in the best sense. Every dog gets a free mini doggie cone. Since dogs can't order for themselves, the owners usually give them vanilla, but the dogs rarely complain. Even if you have several dogs, the owners welcome them all and dole out the goods with a smile. They're especially happy if you buy some ice cream for yourself, of course. The doggie cone tradition has been alive for 20 years. 3142 Noriega Street. (415) 664-2472.

Pompei's Grotto: If your dog likes the smell of seafood, he probably won't mind joining you at an outdoor table here. The fish is fresh and the pasta delicious. And if your dog is thirsty, she'll be offered a cup of water. 340 Jefferson Street. (415) 776-9265.

Real Food Deli: You'd think a place like this would have only the healthiest, most vegetarian cuisine. It does have gourmet natural food, like grilled tofu brochettes, but it also has decadent dishes, like prosciutto sandwiches. Desserts soar to the same extremes. Two outdoor tables make eating with your dog a pleasure. 2164 Polk Street. (415) 775-2805.

Savoy Tivoli: Come to this North Beach bar/cafe on weekday afternoons if you want your dog to be your date. Otherwise, it's too crowded for dogs to be comfortable. 1434 Grant Avenue. (415) 362-7023.

SF Coffee Company: Strong coffee on a hard bench may not be an ideal way to start the day, but it will wake you up enough to take your dog for a long walk. 3868 24th Street. (415) 641-4433.

Simple Pleasures Cafe: This is a quaint cafe with a warm and cozy atmosphere, and food to match. You and your dog can sit at the outdoor tables and catch live folk and jazz music Tuesday through Friday nights. It may be cold, so bring lots of money for hot chocolates. 3434 Balboa Street. (415) 387-4022.

Tart to Tart: If you want to satisfy a sweet tooth with high-quality decadence, with your dog as accomplice, this is the place to do it. Outside, of course. 641 Irving Street. (415) 753-0643.

Tassajara Bread Bakery: The goods here are as wholesome and natural as the bread Tassajara made famous. Although the place is usually crowded, there are plenty of outdoor tables. 1000 Cole Street. (415) 664-8947.

Toy Boat Dessert Cafe: You may not be able to say it 10 times fast, but you and your dog won't feel a need to speak when you're at the outside bench eating rich and creamy desserts. 401 Clement Street. (415) 751-7505.

Trio Cafe: Sandwiches, soups and salads—the basics here are some of the best. 1870 Fillmore Street. (415) 563-2248.

Lodgings & Campgrounds

Best Western Civic Center Motor Inn: One and one-half blocks north of Harrison Street off-ramp. Average cost for a double is $70. 364 9th Street, San Francisco, CA 94103. (415) 621-2826.

Campton Place: Dogs over 25 pounds are not allowed at this luxury hotel one block from Union Square. For small pooches, the fee is $25 per night. "We have to clean the room extra thoroughly, deodorize it, and put flea powder around—so it costs money," a manager explained. "We love dogs, but we want the people who stay in the room after them to be happy, too." Average cost for a double is $200. 340 Stockton Street, San Francisco, CA 94108. (415) 781-5555.

Four Seasons Clift Hotel: They prefer small dogs here, but large ones are welcome if they're subdued. After all, the hotel recently had a pig as a guest. Your dog can get on the Very Important Pet list, and will be greeted with a biscuit next time. Double rooms average $250. 495 Geary Street, San Francisco, CA 94102. (415) 775-4700.

Laurel Motor Inn: As long as you don't leave your dog alone in the room, he may be a guest here. Double rooms average $85. 444 Presidio Avenue, San Francisco, CA 94115. (415) 567-8467.

Mansion Hotel: Step back in time in this mysterious old mansion, circa 1890. It's full of art treasures and beautifully attired mannequins, and people tell tales of a resident ghost. Dogs are allowed in a few of its 16 rooms, but because the hotel itself is a work of art, bring only a very docile dog. Average price for a double room is $140. 2220 Sacramento Street, San Francisco, CA 94115. (415) 929-9444.

Rodeway Inn: The only requirement for dogs here is that they not bark as people walk by their rooms. A $20 deposit is required. Double rooms average $95. 1450 Lombard Street, San Francisco, CA 94123. (415) 673-0691.

San Francisco Marriott: If you've got $200 extra on your credit card, you can bring your dog. That's what the damage deposit costs. You'll get it back as soon as they see your dog didn't shred the beds. Average cost for a double room is $169. 55 Fourth Street, San Francisco, CA 94103. (415) 896-1600.

Sheraton at Fisherman's Wharf: Only one and one-half blocks from the wharf area, this is an ideal hotel for tourists with dogs. Average price for a double room is $160. 2500 Mason Street, San Francisco, CA 94133. (415) 362-5500.

The Westin St. Francis: At this luxurious Union Square hotel, "small, well-behaved dogs are as welcome as anybody," according to a manager. The average price for a double room is $150. 335 Powell Street, San Francisco, CA 94102. (415) 397-7000.

Fairs & Festivals

Cherry Blossom Festival: You'll run into lots of Akitas at this late April festival at the Japan Center. You'll also encounter Japanese food, dance and martial arts demonstrations. It's one of the largest celebrations of Japanese culture this side of the Pacific. Dogs must be leashed. Call (415) 922-6776.

Folsom Street Fair: Proceeds from this South of Market fair always go to a worthy local charity. From rock and roll to new wave, this large street party in autumn has music for the modern, leashed dog's ears. (415) 648-FAIR.

Nihonmachi Street Fair: Another big affair in Japantown, this time in August. It's a lively festival, with music, dance and food from all of San Francisco's Asian communities. Bring your leashed dog and an appetite. (415) 922-8700.

Diversions

Be a stage parent: Anyone who watches KOFY-TV 20 is familiar with the hairy beasts who sit in easy chairs every half-hour for station identification. Maybe you've longed to launch your own dog into the living rooms of thousands of viewers, but never thought you had a chance.

The good news is that your dog doesn't need connections, an agent or a Screen Actors Guild card to be a star. Just send KOFY-TV a photo of your dog, along with your daytime phone number. If they're interested—and they usually are, since they need 45 dogs per month—they'll call and set up a taping date. Don't worry if your dog is the nervous, squirmy type, advises Jeff Fisher, aka The TV-20 Dog

Guy. "We've got tricks to get just about any dog to look at the camera."

An added benefit to being taped is that you can finally find out just what makes those TV dogs whirl their heads toward that TV set at the perfect moment. Write to KOFY-TV 20, Attention: Pets, 2500 Marin Street, San Francisco, CA 94124.

Celebrate great music and dance: Your dog's in for culture shock if you bring him to Golden Gate Park to catch top artists Saturday afternoons in the summer. Grab a picnic blanket, a leash and lunch and head for the Golden Gate Park Music Concourse, in front of the Academy of Sciences. You'll see top dancers from around the world and hear some of the best jazz, classical and ethnic music around. Just be considerate, and if your dog is the barking type, leave her at home. Admission is free. For more information, call Summer Festival at (415) 474-3914.

On Sundays from 1 p.m. to 3 p.m., the Golden Gate Band serenades parkgoers with a wide range of music. They're a lively group with talent for both oom-pah rhythms and delicate tunes. For more information on the band, call (415) 666-7200.

Explore a military pet cemetery: If only human cemeteries were so full of bright flowers (albeit many of plastic or silk) and thoughtful epitaphs, death might not seem so somber. When you enter the little cemetery, surrounded by a white picket fence, a sign tells you, "The love these animals gave will never be forgotten." You'll want to bring your leashed dog friend with you.

"Sarge," reads one epitaph. "Our pet George. George accepted us people," says another. Several markers bear only a large red heart, which means the pet was unknown but loved even after death. This is where cats, birds, dogs and even Freddy Fish—whose grave is marked by a lone plastic rose—can live together in harmony. Take Lincoln Boulevard and turn north onto McDowell Avenue. The cemetery is just south of the corner of McDowell and Crissy Field Avenues. (415) 561-2211.

Go organic: The California Harvest Ranch Market, known for its wide selection of fresh organic produce, has a healthy attitude toward dogs. The owners recently installed two clamps in the front just for dogs. The idea is to hook your dog's leash to the clamp and go shopping, knowing your dog is safe and secure. As always, though, don't leave him unchecked for long. 2285 Market Street. (415) 626-0805.

Help someone with AIDS: PAWS (Pets Are Wonderful Support) is dedicated to preserving the relationship of people with AIDS and their pets. If you've ever been comforted by your dog while ill, you have a glimpse of the importance of the work PAWS does. PAWS needs people to do office work, deliver pet food, and walk and care for pets. And if you have room for another dog in the house, PAWS usually has some special animals for adoption. (415) 824-4040.

Pay homage to a teacup poodle: One of the oddest pieces of art in the city is near the foot of the Filbert steps, at Montgomery Street. It's a mural, at dog's-eye level, of a tiny poodle in a semi-desert setting. A sign in the painting says, "No dogs. Teacup poodles OK." The exhibit also contains a real fire hydrant, lots of real live ferns, and a brass plaque about Ginger the poodle. Among the biographical details is that Ginger flunked out of obedience school. Tsk, tsk. And such a polite-looking thing, too. To drive to the mural, go to the end of Union Street and turn left on Montgomery Street. The art is easy to miss, so keep your eyes low to the ground.

Shop on Beach Street: You can shop for baubles, bangles and T-shirts with your leashed dog at any of dozens of little stands up and down this Fisherman's Wharf area street. You can even get your dog's caricature done by a local artist. Make sure to take him to nearby Aquatic Park while you're there, especially if he's sat patiently for the artist's rendition. The bulk of the stands on Beach Street are between Hyde and Polk Streets.

Hop on a bus: Dogs are allowed on Muni buses and cable cars from 10 a.m. to 3 p.m. and from 7 p.m. to 5 a.m. on weekdays. On weekends and holidays, no time restrictions apply. Only one dog is permitted per bus. Dogs must be on a short leash, and muzzled, no matter how little or how sweet. Bus driver Tom Brown told us about the creative, but ineffective, ways some people muzzle their dogs. "This one man had a part pit-bull dog, and he put a little rubber band around its mouth," said Brown. "No way that dog was getting on my bus."

Dogs pay the same fare as owners. If the owner is a senior citizen, the dog pays senior citizen rates. Because the dog is a paying passenger, he is entitled to his own seat. Keep your dog from getting underfoot, and be sure he's well walked before he gets on. Call (415) 673-MUNI for more information.

I had my 85 cents, Joe had his. We both sat on a bench on Fulton Street, waiting nervously for the bus to take us to the ocean. The man at the Muni information line was plenty amused when I called about taking a dog along. "I guess you'd better take him to the back of the bus—if he even gets up the steps!" he said, and laughed one of those laughs you only hear in B-grade horror films. "Good luck!" Click.

We were already having a problem. Joe didn't want to wear his muzzle, and succeeded in getting the mouth strap off three times in our 10-minute wait. But rules are rules.

In the distance, dull yellow Muni bus lights glowed through the fog. We flagged down the bus, and its doors flew open with a great hiss. Joe ran as far as his leash would allow, but when he saw me being brave and entering the mouth of the giant creature, he followed. We paid our fares, got our transfers and made our way to the back of the bus. So far, so good. The bus driver didn't even blink. And the people in the back of the bus were all smiling at Joe.

Joe got his bus legs while standing in the middle of the aisle. Then, he quickly made friends, and even got two teenagers to give him half of a Milky Way bar.

This is a pretty good spot, thought Joe, and started sniffing the rubber floor for further goodies. An elderly woman wearing a plastic bonnet got on and sat in the seat ahead of us. Joe checked, but she had no food to interest him. He came back and lay down on the floor.

I was staring out the window, happy that Joe was doing so well on his first Muni ride, when out of the corner of my eye, I noticed Joe's head making a strange up-and-down motion. The old woman's hand was grasping a strip of paper, and Joe was nibbling away at the end of it as enthusiastically as the muzzle would allow. I looked closely and saw—horror of horrors—that the now-soggy and torn strip of paper was her Muni transfer.

I explained, apologized and gave her another transfer—Joe's. Since I hadn't brought any extra cash, Joe and I had to wait at the end of the route and come back on the same bus. He hung his head in guilt, or in an attempt to sniff out more snacks.—M.G.

Ride halfway to the stars: As far as cable cars are concerned, opinions vary widely about whether dogs should ride inside or outside. Some drivers feel the outside is better because the cable noise isn't so amplified, and dogs don't get so nervous. Others say the outside is too dangerous—that a dog could panic and jump off.

If you do decide to do the full San Francisco experience and ride outside, have your dog sit on a bench, and hold her securely by the leash *and* by the body. The standing area is very narrow and precarious. And you never want to go on a crowded cable car with your dog, so stay away from the popular tourist areas during the peak seasons. (For rules, see "Hop on a bus," page 173.) Call (415) 673-MUNI for more information.

Joe was so terrified when he first boarded a cable car that he got in no trouble at all after barking at the bell. How much mischief could he get into hiding his head under my coat?

But after a while, with the coaxing of our personable California Street cable car drivers Louie and Dave, he started peeking out at the sights. As they regaled us with stories of dogs they'd known, and flea remedies that work, Joe loosened up. He got so relaxed by the middle of our trip that he fell off his seat as the cable car descended the steep hill in Chinatown. Fortunately, we were seated inside.

No one seemed to want to sit next to Joe. In fact, the deeper we rode into the financial district and the more suits and ties we encountered, the more people avoided even looking at him. Joe got off at the end of the line with his feelings hurt, but his bravery intact.—M.G.

Take a dog to the animal fair: The Great San Francisco Cat and Dog Fair is one of the few indoor dog events that actually welcomes the dog himself. Unfortunately for the owners of dogs who like to eat cats, felines are also invited. But dogs have to wear short leashes, and cats must attend in a box or cage.

Actually, there's plenty of legitimate food for dogs at the fair. They can eat at the Dogitessan, or in a separate dog dining area called the Bow House—which is not too close to the Meow House. Dogs are not allowed to eat anything, or anyone, in the Meow House.

Dogs may participate in dozens of events, or just watch, from dachshund races to dog glamour parades. The fair benefits the San Francisco SPCA. For more information, call the hotline at (415)

554-3096. If the hotline is giving information about a different event, call the SPCA at: (415) 554-3000. The fair is at Pier 2, Fort Mason's Herbst Pavillion.

Walk with thousands of dogs: Get your dog's walking shoes and stroll from one to five miles in what's probably the largest dog walkathon in the world. Dogs and people of all shapes and breeds gather for the PetWalk every May in Golden Gate Park to raise money for the San Francisco SPCA. The walks can get very crowded, so think twice if your pooch can't handle thousands of dog and human legs strutting by. Otherwise, it's probably one of the most fun dog events in the country. After the walk, there are howling contests, athletic competitions and owner/pet lookalike events. And lots of refreshments. For an application, write the San Francisco SPCA PetWalk, 2500 16th Street, San Francisco, CA 94103. The number is (415) 554-3000. A few months before the event, a special hotline can answer your basic questions: (415) 554-3096.

Wash your socks with your dog: A jug of wine, a loaf of bread, your dirty laundry, your dog and you. Bring all this and feast at one of four tables outside Star Wash Laundry, while your wash is in the rinse cycle. This is a very popular spot among dog owners with dirty clothes, and since the laundromat owners adore dogs, chances are your pet won't be alone. It's especially enjoyable for your dog after a sprint in Dolores Park. Don't forget water for her. 392 Dolores Street. (415) 431-2443.

Watch a big-screen flick: Picture this—you, your date, a romantic drive-in movie. The plot thickens, your date takes your hand, the lead characters start to kiss, lips locking.... You feel hot breath on your neck and turn in dreamy anticipation. And there, only millimeters from your face, is your dog's big black nose, sniffing away and asking for more popcorn.

Still, taking a dog *can* be fun. At the Geneva Drive-In Theater, a resident cat prowls around cars looking for a handout, or a dog to tease. The Geneva is on Carter Street, off Geneva Avenue, next to the Cow Palace. (415) 587-2884.

MORE INFO

WHERE YOUR DOG CAN'T GO

- Alcatraz
- Angel Island

- Aquatic Park's beach
- Coit Tower, inside. They're allowed on the grounds, leashed.
- Conservatory of Flowers gardens at Golden Gate Park
- Great Halloween and Pumpkin Festival
- Hyde Street Pier
- Japanese Tea Garden in Golden Gate Park
- North Beach Fair
- Stow Lake's lake. They're allowed on land only.
- Strybing Arboretum, Golden Gate Park
- Union Street Spring Fair
- University of San Francisco campus

USEFUL PHONE NUMBERS & ADDRESSES

San Francisco Recreation & Park Department: McLaren Lodge, Golden Gate Park, San Francisco, CA 94117. (415) 666-7200.

Golden Gate National Recreation Area: Fort Mason, Building 201, San Francisco, CA 94123. (415) 556-0560.

·San Mateo County·

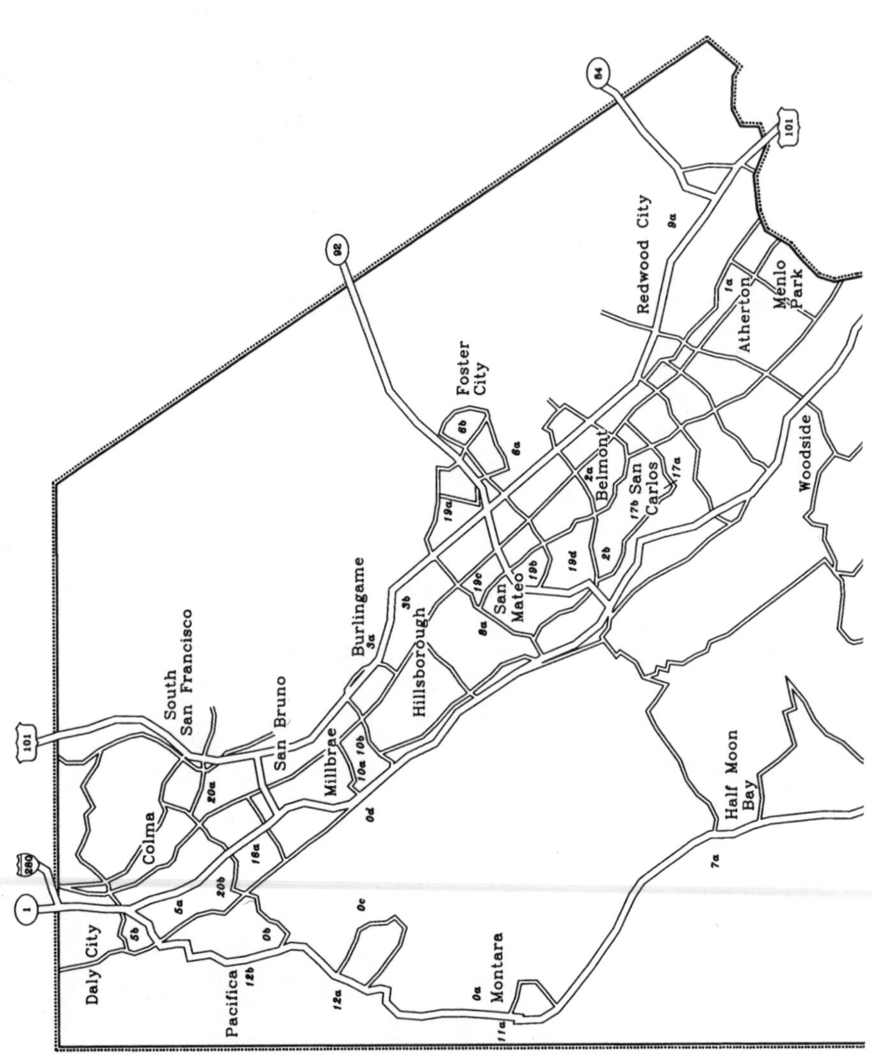
84
101
92
Redwood City
9a
1a
Atherton
Menlo Park
Foster City
6b
6a
Belmont
2a
San Carlos
17a
17b
Woodside
19a
Burlingame
3a
3b
19c
19b
19d
2b
San Mateo
8a
South San Francisco
San Bruno
Hillsborough
Millbrae
10a
10b
0d
20a
Colma
18a
280
20b
5a
1
5b
Daly City
0b
0c
Pacifica
12b
12a
0a
Montara
11a
Half Moon Bay
7a

6. SAN MATEO COUNTY (map page 180-181)

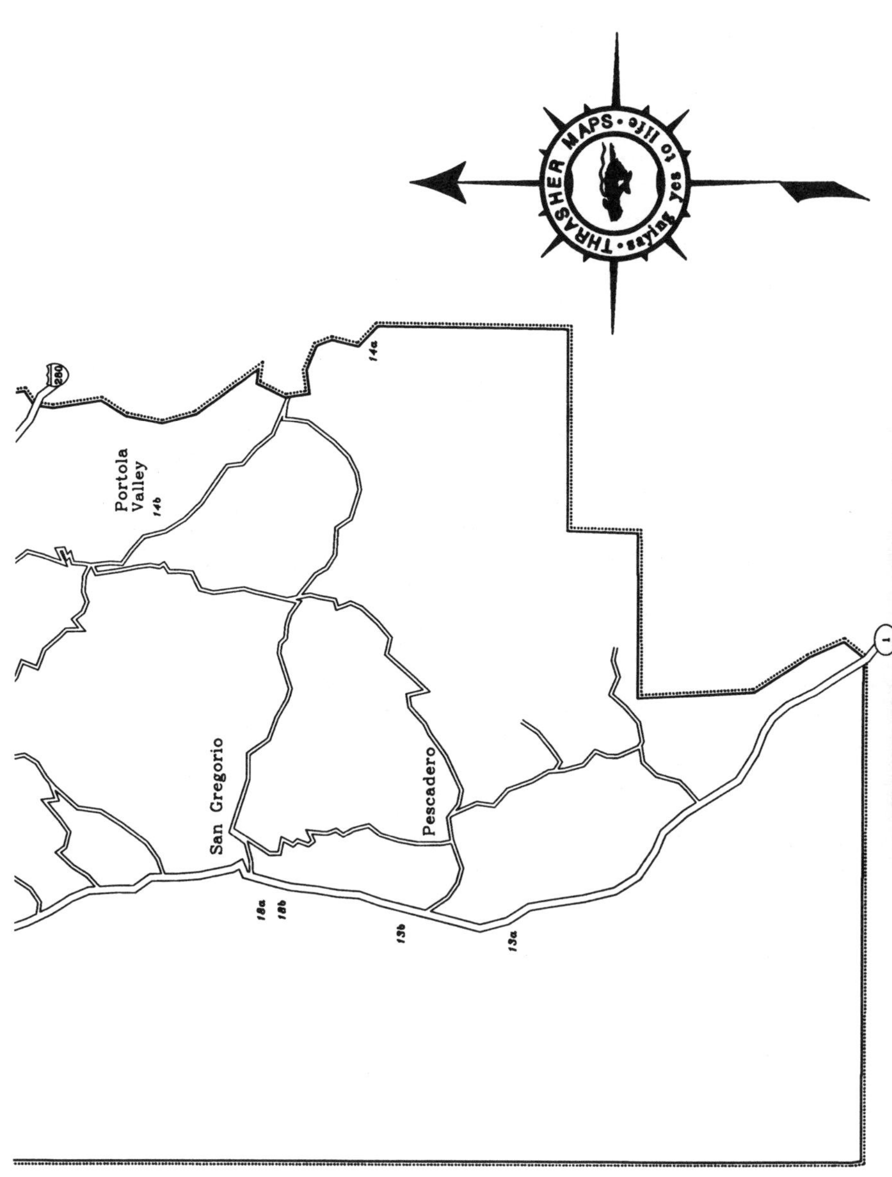

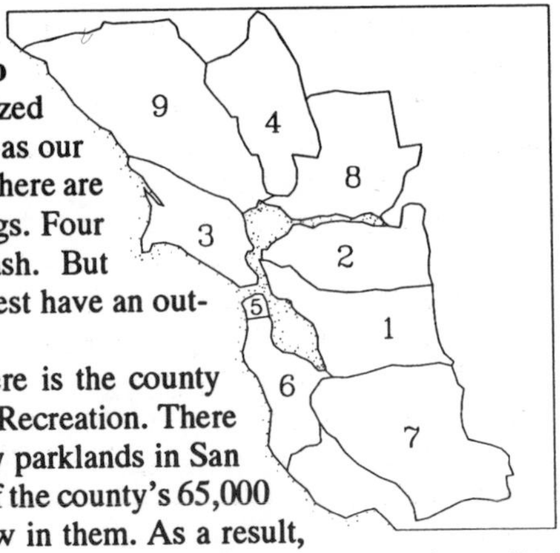

6 Once we started exploring **San Mateo County**, we realized that it wasn't quite as bad as our first impression seemed. There are many parks that allow dogs. Four even allow them off-leash. But some of the biggest and best have an outright ban on canines.

The worst offender here is the county Department of Parks and Recreation. There are 15,000 acres of county parklands in San Mateo County, but none of the county's 65,000 licensed dogs may set paw in them. As a result, dozens of desperate dog owners have formed an organization called DOGS—Dog Owners for Green Space. Their goal is modest: to get the county to open one or two of its parks to dogs on-leash. Thousands of residents have signed a petition requesting this. Members of DOGS are even willing to pay an annual user's fee to help defray costs.

But county officials have continued to stubbornly deny their request. They fear liability, they say. They fear for wildlife. They fear the expense of signs and enforcement.

DOGS members are themselves concerned about wildlife, saying that dogs should be allowed only in areas where people, and even bikes and horses, are already allowed. As for the other worries the commissioners have, DOGS members remind them that San Mateo County is the only regional park district in the Bay Area that bans dogs.

"It's time to give dog owners the same rights as bikers and hikers and horses," says Terry Robertson, chairman of DOGS. "This county is just full of bad excuses. For the sake of our dogs, I hope these excuses crumble soon."

A vote by the Parks and Recreation Commission in late 1991 has given the county's dog owners hope. Commissioners agreed to open a half-mile trail for a year—on a trial basis. While DOGS members were grateful for the chance to prove their good dog etiquette to county officials, they were surprised at the location of the trail: It runs through the San Francisco watershed.

"It's a foot in the door, even though it's not a foot in a gate of a county park," says Robertson. "But we'll take what we can get, because making even this much progress in San Mateo County is truly a victory."

The new dog trail, **Sheep Camp Trail**, is west of Belmont. It's slated to be open to dogs through December 1992. Going south on Interstate 280, exit at the first vista point exit after Highway 92. Follow the road toward the vista point. Park at the foot of the hill just before you get to the vista point. You'll see a sign marking the wide, unpaved Sheep Camp Trail. Your dog must wear a six-foot leash and his license. You must bring a pooper scooper. Be a responsible dog owner here, and the county just may start opening some of its park gates to dogs. For more information, call the county Department of Parks and Recreation at (415) 363-4020, or Terry Robertson, of DOGS, at (415) 595-1026.

Joe and I were stuck in Redwood City on business all day. After a while, he began to glare at me. His brow wrinkled. His eyes got wide and seemed to float in extra liquid. Then he started groaning like a door in a bad horror movie. It was all too clear. This was a dog urgently in need of a park.

So we got in the car and drove until we found a little city park. I let Joe out and he bounded for a private spot behind a bush. But just as he was getting into position, a woman with a baby stroller bustled up. "No! Bad dog! No dogs allowed. Tell your mother that," she yelled, and shot us an angry look.

Joe ran back to the car in a more cowardly manner than I care to admit, tail down, head low. Instead of arguing, we left. Besides, there was a big county park at the other end of Redwood City that looked even better.

Joe was so desperate that by the time we got there he was crossing his legs. But it seemed worth the wait. The park was big and grassy with lots of pine trees and bushes essential for Joe to do his thing. Birds and wildflowers were everywhere. It was one of the more alluring parks we'd ever seen.

But just as we entered, three words on a sign stopped us in our tracks. They were big, bold and mean.

NO DOGS ALLOWED

Joe lifted his leg on the sign and we were gone. Thus was our unsavory introduction to San Mateo County. —M.G.

STATE PARKS

State parks usually ban dogs completely, or at least from all but paved roadways, but there's a refreshing exception to the rule in San Mateo County.

McNee Ranch State Park 

At McNee, you can hike at the same level as the soaring gulls and watch the gem-blue ocean below. The higher you go up Montara Mountain, the more magnificent the view. Hardly a soul knows about this park, so if it's peace you want, it's peace you'll get.

And if it's a workout you want, you'll get that, too. Just strap on a day pack and bring lots of water for you and your dog. If you do the full hike, you'll ascend from sea level to 2,100 feet in a couple of hours. As you hike up and away from the ocean and the road, you lose all sounds of civilization, as Highway 1 fades into a thin ribbon and disappears below.

As soon as you go through the gate at the bottom of the park, follow the narrow trails to the left up the hills. You may be tempted to take the wide and winding paved road from the start, but to avoid any bikers, take the little trails. Besides, they lead to much better vistas.

Eventually, you'll come to a point where you have a choice of going left or right on a wider part of the trail. It's a choice between paradise and Eden. Left will lead you to a stunning view of the Golden Gate Bridge and the Farallon Islands. Right will bring you to the top of the ridge, where you see Mount Diablo and the rest of the bay.

This would be Joe's favorite park, but dogs are supposed to be leashed. Still, he always manages to slide down several steep grassy hills on his back, wriggling and moaning in ecstasy all the way.

6-0a It's easy to miss this park: There aren't any signs, and there's no official parking lot. From Highway 1 in Montara, park at the far northern end of the Montara State Beach parking lot and walk across the road. Be careful as you walk along Highway 1, because there's hardly any room on the shoulder. You'll see a gate on a dirt road just north of you, and a small state property sign. That's where you go in. A few cars can also park next to the gate, on the sides of the dirt road. But don't block the gate, or your car probably won't be there when you get back. Open dawn to dusk. (415) 726-6203.

GOLDEN GATE NATIONAL RECREATION AREA PARKS

Milagra Ridge

Follow the trail up to the top of the tallest hill, and you'll end up with both an incredible view of the Pacific and a perfect plateau for a picnic. There are hillsides covered with ice plant and even a few small redwoods along the way. Despite the leash law, dogs really seem to enjoy this park. Make sure to keep them on the trail, as the environment here is fragile. And keep your eyes peeled for the Mission Blue butterfly: This park is one of its last habitats.

Milagra Ridge is especially magical at night. You've never seen the full moon until you've seen it from here.

6-0b Enter on Sharp Park Road in Pacifica, between Highway 1 and Skyline Boulevard. Open 24 hours. (415) 556-0560.

Sweeney Ridge

If your dog appreciates breathtaking vistas of the Bay Area, with a rainbow assortment of wildflowers in the foreground, this 1,000-acre park is a rare treat. But if your canine is like most, he can take or leave such a magnificent panorama.

If you like a vigorous uphill climb, take the Sneath Lane entrance. It may be toasty when you start, but bring a couple of thick wool sweaters if you plan to hike along the ridge—it's cold and often foggy up there. The furrier your dog, the more she'll take to the invigorating conditions.

The Skyline College entrance is ideal if you want a more moderate grade, but both trailheads will take you to the same place. The leash law here can come in handy if your dog is of the pulling mentality. Just say "mush" on those steep slopes.

From different parts of the ridge, you'll be able to see the ocean—and the Farallon Islands, on a good day—Mount Tamalpais in Marin, Mount Diablo to the east, and Montara Mountain to the south. Judging by all the canines with flaring nostrils, the scents from all four directions must be as enticing as the views.

6-0c For the Sneath Lane entrance, take San Bruno's Sneath Lane all the way to the end. There's usually plenty of parking. The Skyline College entrance, off College Drive, is in the southeast corner of campus, near Lot 2. Open 24 hours a day. (415) 556-0560.

STATE FISH & GAME REFUGE

San Andreas Trail

We should probably feel lucky to even be allowed inside the **Crystal Springs Reservoir** area with dogs. But though this two-mile trail past sparkling **San Andreas Lake** provides a view of nature at its best, it's probably not a place your dog will long to return to. He's got to be on a leash, and the trail is often so crowded with joggers, walkers and bikers that you'll have to keep the leash very short. Besides, you're separated by fence from all but a narrow strip of land and you're right next to the roaring freeway for most of the trail.

But on the good side, the San Andreas Trail is a stone's throw from several areas with a distinct shortage of parks that allow dogs. And you can still see eagles here, if you're lucky.

6-0d There are a few entrances off Highway 280. We prefer to exit at Highway 35 (Skyline Boulevard). Some like the Millbrae Avenue exit. For either, get as close to the trail (to the west) as you can and park on the side of the road. Open from dawn to dusk. We don't list a phone number because responsiblity for the trail is unclear.

6-1

ATHERTON

PARKS, BEACHES & RECREATION AREAS

Holbrook-Palmer Park

Roses. Gazebos. Bathrooms that look like saunas. Trellises. Jasmine plots. Tennis courts. Buildings that belong in a country club. People in white linen love it here. Dogs are often just plain intimidated. Joe didn't lift his leg once last time we visited.

"Don't put it in your book that we allow dogs," a woman with the Atherton Parks and Recreation Department told us. "We have too many weddings and banquets going on, and the people don't want to be disturbed."

Don't forget a leash.

6-1a On Watkins Avenue, between El Camino Real and Middlefield Road. Park at one of several lots in the park. Open dawn to dusk. (415) 688-6534.

6-2
BELMONT

PARKS, BEACHES & RECREATION AREAS

Twin Pines Park

This park is a hidden treasure, nestled among eucalyptus trees just outside the business district of Belmont. You'd never guess the dog wonders that await within. Your dog may hardly notice she's leashed.

The main trail is paved and winds through sweet-smelling trees and brush. A clear stream runs below. In dry seasons, it's only about two feet deep, but in good years it swells to several feet. Dogs love to go down to the stream and wet their whistles. Past the picnic area are numerous small, quiet dirt trails that can take you up the woodsy hill or alongside the stream.

6-2a 1225 Ralston Avenue, behind the police department. Open sunrise to sunset. (415) 595-7441.

Water Dog Lake Park

Dogs and their people seem drawn magically to this large, wooded park with a little lake in the middle. Maybe it's the way the moss drips off the trees at the bottom of this mountainous area, or the way the lake seems to create a refreshing breeze on the hottest days.

Or maybe it's got something to do with the name. We asked several dog owners how the park came to be called Water Dog Lake Park.

"I think the lake is kind of shaped like a dog. Actually, it's more like a kangaroo, isn't it?" said the proud owner of a beagle/terrier mix.

"It would be a good place to water your dog, if that were allowed," said a woman with a black lab.

"When dogs and people were allowed to swim here, you couldn't get the labs and all those water dogs out of this lake," explained a man with an Irish setter.

We hate to burst the romantic fantasy that a park as alluring as this one is named after man's best friend. But after some searching through historical records, we discovered the biting truth: Water Dog Lake Park is named after salamanders. A colloquial name for a salamander is water dog, and, apparently, the little critters used to wriggle all over the place around here.

We still think the park is great. Too bad dogs have to be leashed.

One other thing that we discovered about this park: If people would follow their dogs, perhaps a lot fewer would stumble onto the wrong trail—the one that goes up to the top of the park, never comes near the lake, and comes out more than a mile away from where you started. Joe tried tugging in the other direction, but we ignored him. We got a ride back to the entrance from a teenage boy who felt sorry for us.

On entering the park from the Lake Road entrance, take the wide path that goes straight in front of you. It will lead you down to the lake. Neither you nor your dog can go in the water, but you can have a great picnic there, or even go fishing off the little wooden pier.

If you start off taking the smaller trail that veers to the right, you'll get good exercise and a great view of the bay, but we don't recommend it, unless you enjoy getting lost and suffering heat fatigue in the summer. A final word of warning: Watch out for bikers. They're fast here.

6-2b Enter on Lake Road, just off Hallmark Drive. Try to come back to the same place. Open sunrise to sunset. (415) 595-7441.

RESTAURANTS

Cafe del Pollo: You can get fast food chicken in a slow-paced setting. One or two outdoor tables. 2040 Ralston Avenue. (415) 591-3262.

The Coffee Club: This is an international coffee nook with a wooden bench in front. It's a great place to visit on a morning walk in Twin Pines Park. 1035 Ralston Avenue. (415) 591-9888.

Yumi Yogurt: With a few chairs outside, and ample portions of yogurt, this place is especially refreshing after taking the wrong trail at Water Dog Lake Park. You can scoop off the top for the dog in your life and still have plenty for yourself. 2040 Ralston Avenue. (415) 592-9864.

FAIRS & FESTIVALS

Belmont Art & Wine Festival: This festival is held each May in Twin Pines Park. Dogs must be leashed. With roughly 10,000 people attending, this festival isn't as crowded as some, but it's not for dogs who are squeamish about masses of people. To get this year's date or more information, call (415) 595-7441.

6-3
BURLINGAME

PARKS, BEACHES & RECREATION AREAS

Bayside Park

Between the airport hotels and the local sewage disposal plant lies this nondescript patch of land. While it might be fun for baseball players and kids (there are three large baseball fields and a children's park), it's only ho-hum for dogs. They have to be leashed, there aren't many trees, and the constant drone of the highway seems to obliterate the natural sounds that dogs thrive on.

Slightly better, and directly across the street from Bayside Park, is a gravel jogging path that runs along the bay. While the bay looks particularly gray here and smells like a combination of swamp and diesel fuel, it's still the bay, and dogs seem to enjoy just being near it—leashed, of course.

6-3a On Airport Boulevard and Bayshore Highway, behind the Sheraton Hotel. Both areas are open from dawn to dusk. (415) 342-8931.

Washington Park

This relatively small park has the look of an old college campus. Its trees are big and old and mostly deciduous, making autumn a particularly brilliant time. Bring a lunch and eat it on the thick, knotty old redwood picnic tables. They're something out of the Enchanted Forest. Joe is intrigued by the abundance of squirrels, but doesn't get too far with his pursuits, since leashes are the law.

6-3b Corner of Burlingame and Carolan Avenues. Open dawn to dusk. (415) 342-8931.

RESTAURANTS

Coffee Bistro: A charming little cafe below street level, Coffee Bistro is just a few blocks from Washington Park. Dogs must be tied to something sturdy when you dine at any of the outdoor tables. A good snack is the strawberry fruit shake. At the Avenue Arcade, 1110 Burlingame Avenue. (415) 347-1208.

LODGINGS & CAMPGROUNDS

Days Inn: Southbound on Highway 101, take Broadway-Burlingame exit; northbound, exit East Anza Boulevard. 777 Airport Boulevard, Burlingame, CA 94010. Doubles cost about $65. Dogs are $4 extra. (415) 342-7772.

San Francisco Airport Marriott: Exit Highway 101 at Millbrae Avenue East. 1800 Old Bayshore Highway, Burlingame, CA 94010. Small pets only. Double rooms are about $125. (415) 692-9100.

Sheraton International: Southbound on Highway 101, take the Broadway-Burlingame exit; northbound, Old Bayshore Highway. 1177 Airport Boulevard, Burlingame, CA 94010. "Very tiny pets only," says a clerk. Doubles average $80. (415) 342-9200.

Vagabond Inn, Airport: Exit Highway 101 at East Millbrae Avenue. 1640 Bayshore Highway, Burlingame, CA 94010. Double rooms are about $55. Dogs are $8 extra per night. (415) 692-4040.

Fairs & Festivals

Broadway Merchants Street Festival: If your dog appreciates an old-fashioned, small-town atmosphere, he'll like this festival. Strolling musicians, barbershop quartets and dozens of locals fill Broadway during early August. Call (415) 588-2933.

Diversions

Slurp it up: Does your dog get the urge to down a cold one with the boys while you're strolling down Broadway together? We've got just the oasis for him. There are two popular "pet fountains" in front of the pet store Feast Your Beast. Dogs are welcome to drink all the fresh water they can hold, and there's no cover charge.

And if your dog's birthday is coming up, the folks at the store will put together all the fixings for a dog party—including a meatloaf birthday cake with mashed potato frosting. At 1205 Broadway. (415) 343-2378.

6-4

COLMA

There aren't any parks here, but there are plenty of cemeteries. We were told by more than one cemetery manager that unless the dog is a friend of the deceased, she's not allowed.

6-5

DALY CITY

We called the Daly City parks department to find out what its rule is regarding leashes. A helpful woman read the city ordinance:

Animals must be "*under control of owner by being saddled, harnessed, haltered or leashed by a substantial chain, lead rope or leash, which chain lead rope or leash shall be continuously held by some competent person capable of controlling such an animal.*"

So Joe wore a leash during our Daly City visits. But he put his paw down when it came to donning the saddle and halter.

Parks, Beaches & Recreation Areas

Gellert Park 

The best feature of this flat, square park is that it's right behind the Serramonte Library. It's also conveniently located if you are going to pay homage to someone at the Chinese Cemetery, right across the street. The park is made up of a few sports fields—watch out for flying baseballs, soccer balls and softballs. The park's trees, which surround two sides, aren't even accessible—they're on top of a very steep little ridge. Your dog may become frustrated, especially since he must wear a leash through all this.

6-5a On Wembley Drive at Gellert Boulevard. Open sunrise to sunset, or until night sporting events are over. (415) 991-8006.

Westmoor Park 

Another flat park in Daly City. This one is surrounded on most sides by chain-link fence. Nearly all the intriguing vegetation and big trees are fenced off, leaving just a few saplings for the sniffing of your poor leashed friend.

6-5b On Edgemont Drive at Lincoln Avenue. Open sunrise to sunset, or until night sporting events in adjacent field are over. (415) 991-8006.

Fairs & Festivals

Daly City Fall Festival: Take your dog for a stroll *and* get your Christmas shopping done early. This crafts fair is held each autumn outside the Westlake Shopping Center. Call (415) 755-8526 for more information.

Diversions

Ask your dog for a date to a movie: It's greasy. It's hokey. But going to the Burlingame Drive-In Theater is a great way to catch a movie and spare yourself the guilt of leaving your dog home alone. And it's cheap. Dogs are free—unless, like ours, they have a thing for popcorn. We saw a real classic here: *Don't Tell Mom the Babysitter's Dead.* Joe loved it. He couldn't take his eyes off the screen, except to lick the sound box. 350 Beach Road. (415) 343-2213.

6-6

FOSTER CITY

John Oliver, former mayor of Foster City, isn't the sort to beat around the bush. When he describes the older women who set out to improve the town by getting recreational vehicles off the streets and enforcing the leash law, he's not kind.

"They are the forces of darkness," he says. "They're a couple of little old ladies right from central casting for their nit-picking roles."

Oliver's feathers are ruffled for good reason. In 1988—a year after he stopped being mayor, and shortly after the "forces of darkness" started crusading for more dog patrols—a cop cited him for walking his little dog Topper off-leash. The ticket was only $25. It was the principle that distressed him—not to mention the newspaper story. "Topper was an angel of a dog and in a totally empty park. Come on, let's get sensible here," he says.

This is the dog who used to break out of Oliver's truck and run into city council chambers to find him during meetings. She's the same 20-pound mutt who stayed by Oliver's side during a recent bout of bad luck that forced them into homelessness. "She made life a lot easier when we were living in that truck," he says.

Oliver has always voted for leash laws, but he believes the real issue is control. "If you can control your dog in a safe area, and there's no one around to disturb, why not let her loose for a few minutes?" he asks. "It's a shame it has to cost you if you're caught."

PARKS, BEACHES & RECREATION AREAS

Boothbay Park 

It's off with the leash once you find the right section of this park, which is the grassy area behind the tennis courts. It's surrounded on two sides by a tall wooden fence, and is comfortably far from the road. This little corner of the park is nothing fancy, but it does allow dogs some freedom.

6-6a On Boothbay Avenue and Edgewater Lane. Open dawn to 10 p.m. (415) 345-5731.

Foster City Dog Exercise Area 

This enclosed dog run area has great potential, but it's a disappointment. Dogs are allowed off-leash here, but as soon as they get down to having fun with each other, they kick up clouds of dust. The ground is pretty much packed dirt, with little bits of grass trying to push through.

The view isn't any more attractive, with powerlines overhead, the back of City Hall in the foreground and rows of look-alike townhouses in the distance. What this place needs is a few good trees. And some water for the dogs.

Two good points, though: The fences are very high, so if you have an escape artist for a dog, this place is about the safest around. And there are plenty of large trash cans—six, to be exact—and no shortage of pooper scoopers.

6-6b At 600 Foster City Boulevard. Park in the lot behind City Hall. Open dawn to 10 p.m. (415) 345-5731.

FAIRS & FESTIVALS

Foster City Art & Wine Festival: Ferris wheels, merry-go-rounds, crafts, food and wine surround you at this early summer event in Leo J. Ryan Park. Dogs must be leashed and can't go on the rides, but there's plenty to interest them on the ground. (415) 573-7600.

Fourth of July: Start with a pancake breakfast at Leo J. Ryan Park and peruse arts and crafts with your leashed dog for the rest of the day. Make sure to take your dog home before the fireworks start. Even the bravest mutt can fall to pieces hearing all that noise. (415) 573-7600.

6-7 HALF MOON BAY

PARKS, BEACHES & RECREATION AREAS

Half Moon Bay State Beach 

This is the beach air-conditioned by the god of sheepdogs and malamutes. No matter how steaming hot it is elsewhere, you can almost always count on brisk weather here. It's cool and foggy in the summer, wet and windy in the winter, and moderate in the fall and spring.

The three-mile crescent of beach is actually made up of four beaches. From north to south, along Highway 1, they are: **Roosevelt Beach**, **Dunes Beach**, **Venice Beach** and **Francis Beach**.

Dogs aren't permitted on Francis Beach, but they are allowed at the campground above. (For more information about camping here, see listing under Lodgings and Campgrounds.) Dogs are allowed on-leash on all other beaches, but this isn't the place to come for a 15-minute romp: It costs $5 per car and $1 per dog.

The beaches are all clean and each is almost identical to the next, so your choice of beach should depend on which entry is most convenient. Rangers roam year-round. If you're thinking of breaking the leash law, this is a bad place to try it.

6-7a From Highway 1, follow the brown and white signs to the appropriate beach. Open sunrise to sunset. (415) 726-6203.

RESTAURANTS

Big I's Cream Parlor Restaurant: Rich and creamy fountain treats are the specialty here, but burgers are big sellers, too. There are two outdoor picnic tables for dining with friends and dogs. Located just south of Venice Beach on Highway 1. (415) 726-5705.

Cosmic Charlie's: A sign inside reads, "Over 4,800 tofu burgers sold!" This charming vegetarian restaurant you'd expect to find in Santa Cruz has a wooden patio with tableside service and a large menu. The nutloaf with mushroom sherry sauce is exquisite, though your dog may prefer meatloaf. After your meal, visit Moontown Pottery at the back lot. They'll custom-make a clay steamer for you, with dog biscuits for handles and a replica of your dog—in howling position—on top. When the water boils, the steam shoots out your dog's mouth. Cosmic Charlie's is at 510 Kelly Avenue, near the Francis Beach Campground entrance. (415) 726-0239.

Taqueria La Mexicana: Fast burritos, tacos, enchiladas, burgers and fried chicken are just a few of the items you can eat at picnic tables under a bright orange awning. On Highway 1 just north of Kelly Avenue. (415) 726-1746.

Pasta Moon: This restaurant offers several sidewalk tables and every type of pasta imaginable. 315 Main Street. (415) 726-5125.

LODGING & CAMPGROUNDS

Francis Beach Campground: If you can ignore all the RVs and crowds of tents, this is a stunning camping spot. Perched on iceplant-covered dunes above the Pacific, it's one of the most accessible beach camp areas in the Bay Area. There are cold outdoor showers near the restrooms. You can make reservations through MISTIX by calling (800) 444-PARK. In the summer, you'll need to make them at least eight weeks in advance. Off Highway 1 and Kelly Avenue.

Old Thyme Inn: The herb theme runs deep in this homey 1899 Victorian. You and your dog can stay in any of six rooms, all named—and fashioned—after herbs, and filled with antiques. One of the best is the Mint Room. It's painted a cool green and comes with fireplace, claw-foot tub and a view of the ocean. "San Mateo County is ridiculous when it comes to hospitality to dogs," laments owner Simon Lowings. "I'm doing my part to make them feel more welcome." Hurray for Simon. 779 Main Street, Half Moon Bay, CA 94019. Room rates vary signifcantly, but average about $80. (415) 726-1616.

The Zaballa House: This 1859 country Victorian is the oldest standing house in Half Moon Bay. It's tops on Joe's list of bed and breakfast inns. Some of the nine quaint bedrooms have fireplaces and Jacuzzis. Breakfasts are fresh and out of this world. Cats are occasionally guests here, so if your dog likes cats for lunch, you may want to inquire as to their presence when you make your reservation. Average double room is $90. 324 Main Street, Half Moon Bay, CA 94019. (415) 726-9123.

6-8

HILLSBOROUGH

PARKS, BEACHES & RECREATION AREAS

Vista Park

You can visit this park only if you live here, unless you choose to walk miles to get to it: There's no street parking for blocks, and no parking lot. And chances are that if you live in this town, your back yard is bigger anyway. There's a little section in the back with several tall eucalyptus trees that leashed neighborhood dogs call their own. It's good for sniffs when you can't get to a better park.

6-8a At Vista Road and Culebra Road. Open dawn to dusk. (415) 579-3800.

6-9

MENLO PARK

PARKS, BEACHES & RECREATION AREAS

Bayfront Park

This place used to be a dump—literally. It was the regional landfill site until it reached capacity in 1984. Then the city sealed the huge mounds of garbage under a two-foot clay barrier and covered it with four feet of soil, planted grass and trees, and *voila*—instant 160-acre park!

Now it's a land of rolling hills with a distinctly American Indian flavor. The packed dirt trails take you up to majestic views of the bay and surrounding marshes. There's no sign of garbage anywhere, unless you look down from the top of a hill and spot the methane extraction plant. Fortunately, very few vista points include that.

Our favorite part of the park is a trail studded with large, dark rocks arranged to form symbols, which in series make up a poem. The concept was inspired by American Indian pictographs— a visual language system for recording daily events. At the trailhead, you'll find a sign quoting part of the poem and giving a map of the trail, showing the meaning of each rock arrangement as it corresponds to the poem.

Here's the entire poem:

Evening good
weather clear with stars.
I walk with the wind behind me
inspired with glad heart.
Come,
discover many animals,
grass, sun, canyons, and earth.
No hunger, war, no fear
Making peace and strong brothers.
Climb this way,
over mountain or hill.
Go in four directions —
up, down, close or far away,
to places hidden or bright,
under rain or cloud, night or day,
reaching to see
birds, plants, water and trees,
as you walk this trail and cross this path.
Rest here.
Talk here.
Flee your troubles to the sky
holding firm to harmony, virtue and peace,
barring evil,
strong with wisdom and healing,
reaching out with supplication
to the Great Spirit everywhere.

Although leashes are required, dogs seem really fond of this park, sniffing everywhere, tails wagging constantly. Perhaps they can sense the park's less picturesque days deep underground. Or they may be touched by the Indian magic that imbues these hills.

6-9a The park starts at the end of Marsh Road, just on the other side of the Bayfront Expressway. To get to the beginning of the rock poem trail, continue past the entrance on Marsh Road to the second parking lot on the right. Open sunrise to sunset. (415) 858-3470.

RESTAURANTS

Garden Grill: This is one of our top choices. In an old English garden, under the canopy of an enormous 400-year-old oak tree, you can eat like a king—literally. While the Garden Grill specializes in traditional English dishes and a charming afternoon tea, it's especially proud of its medieval cuisine. Try the 14th-century soup. It was one of King Richard II's favorites. And your dog will salivate when your server brings you elk, venison or squab with a hearty fruit and wine sauce. Unlike medieval tourist traps, the Garden Grill encourages use of fork and knife. There are 18 tables outside this English cottage restaurant. 1026 Alma Street. (415) 325-8981.

6-10

MILLBRAE

PARKS, BEACHES & RECREATION AREAS

Central Park 

A long, inviting line of redwood trees runs down the middle of this park. Leash your dog and explore. Other than the trees, Central Park isn't too distinctive, except for a popular children's playground at one end.

6-10a On Lincoln Circle at Laurel Avenue. Open dawn to dusk. (415) 259-2360.

Constitution Park

This is a thumbnail of grass adjacent to the Millbrae Museum. Your dog won't get much exercise here, but he may get other benefits: Local dog owners call it Constitutional Park. Don't forget a leash.

6-10b On Poplar Avenue at Lansdale Avenue, in back of the city library. Open dawn to dusk. (415) 259-2360.

RESTAURANTS

Angela's Italian Deli: "Mamma mia!" was Joe's reaction to the side order of pesto pasta spilled all over the sidewalk. He must have looked thirsty after he wolfed it down, because the cashier came out and gave him a bowl of water. Only two sidewalk tables here. 310 Broadway Avenue. (415) 697-2617.

Leonardo's Delicatessen: Just a few blocks from the parks, this truly Italian deli has plenty of outdoor tables, all comfortably far from sidewalk traffic. 540 Broadway Avenue. (415) 697-9779.

LODGINGS & CAMPGROUNDS

Clarion Hotel: East off Highway 101 at Millbrae exit. 401 East Millbrae Avenue 94030. Dogs must be brought in via cage, so think twice if your Saint Bernard needs a place to stay. Average price for a double is $110. (415) 692-6363.

FAIRS & FESTIVALS

Millbrae Art & Wine Festival: Every Labor Day weekend, 100,000 people flock downtown to see the works of 250 artists and sample the goods of dozens of wineries. It's fun only for the most crowd-loving dogs—200,000 is a lot of legs. Call (415) 697-7324 for more details.

6-11

MONTARA

PARKS, BEACHES & RECREATION AREAS

Montara State Beach 

This long, wide beach has more nooks and crannies than your dog will be able to investigate. Around mid-beach, you'll find several little inlets carved into the mini-cliffs. Take your dog back there at low tide, and you'll find all sorts of water, grass, mud and *objets de beach*. It's a good place for her to get her paws wet, while obeying the leash law.

The water is very still back there. This is where Joe first dared to walk in water. It was only a centimeter deep, but he licked his paws in triumph all the way home.

6-11a Off Highway 1, park in the little lot behind the Chart House restaurant. There's also a parking area on the north side of the beach, off Highway 1. Open sunrise to sunset. (415) 726-6203.

6-12

PACIFICA

Parks, Beaches & Recreation Areas

Pacifica State Beach 

This surfer's paradise rates just so-so in the canine world. Dogs must be leashed, picnickers abound, and the temptation to sneak a chicken leg can be too much for even the best of dogs. The beach isn't very wide, leaving little room for exploration. The setting alone, however, warrants good marks: green rolling hills in the distance behind you, the pounding sea before you.

6-12a On Highway 1, park between Crespi Drive and Linda Mar Boulevard. Open sunrise to sunset. (415) 726-6203.

Sharp Park Beach 

Don't make the mistake several people have told us they've made—get up at an ungodly hour, gather your fishing gear, and march out to the pier with your dog to catch your supper. Dogs aren't allowed on the pier, perhaps because they tend to eat the bait and the catch of the day. But you may take them to the beach 30 feet below, as long as they're leashed. It's a narrow beach, though, so make sure you go when the tide is out.

6-12b Enter at San Jose and Beach Boulevards, or Beach Boulevard at Clarendon Road. Open sunrise to sunset. (415) 738-7380.

Sweeney Ridge

(See page 185 for a description.)

Restaurants

Beach Cafe: After a walk on the chilly beach, there's nothing like a hot espresso and homemade croissant at the outdoor tables here. The owners have two samoyeds, so it's a very dog-friendly place. Highway 1 at Rockaway Beach Avenue, next to Kentucky Fried Chicken. (415) 355-4532.

Sam's Deli: A refreshing spot to hit after an afternoon at Pacifica State Beach. Good sandwiches at low prices and two outdoor tables. At the Linda Mar Shopping Center, just behind the beach. It's on the same side as Denny's and the shoe stores, about halfway down the row of shops. 1261 Linda Mar Shopping Center. (415) 359-5330.

6-13

PESCADERO

PARKS, BEACHES & RECREATION AREAS

Bean Hollow State Beach 

The rocky intertidal zone here is terrific for tidepooling, but only if you and your dog are sure-footed. To get to the best tidepools, you must perform an amazing feat of team coordination—climbing down 70-million-year-old rock formations while attached to each other by leash. It's not that steep, just awkward. The pitted rocks can be slippery. This maneuver is not recommended for dogs who go deaf and senseless when the alluring ocean beckons them to swim. Besides, the surf can be treacherous in this area.

If you reach the tidepools, you're in for a real treat. But make sure your canine companion doesn't go fishing—we've seen a dog stick his entire head in a tidepool to capture a little crab. Fur and fangs aren't natural in the delicate balance of this wet habitat, so please keep dogs out of the tidepools. The mussels will thank you.

If you decide to play it safe and stay on flat land, you can still see the harbor seal rookery on the rocks below the coastal bluffs. Bring a pair of binoculars, and you can really get a view of them up close and personal.

6-13a Off Highway 1 at Bean Hollow Road. Open sunrise to sunset. (415) 726-6203.

Pescadero State Beach 

There are three entrances to this two-mile-long beach, and each one leads to a unique setting on the Pacific. The prime attractions at the southernmost entrance, on Highway 1 at Pescadero Road, are the small cliffs that hang over the crashing ocean. There are even a few picnic tables on the edges of the mini-cliffs, for those who like lunch with a built-in thrill. Hold onto your leash!

The middle entrance, reached from the small parking lot, will lead you to a secluded and untamed rocky area. Take one of the less steep trails down, and you'll find yourself in the middle of lots of rocks, rotting kelp, driftwood and a few small tidepools. This is an eerie place to come on a very foggy day. Joe loves it here during pea-soupers.

Perch atop the vista point at this central entrance, and you'll get a great view of the **Pescadero Marsh Natural Preserve**, just across

Highway 1. Unfortunately, you can't explore the preserve with your dog.

The north entrance is the only one that charges a fee for use—$5 per car and $1 per dog. But many people park beside the road and walk over the sandy dunes to escape the cover charge. This is the most civilized—and mundane—entrance, with a wide beach and lots of kite fliers. Dogs must wear leashes on all parts of the beach.

6-13b The south entrance is at Pescadero Road and Highway 1. Follow the signs to the north for the other entrances. Open sunrise to sunset. (415) 726-6203.

RESTAURANTS

Arcangeli Grocery Company: There's always fresh-baked bread here—still hot—waiting for you after a cold day at the beach. We like to buy a loaf of steaming herb-garlic bread and eat it on the bench out front. 287 Stage Road. (415) 879-0147.

Dinelli's: For homemade pies, Greek food and french-fried artichokes, this diner with three big wood tables outside is the best. If you tie your dog to a table with a short leash, she's welcome. 1956 Pescadero Road. (415) 879-0106.

LODGINGS & CAMPGROUNDS

McKenzie House: This enchanting 1840s cottage—with spa tub and wood-burning stove—is the place your dog would visit every weekend if he had a choice and $95 a night. Owner Christie Keith has created the most dog-friendly lodging possible. The three acres around the cottage are surrounded by fences. There's also a one-acre dog run, for dogs who are cat crazy (Keith has two cats in addition to her four dogs, and the cats know the run is off-limits). In addition, Keith can tell you about some superb private areas nearby that allow the occasional off-leash dog. 443 Dearborn Park Road, Pescadero, CA 94060. (415) 879-1240.

6-14 PORTOLA VALLEY

PARKS, BEACHES, & RECREATION AREAS

Long Ridge Preserve

Although the park is 980 acres of oak and madrone forests, grassy hills, miles of trails and great expanses of open land with incredible views, dogs are confined to a tiny, boring strip in the north end of the park.

It's a real disappointment. Just when you get going, you have to turn around. The part that really kills dogs, though, is a refreshing little creek: No dogs are allowed near it. But we've seen many a thirsty leashed dog pull a protesting owner to the creek's edge as he dips his paws.

6-14a The park is on Highway 35 (Skyline Boulevard), about three miles north of the intersection of Highways 9 and 35. It's actually several miles south of Portola Valley, the nearest town. Use the Grizzly Flat parking area to the east. Signs will tell you where dogs are allowed. Open dawn to dusk. (415) 949-5500.

Windy Hill Preserve 

You can look out from the top of the first big hill you come to and see for miles all around—and though you're on the edge of the suburbs, you'll see hardly a house. This 1,130-acre preserve of the Midpeninsula Regional Open Space District has as many different terrains as it has views—grassland ridges and lush wooded ravines with serene creeks.

There are more than three miles of trails that allow you with your leashed canine companion. But watch out for foxtails. The park is so dry that foxtails seem to proliferate all year. Bring lots of water, because it can get very hot here, and there isn't any shade for the first mile.

Start at **Anniversary Trail,** to your left. The hike is a vigorous three-quarters of a mile uphill, and that may be enough, especially when it's baking. But you can continue down the other side of the hill and loop right, onto **Spring Ridge Trail.** Near the end of this 2.5-mile-long path, you'll come to a wooded area with a small, very refreshing creek. This is a good place to sit a spell before heading back.

6-14b Park at the lot on Skyline Boulevard, two miles south of Highway 84 and five miles north of Alpine Road. You'll see the big sign for the preserve, and three picnic tables. Open sunrise to sunset. (415) 949-5500.

6-15

REDWOOD CITY

No dogs are allowed in any of Redwood City's parks. But if you happen to be passing through, there are a couple of dog-friendly restaurants and lodgings.

RESTAURANTS

Cafe Figaro: Polenta and risotto are big here. So is opera. From your table outside, you and your dog can feast your ears on recordings of some of the best vocal cords in the world. 2639 Broadway. (415) 365-1223.

LODGINGS & CAMPGROUNDS

Howard Johnson Motor Lodge: West of and adjacent to Highway 101. Exit at Whipple Avenue. 485 Veterans Boulevard, Redwood City, CA 94063. Average price for a double is $65. (415) 365-5500.

FAIRS & FESTIVALS

Sunflower Festival: Considering Redwood City's anti-dog attitude in its parks, this is as close as your dog will ever come to having a good time in a public place here. Sunflowers are the theme, but there's plenty of wine tasting and food sampling. The festival is usually held on Broadway in late September. Call (415) 365-0718 for more details.

6-16

SAN BRUNO

PARKS, BEACHES & RECREATION AREAS

San Bruno Dog Exercise Area 

This is a gem of a fenced-in park, where dogs can run their tails off—without a leash. The grass always seems to be green; there's plenty of water, pooper scoopers galore and benches for two-legged beasts. As an extra bonus, it has a great view of the bay. And for those who can't get enough of it while driving north on Highway 101, there's an unparalleled view of that strange sign:

"SOUTH SAN FRANCISCO—THE INDUSTRIAL CITY"

The park opened in 1989 after local dog trainer Mal Lightfoot was fined for walking his notoriously obedient dogs off-leash. "I spend all my life training dogs to be good citizens, and I was treated like a criminal," says Lightfoot, who runs the San Bruno Dog Training School. "It was the last straw." It took him and dozens of other frustrated dog owners nearly two years of working with—and against—city officials to get the park of their dreams.

6-16a Some detailed directions are necessary for finding this out-of-the-way park, even for locals. From El Camino Real, take Sneath Lane west. Just past Highway 280, turn right on Rollingwood Drive. Go right again at the first possible right, Crestwood Drive. Go left on Valleywood Drive, and take a sharp right at Evergreen Drive. The park is in a few blocks, at Maywood and Evergreen Drives in back of the old Carl Sandburg School. Once at the school driveway, take the first road to the right and drive until you see the dog park. Open sunrise to sunset. (415) 877-8868.

6-17

SAN CARLOS

Parks, Beaches & Recreation Areas

Big Canyon Park

The big canyon here is more like two steep hills, which you're sandwiched between. There's a short trail that takes you and your leashed dog to the back of the park, but it's barely worth the walk, unless the creek is dry. If it is, you can keep walking beyond the trail, along the creek bed. Bring your insect repellent, because the farther back you go, the more voracious the mosquitos.

6-17a On Brittan Avenue, just east of Crestview Drive. Open dawn to dusk. (415) 593-8011.

Heather Park

This is the only fenced-in dog park we've ever seen that comes complete with rolling hills, wildflowers, old gnarled trees and singing birds. Your dog will have the time of his life here, bounding up and down hills or trotting down the winding paved path to the bottom of the park—*sans* leash. You may be tempted to take some of the tiny dirt trails up the steep hills, but they tend to end abruptly, leaving you and your dog teetering precariously. The only thing the park lacks is water, usually a given at dog runs.

If you have a dog who likes to wander, watch out: There are a couple of potential escape routes near the park's two gates. They're at the far ends of the park, so you may not encounter them until you're ready to leave. Also on the down side: We've been told the place is infested with ticks, although we've never had a problem.

6-17b At Melendy and Portofino Drives. Open dawn to dusk. (415) 593-8011.

RESTAURANTS

Coffee Club Two: Lots of dogs come here with their owners for a sip of coffee and a pastry on weekend mornings, sitting in any of several chairs outdoors. There's heavy socializing among dog people. 749 Laurel Street. (415) 592-9888.

6-18

SAN GREGORIO

PARKS, BEACHES & RECREATION AREAS

San Gregorio State Beach 

This place is usually a little too crowded with families for a comfortable dog walk, even a leashed one, which is the rule. It's sometimes just too difficult to negotiate through all the barbecuers, sunbathers, children and sand castles. The beach is so popular in part because of a lagoon that often forms at the mouth of **San Gregorio Creek**. The still water is an ideal depth for children, but dogs tend to enjoy wading through too. Watch out for crumbling cliffs above. And don't forget the $5 entry fee, plus $1 per dog.

6-18a On Highway 1 just south of Highway 84. Open sunrise to sunset. (415) 726-6203.

Pomponio State Beach 

This 1.5-mile-long beach is fine for sunbathing, but you can also go surf fishing for striped bass, search for driftwood or walk to the south end of the beach and watch nesting ravens along the craggy bluffs. Dogs must be leashed, but they seem to feel right at home here. One of Joe's favorite pastimes is picking up long pieces of driftwood and "accidentally" tripping whoever is walking him as he trots merrily along. $5 fee per car, $1 extra per dog.

6-18b On Highway 1, just south of San Gregorio State Beach. Open dawn to dusk. (415) 726-6203.

6-19

SAN MATEO

PARKS, BEACHES & RECREATION AREAS

Bayside-Joinville Park 

Human olfactory senses may be mildly offended by the scents in this park, but dogs seem to thrive on them. Depending on which way the wind is blowing, the odor is bound to hit you at some point. It's a stale smell, like a dishrag that's still in the sink a week after Thanksgiving. Sometimes it's even worse. The alleged culprit is an old compost site across the street, where **Shoreline Park** will be built in the future. When it's potent, Joe stands nose to the wind, tail trembling, glued in homage.

But the park has some notable qualities. It's just across the street from San Francisco Bay, it's on the **Marina Lagoon** (no swimming allowed) and it's well maintained.

6-19a The park has two parts. If you're the type who likes the bad news first, start at the Anchor Road entrance and take the path along the lagoon, over a guano-covered footbridge, past the big gray pump station and onto a little dirt path on the edge of the lagoon. Then go left and take the second, cleaner footbridge over to the better half of the park. It's got a decent-sized field, young trees and tennis courts. Or you can enter at Kehoe Avenue and Roberta Drive and reverse the path. Open sunrise to sunset. (415) 377-4640.

Beresford Park 

The bulk of this park is made up of sports fields. But venture behind the garden center, and you and your pooch can enjoy a pleasant little leashed romp on a large grassy field. A dozen or so adolescent pine trees are trying to grow despite dozens of daily assaults from male dogs. Several picnic tables and a children's play area near the field make this an adequate spot for a weekend afternoon with the family. People are friendly here—we were twice offered soda and beer by locals, who wanted Joe to "hang" with them.

6-19b On Parkside Way at Alameda de las Pulgas. Open dawn to dusk, or until night sporting events are over. (415) 377-4640.

Central Park 

Bring plenty of quarters if you want to fully experience this strange park on the edge of downtown. It costs a quarter to park in the underground lot; a quarter to put your finger in the pulse machine; a quarter to watch the chicken lay a plastic prize egg; a quarter for the Pen Vendorama; it even costs a quarter for a cup of water at the refreshment stand, although a water fountain is within 20 feet.

As you enter the park from the 5th Avenue side, you immediately encounter the concession stand and surrounding dispensers that rival any at state fairs. The stand has good ice cream and tolerable pizza.

The rest of the park is a lush green miniature version of Golden Gate Park. There's a Japanese garden, and although no dogs are allowed inside, the Japanese ambiance spills outside. The days we've visited, there has usually been something going on at the outdoor stage in back of the recreation center. A couple of large meadows are bordered by big shady redwoods. There's even a pint-sized railroad that takes up part of a small field. Someone told us that dogs have been known to chase the cars as they chug along the track. Leashes are a must, a rule you'd be well-advised to follow: The fine for loose dogs is not a quarter.

6-19c East 5th Avenue at El Camino Real. Open sunrise to sunset. (415) 377-4640.

Laurelwood Park 

A small, clear stream winds the length of this rural park in the suburbs. Joe won't have anything to do with the water and jumps from one side to the other without getting a toenail damp. But normal dogs delight in its fresh scents and enticing sounds. Follow the bike trail—heeding the leash law, as this is a popular spot for bikers—along the stream, and enjoy tree-covered hillsides in a virtually suburb-free environment. Only a few blocks from the Laurelwood Shopping Center, this park is an ideal getaway after a quick shopping trip. The kids can use the playground at the foot of the bike trail.

6-19d Glendora Drive at Cedarwood Drive. Open sunrise to sunset. (415) 377-4640.

Restaurants

Norby's Frozen Yogurt: If you'd rather indulge in yogurt than Central Park's ice cream, this shop has some of the best. Two benches on the sidewalk. 239 East 3rd Avenue. (415) 344-3863.

Rigoletto Caffe/Ristorante: A classic Italian courtyard with several tables, 17 pastas at dinner and warm tableside service. 50 East 4th Avenue. (415) 344-6326.

Lodgings & Campgrounds

Dunfey San Mateo Hotel: Exit Highway 92 at Delaware Street; go east on Concar Drive. 1770 South Amphlett Boulevard, San Mateo, CA 94402. Average double price is $110. (415) 573-7661.

Residence Inn by Marriott: Exit Highway 92 at Edgewater Boulevard. 2000 Winward Way, San Mateo, CA 94404. Doubles cost about $150. Dogs are $6 extra a day, plus a $50 deposit. (415) 574-4700.

Villa Hotel: Exit Highway 101 at Hillsdale Boulevard West, 1.5 miles. 4000 South El Camino Real, San Mateo, CA 94403. Average double price is $100. (415) 341-0966.

Fairs & Festivals

Victorian Days: You and your dog may feel as though you've traveled back in time a century or so. This fair has mock Civil War skirmishes, duels, historic plays and entertainment and, of course, arts and crafts. Victorian Days is held at the end of August at Central Park. Call (415) 574-6441 for more information.

6-20 SOUTH SAN FRANCISCO

Parks, Beaches & Recreation Areas

Orange Memorial Park

Hidden behind the park's large baseball field is a big square of land surrounded on all sides by tall trees. It's good for a quick romp on-leash. There seem to be all kinds of sniffs around the large weeping willow tree in the middle of the field.

6-20a Orange Avenue at Tennis Drive. Open dawn to dusk. (415) 877-8560.

Westborough Park

This is a hilly little park with many picnic tables, a tennis court and a children's playground. Your best bet is to take the narrow, paved path along the back of the park. It's lined with trees, and far from the madding baseball field below. Leashes required.

6-20b Westborough Avenue at Galway Drive, just west of Highway 280. Open dawn to dusk. (415) 877-8560.

Lodgings & Campgrounds

Holiday Inn San Francisco International: Exit Highway 101 at South Airport Boulevard. 245 South Airport Boulevard, South San Francisco, CA 94080. Doubles are about $80. (415) 589-7200.

La Quinta Motor Inn: Take the Highway 101 exit at South Airport Boulevard. 20 Airport Boulevard, South San Francisco, CA 94080. Doubles are about $75 a night. Small pets only. (415) 583-2223.

Fairs & Festivals

South San Francisco Art & Wine Festival: Usually held in late August on Grand Avenue. Call (415) 588-2933 for information.

6-21

WOODSIDE

Restaurants

Alice's Restaurant: You can get almost anything you want at this restaurant, including a table for you and your dog on the large porch. Weekends here are packed with bikers, especially for Alice's colossal breakfasts. If your dog rides in your motorcycle sidecar, this is the place for you. At 17288 Skyline Boulevard, the corner of Highways 35 and 84. Just two miles north of Portola Valley's Windy Hill Preserve. (415) 851-0303.

King's Mountain Country Store: Owner Sheri Fisher loves dogs. In fact, she's soon going to start making homemade dog biscuits. Inside there are candles, books, dog food, crafts, camping items and a deli. Classical music plays all the time. Grab a sandwich and a dog biscuit and step outside to a table, and you and your dog can break bread together. 13100 Skyline Boulevard, adjacent to the Purisima Creek Open Space Preserve (no dogs allowed there). (415) 851-3852.

More Info

Where Your Dog Can't Go

- Any county parks
- Any Redwood City Parks
- Any open space preserves, except Long Ridge and Windy Hill (see pages 201 and 202)
- Any marine reserve or wildlife refuge
- Unpaved trails at any state parks, except for McNee Ranch State Park (see page 184)
- Pacifica Pier
- Sawyer Camp Trail, at San Andreas Lake
- Several Daly City parks: Alta Loma Park, Arden Court Park, Camelot Park, Canterbury Park, Cameo Park, Frankfurt Park, Hampshire Park, John Daly

Park, Longview Park, Lycett Park, Mission Hills Park, Norwood Park and Polaris Park

- Two major festivals: Pacifica's Fog Fest and Half Moon Bay's Pumpkin Fest

USEFUL PHONE NUMBERS & ADDRESSES

California Department of Parks & Recreation: San Mateo Coast District, 95 Kelly Avenue, Half Moon Bay, CA 94019. (415) 726-6203.

Midpeninsula Regional Open Space District: 201 San Antonio Circle, #C-135, Mountain View, CA 94040. (415) 949-5500.

Dog Owners for Green Space (DOGS), Terry Robertson, chairman: (415) 595-1026.

Note: Dogs are allowed on SamTrans buses, but only if they're in a box or cage. There's no extra charge for them. Call (800) 660-4287 for details.

MISTIX: (800) 444-7275.

Santa Clara County

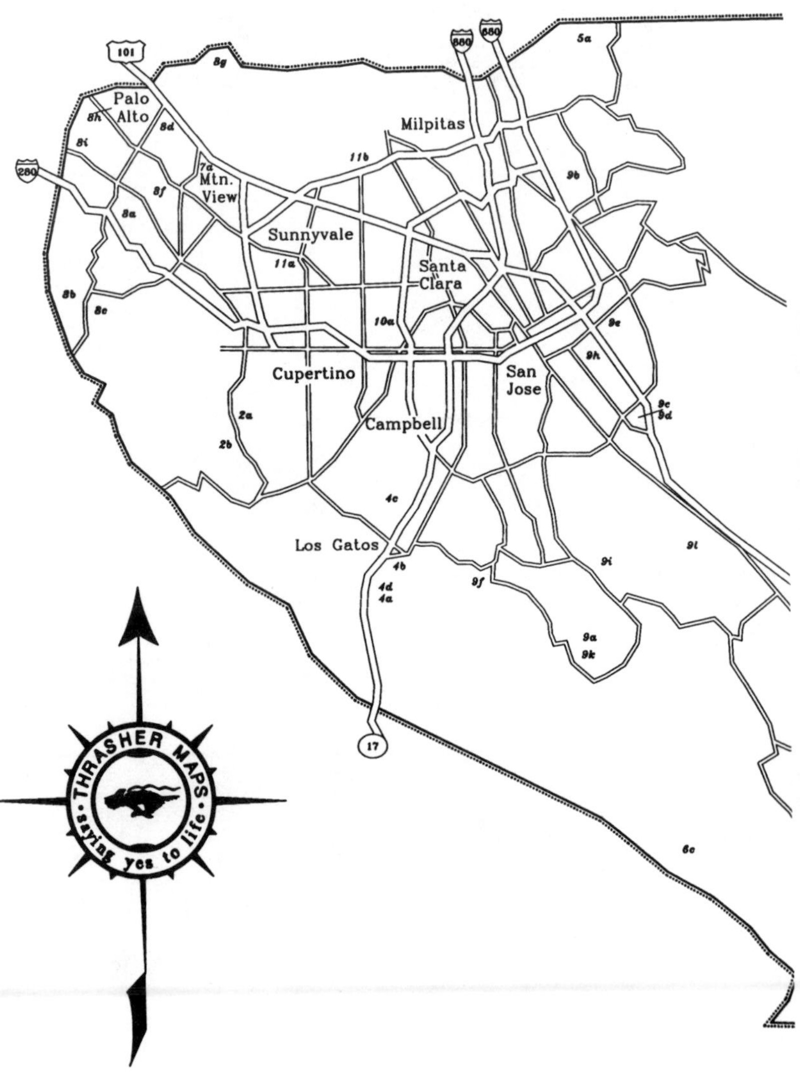
101
8g
680
880
5a
Palo
Alto
8h
8d
8i
Milpitas
11b
280
7a
Mtn.
View
8f
9b
8a
Sunnyvale
11a
Santa
Clara
8b
8c
10a
9e
9h
Cupertino
San
Jose
9c
9d
2a
Campbell
2b
4c
Los Gatos
9l
9i
4b
4d
4a
9f
9a
9k
17
THRASHER MAPS
saying yes to life
6c

9g
9j
6a
6b
3a
3b
Morgan Hill
Gilroy
152
156
101

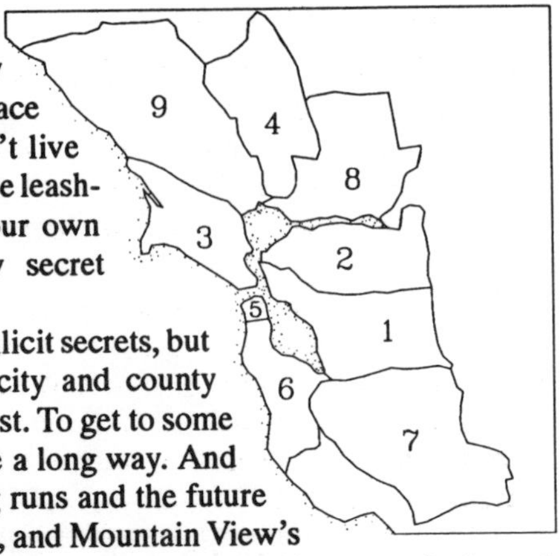

7

The 1,316 miles of **Santa Clara County** can be a miserable place to own a dog—if you don't live in Palo Alto, which has three leash-free dog runs, or have your own acreage, or know a few secret places.

We won't tell you any illicit secrets, but we'll tell you about the city and county parks your dog will like best. To get to some of them, you have to drive a long way. And except for Palo Alto's dog runs and the future run planned for Sunnyvale, and Mountain View's parks if you have a permit, dogs must be leashed in every single park and recreation area in the entire county. For this county, a high Paws Scale rating isn't necessarily based on accessibility or leash-freedom.

You and your dog can have fun in imaginative ways here, though. For instance, you can turn Santa Clara County's infamous 150 shopping malls into an asset. Several of the larger malls that are open to the air allow dogs in the corridors. (The huge Eastridge Mall doesn't, but the Stanford Shopping Center does.) Check with the business office of your usual shopping center before leaving that poor sad pup at home.

The county's ethnic variety affords a wealth of festivals, and its rural past survives in various farm industry fairs. All furnish music, food and terrific smells, and your dog will love to go along.

Farming is by no means dead in the county, either. Especially around Watsonville, just over the line in Santa Cruz County, U-pick farms do a good business. Call before you go to see if a well-picked-up-after dog will be allowed.

Santa Clara County's wineries, often neglected in favor of those to the north, might be so grateful to see you that they'll let you bring the dog along. (See the discussion of wine-tasting in chapter 10, Sonoma County.)

STATE PARKS

- California State Parks in Santa Clara County
- Henry Coe State Park, 14 miles east of Morgan Hill

MIDPENINSULA REGIONAL OPEN SPACE DISTRICT

The Midpeninsula Regional Open Space District runs close to 30 preserves in San Mateo and Santa Clara counties (see San Mateo County, page 179), but only three in Santa Clara County allow dogs: **St. Joseph's Hill Open Space Preserve**, Los Gatos; **Fremont Older Open Space Preserve**, Cupertino; and **Foothills Open Space Preserve**, Palo Alto.

These open spaces all require your dog to be leashed, and they have no toilets or potable water sources. Always carry your own. They're open from sunrise to sunset. We've supplied directions to the main entry point of each, listed under its nearest city. For maps (unfortunately, fairly hard to follow) and further information, call the district: (415) 949-5500.

SANTA CLARA COUNTY PARKS

The county-run parks are definitely the nicest developed parks in the county. **Mount Madonna** and **Coyote-Hellyer** are the jewels in the Santa Clara dog's crown, such as it is. The county's rules are confusing, though: Most of the park brochures say "Dogs prohibited except in designated areas," which doesn't help. You might see a "No Pets" sign on a given trail, while a recently printed dog information sheet tells you that dogs are allowed on all trails in that park. If you find a ranger, he or she may tell you something else entirely.

The confusion stems from the system's history. For years, dogs weren't allowed in most of the county's parks at all. Then, in 1991, a year-long trial period was launched, allowing dogs on-leash on many trails. Rangers complained that during this period, they had problems getting leash scofflaws to comply, issuing many multiple citations. In June of 1992, they'll report to the parks board, which will decide whether to continue the dog-access policy.

Sadly enough, it's quite possible that dogs will lose their access. The other chief complaint has been that dog owners don't clean up after their dogs. To help, the park system plans to install some scooper dispensers on an experimental basis. While all these rules are up in the air, call the individual park or headquarters, (408) 358-3741, before setting out.

Most of the parks are open from 8 a.m. to dusk and charge a $3 vehicle fee on weekends, or whenever the entrance kiosks are staffed. Dogs must be leashed everywhere, and they mean it. In this chapter, county parks are listed under their nearest city.

7-1

CAMPBELL

Lodgings & Campgrounds

Campbell Inn: Exit Highway 17 at Hamilton Avenue East. Go one-quarter mile south on Bascom Avenue, then go one-quarter mile west on Campbell Avenue. 675 East Campbell Avenue, Campbell, CA 95008. $100 to $150 for a double. Dogs $10 extra. (408) 374-4300.

Fairs & Festivals

Highland Games: Put on her tartan collar and dance a fling with your dog. Scotties and other breeds are welcome to attend Campbell's Highland Games. The bagpipe competitions may be hard on the ears, but the meat pies make up for that. Leash, of course. Adults $7, children $5. Held on the third Saturday in August at the Campbell Community Center Stadium, corner of Campbell and Winchester Boulevards. (408) 378-6252.

Diversions

Bathe your own dog for more fun (his): Even if your dog hates a bath more than anything, he'll surely like it a bit better if you work him over, and not some stranger. Shampoo Chez (pronounced "Shampoochers") is a wash-him-yourself dog grooming establishment with three branches in the Bay Area, looking to expand. The owners say they've done 40,000 self-service washes in the eight years they've been in business. A shampoo for any size dog is $12 for 20 minutes of wash time, an additional $1 for each five minutes after that. 523 East Campbell Avenue. (408) 379-WASH.

7-2

CUPERTINO

Parks, Beaches & Recreation Areas

Fremont Older Open Space Preserve 🐾🐾🐾

This park smells sweet and clean, but that doesn't disappoint dogs. They've got enough trees and ground-level odors to keep them happily trotting along on their mandatory leashes.

Once you park in the small lot, you'll walk several hundred feet on a paved roadway, but be sure to turn right at the first sign for hikers. Otherwise you'll find yourself in the middle of a bicycle freeway. The narrow dirt trail to the right takes you on a three-mile loop through cool woodlands and rolling open hills up to Hunters Point via the

Seven Springs Loop Trail. The view of Santa Clara Valley from the top is incomparable.

Signs at the entrance warn of ticks, so be sure to give your dog (and yourself) a thorough inspection after your hike.

7-2a From Highway 101 or Interstate 280, take Highway 85 (Saratoga-Sunnyvale Road) south to Prospect Road. Go west on Prospect Road to the park entrance. Open sunrise to sunset. (415) 949-5500.

Stevens Creek County Park

Dogs are allowed only in the **Villa Maria picnic area**. It's not large, it's heavily patrolled for off-leash offenders, and it's got more foxtails per-square-foot than Mother Nature should allow. We can recommend it only as a place to let your dog relieve herself. Try the nearby Fremont Older Open Space Preserve if you want real hiking room.

7-2b From Interstate 280, take Foothill Boulevard south. It turns into Stevens Canyon Road. Follow the signs to the Villa Maria picnic area. Open from 8 a.m. to dusk. (408) 867-3654.

7-3

GILROY

PARKS, BEACHES & RECREATION AREAS

Coyote Lake Park

This county park is full of wildlife no matter how high or low the lake. In fact, when we last visited, we saw foxes, wild turkeys and a grazing deer—and there wasn't a drop of water in the reservoir. The reservoir had been bone dry for so long that it looked like an enormous open field. Brush and a few trees were starting to emerge from the hard, dry ground.

When it's in this drought condition, the lake bed is a favorite stomping ground for leashed canines—who are usually relegated to picnic areas, the campground and a one-mile trail connecting them.

The campsites are roomy. Each has its own picnic table. Several are shaded by large oak trees. Others look out on the lake—or field, depending on the water level. We like to visit the nearby picnic areas after stopping at one of Gilroy's garlic stores for lunch supplies. Joe has a penchant for garlic-flavored pistachios.

7-3a From Highway 101, exit at Leavesley Road and follow the signs to the park. Day-use hours are from 8 a.m. to one-half hour after sunset. (408) 842-7800.

Mount Madonna County Park 🐾🐾🐾🐾

This magnificent park is midway between Gilroy and Watsonville (in Santa Cruz County). No matter where you're coming from, it's worth the drive. The mountain, covered with mixed conifers, oak, madrone and bay and sword ferns, is wonderfully quiet and cool—especially appreciated by San Jose dwellers, whose parks are almost never far from the roar of freeways. You may hear the screech of jays and little else. Try driving on Valley View Road (to the right from the ranger station) to the **Giant Twins Trail**, where you can park in the shady campsite of the same name—at least, when no one is camping there. (When we were there on a perfect Indian summer day in late September, the park was deserted.) Two huge old redwoods, green with lichen, give the trail its name. After one-half mile, the trail becomes **Sprig Lake Trail** and continues for another two miles. **Sprig Lake**, really a pond, is empty in summer, but in winter is stocked for children's fishing. If no one's fishing, your dog will happily plunge in.

This walk isn't much of a strain. If you'd like more exercise, there are plenty of longer and steeper trails—18 miles in all, and as of this writing, your dog may enjoy every one of them. (Warning: See note on dog rules for county parks at the beginning of this chapter.)

From the **Redwood Trail** or the **Blackhawk Canyon Trail**, you'll be rewarded with views of the Santa Clara Valley, the Salinas Valley and Monterey Bay. For a walk nearly completely around the park, try the **Merry-Go-Round Trail**. The park's deer are only one of many reasons you should keep your dog securely leashed, tempting as it might be to let her off. "Dogs have instincts," a friendly ranger said.

Carry plenty of water in summer. The only creek, feeding Sprig Lake, disappears. Your dog might love a camping vacation here (see Lodgings and Campgrounds).

7-3b From Highway 101, exit at Highway 152 west to Gilroy. Continue on 152 (Hecker Pass Highway) through part of the park; the entrance is a right (north) turn at Pole Line Road. Open one hour before sunrise to one hour after sunset. A $3 vehicle fee is sometimes charged. (408) 358-3741.

LODGINGS & CAMPGROUNDS

Best Western Inn: Exit Highway 101 at Leavesley Road and go one-quarter mile west on Leavesley. 360 Leavesley Road, Gilroy, CA 95020. About $60 for a double. (408) 848-1467.

Coyote Lake Park Family Campground: There are 74 sites here, some spacious and shady. Fees for camping are $8 per night, and $1 extra per dog. Dogs must be kept in tents or campers at night. Follow directions to Coyote Lake Park (see listing). (408) 842-7800.

Leavesley Inn: From Highway 101, exit westward at Highway 152. 8430 Murray Avenue, Gilroy, CA 95020. A double is about $50. You shouldn't leave the dog alone in your room. (408) 847-5500.

Mount Madonna County Park Family Campground: There are 117 large, private campsites without showers. First-come, first-served. $8 per night, $1 for each dog (limit of two). Dogs must be confined to your tent or car at night. (408) 358-3741.

Sunrest Inn: From Highway 101, exit westward at Highway 152. 8292 Murray Avenue, Gilroy, CA 95020. About $50 for a double. (408) 848-3500.

7-4

LOS GATOS

PARKS, BEACHES & RECREATION AREAS

Lexington Reservoir County Park

When the reservoir is full, this park is full of life. Birds sing, foliage is bright green. But in drought years, everything here—trees, grass, brush—is covered with silt. This death mask must frighten birds away to better nesting areas, because it's utterly silent, except for a few cars kicking up dust on a nearby road.

It can really bake during summer months, too. And since there's no swimming allowed, dogs get miserable fast. (To cool himself off here, Joe rolled on the dusty ground until his entire body was coated with ash-colored silt and he looked like some kind of odd statue on a mandatory leash.)

7-4a Exit Highway 17 at Montevina Road and drive east. You can stop at any of several parking areas along the road. The entrance fee is $3, but it's sometimes waived, depending on drought conditions. Open from 8 a.m. to dusk. (408) 358-3741.

Los Gatos Creek Trail 

From downtown Los Gatos' East Main Street, this jogging trail runs south to **Lexington Dam**, where you can connect with trails through **Lexington Reservoir County Park** and **St. Joseph's Hill Open Space Preserve.** Be sure to leash up.

7-4b Take the Main Street exit in Los Gatos, off Highway 880 (formerly Highway 17). (408) 358-3741.

Vasona Lake County Park 

This is a perfectly manicured park, with grass like that of a golf course. Dogs find it tailor-made for rolling, although they tend to get tangled in their leashes—a mandatory part of their attire.

Several pathways take you through this 151-acre park and down to the lake's edge. But no swimming is allowed. And dogs aren't allowed to visit the children's playground, either. Our favorite route is to start at the **Willow Point** group picnic area and hike on the paved trail along a grassy hill and down to the lake. You can picnic in the shade of one of the large willows, or lead your dog up to the groves of pines and firs for a relief session.

7-4c From Highway 17, take Highway 9 (Saratoga-Los Gatos Road) west to University. Go right, and continue to Blossom Hill Road. The park will be on your left. Enter at Garden Hill Drive. Fee is $3. Open 8 a.m. to dusk. (408) 356-2729.

St. Joseph's Hill Open Space Preserve 

This small preserve in the foothills just south of Los Gatos allows dogs on-leash. There are no facilities for you here, and no water; bring your own. The grassy meadows are actually overgrown vineyards. From the public parking areas east of the **Lexington Reservoir** dam, you can find the trailhead to St. Joseph's Hill. It starts opposite the boat launch beyond the dam.

You may encounter horses on the dirt trails, but you and your dog will probably have the place to yourselves, with views of the reservoir, the valley and the Sierra Azul range.

7-4d From Highway 17, take the Alma Bridge Road exit and follow signs. Open dawn to dusk. (415) 949-5500.

Lodgings & Campgrounds

Los Gatos Motor Inn: From Highway 17, exit at East Los Gatos. 55 Saratoga Avenue, Los Gatos, CA 95032. A double is about $60. Dogs shouldn't be left alone in your room. (408) 356-9191.

FAIRS & FESTIVALS

Eastfield Ming Quong Strawberry Festival: You and your dog can get just about anything strawberry but a rawhide chew at this festival, held the first weekend in June on the Los Gatos Civic Center grounds. The strawberry pancakes are a great breakfast, and dogs like to get there early, while it's still cool. Lots of dogs line up with their owners. Be sure to leash. 110 East Main Street. (408) 379-3790.

7-5

MILPITAS

PARKS, BEACHES & RECREATION AREAS

Ed R. Levin County Park 

Don't drive to this large, rustic park, except for a picnic with your dog. The picnic spots are all he can set paw in, and he must wear a leash. The park's worth a listing, though, because the picnic grounds around **Sandy Wool Lake** are especially attractive, with willow trees and golden hills for a backdrop.

7-5a From Interstate 880 or Interstate 680, exit at Calaveras Boulevard and drive east to the park. Take a left on Downing Road for the picnic areas. Open 8 a.m. till dusk; vehicle fee is $3. (408) 358-3741.

LODGINGS & CAMPGROUNDS

Best Western/Brookside Inn: At Interstate 880 and Highway 237. Exit 237 at Abbott Avenue. 400 Valley Way, Milpitas, CA 95035. A double is about $60. Dogs are $5 extra. (408) 263-5566.

Economy Inns of America: One-quarter mile southeast of the junction of Interstate 880 and Highway 237. Exit at Calaveras Boulevard and drive east. 270 South Abbott Avenue, Milpitas, CA 95035. A double is about $50. (408) 946-8889.

7-6

MORGAN HILL

Parks, Beaches & Recreation Areas

Anderson Lake County Park 

When there's enough water to keep the reservoir open to the public, dogs love to go along on fishing trips. But when it's low, dogs take solace in dipping their paws in the shady, secluded stream that runs between picnic areas.

Call the rangers to find out if the reservoir is open, because if it isn't, it may not be worth a trip. You can't get anywhere near the lake if it's too low.

The only trail connects picnic areas and isn't even one-half mile long. There are plenty of picnic tables with lots of shade, but dogs tend to get bored unless hunks of hamburger happen to fall from the grills. The picnic areas can be rowdy, with lots of beer and loud music, so if your dog doesn't like rap, take him somewhere else.

7-6a From Highway 101, follow Cochrane Road east to the park. Open from one-half hour before sunrise to dusk. (408) 779-3634.

Henry Coe State Park 

On the map, this park is represented by a spectacular swatch of green that's bigger than all of the parks in the county combined. It's 68,000 acres—105 square miles. But alas, the portion that allows pets is minuscule. It wouldn't even be a speck on a county map. Dogs are allowed only on a half-mile paved road that loops into the park at the entrance, and in the adjacent campground. And they must be leashed.

The ride up to this 2,600-foot elevation is no great joy, either. It's 13 miles from Highway 101, and 10 of those miles are sheer switchback hell. Joe and a fellow passenger were green by the time we reached the park.

The only saving grace for dog owners is the view at sunset. Through the layers of haze, and over mountaintops, the sky turns such vibrant hues of orange and red that you nearly forget about the dizzying ride down that awaits you.

7-6b Exit Highway 101 at Dunne Avenue and follow it for 13 miles to the park entrance. Day use fees are $5 per person and $1 per dog (but there's nothing to do with a dog during the day, unless your idea of hiking fun is pounding pavement alongside cars). The park is open from dawn to dusk for day use. (408) 779-2728.

Uvas Canyon County Park 

The question of which trails in this park allow dogs isn't quite settled yet. The county office says all of them; a ranger says only one—the half-mile **Uvas Creek Trail**, which starts about one mile from the ranger station. You can get a map when you drive through the entrance kiosk.

This is a pretty, clean park of oaks, madrone and douglas firs in cool canyons. The **Uvas Creek Trail** is Dabney's favorite, in any case. He always appreciates a creek on a warm summer day, and this one doesn't dry up in hot weather. If someone gives you permission to take a dog on any trail, you might also try the wide, dirt **Alec Canyon Trail**, one and one-half miles long, within sight of **Alec Creek**; or the **Nature Trail Loop**, about one mile long, beside **Swanson Creek**. There'll be some waterfalls in late winter and early spring.

The dog access question may be resolved in June of 1992, when the county parks board rules on whether to restrict dogs further or to continue its present policy of allowing leashed dogs on some trails in some parks (see Santa Clara County Parks, page 215). Dogs are always allowed in the campgrounds and picnic areas of Uvas Canyon.

7-6c From Highway 101, exit at Cochrane Road; go south on Business 101 to Watsonville Road, then right (west) on Watsonville to Uvas Road. Turn right (north) on Uvas (past Uvas Reservoir) to Croy Road. Go left (west) on Croy to the park. The last four miles on Croy are fairly tortuous. It's open 8 a.m. to dusk; a day use fee of $3 may be charged on weekends. (408) 358-3741.

RESTAURANTS

Country Kitchen: This place has only two or three tables outside, but it specializes in homey dishes like spaghetti, hamburger or Mexican plates. There's a different special every night. 10980 Monterey Road. (408) 779-2928.

A motel manager insisted he accepts only small dogs. How small—what about 50 pounds? Too large, he said. What kind is the 50-pound dog? Collie. His name's Dabney. Aw, why not, he said, melting like butter—he loves collies. (The moral: Always tell the desk something personal about your dog. It sometimes works.)—L.Y.

LODGINGS & CAMPGROUNDS

Best Western Country Inn: From Highway 101 northbound, exit at Tennant Avenue; southbound, exit at East Dunne Avenue. 16525 Condit Road, Morgan Hill, CA 95037. A double is around $65. (408) 779-0447.

Henry Coe State Park Campgrounds: There are twenty primitive family sites (no showers) for $7 a night. (See listing, page 222, for directions to the park.) (408) 779-2728.

Uvas Canyon County Park Campgrounds: The park has 25 family sites, without showers, on a first-come, first-served basis, for $8 a night. $4 is charged for a second vehicle. There's a self-service fee station. Campground is open daily from April 15 to October 31; open Friday and Saturday from November through March. It's crowded on weekends during late spring and summer; arrive early—or camp during the week. (408) 358-3741.

7-7

MOUNTAIN VIEW

PARKS, BEACHES & RECREATION AREAS

Rengstorff Park

This park is typically neat, green and interesting for people, and it has another excellent feature. A sign reads, "Dogs must be on-leash (except by permit)." This means that you can get a permit from the city that allows you to train a dog off-leash, with the understanding that he'll be under control, in any of Mountain View's parks. Another policy handy for dog owners is the city's practice of opening schoolyards to public use (including dogs, on-leash) when school isn't in session.

7-7a Rengstorff Park is at Rengstorff Avenue and Leland Avenue. Open from 6 a.m. to one-half hour after sundown. (415) 903-6331.

RESTAURANTS

Blue Sky Cafe: A popular neighborhood restaurant in a small house with outdoor tables. Ingredients are strictly fresh, with vegetarian dishes a specialty. Meat is served, too. The owners will be happy to seat your dog at your feet outside, so long as he's leashed and quiet. He'll be good if slipped a bite or two. 336 Bryant Street. (415) 961-2082.

Lodgings & Campgrounds

Best Western Tropicana Lodge: 1720 El Camino Real West, Mountain View, CA 94040. A double is about $70. (415) 961-0220.

Fairs & Festivals

California Small Brewers Festival: Mountain View hosts this annual festival late in September. It's open to owners and dogs, even if most of the latter aren't 21 yet. The festival sets up live music, beer-tasting booths and food booths, serving all kinds of dishes with chili predominating. Proceeds from the festival benefit local non-profit organizations. At The Tied House Cafe and Brewery, 954 Villa Street, north of Castro Street. (800) 300-BREW.

7-8 PALO ALTO

For dogs, this town is the county's garden spot. Here, you'll find lots of other dog lovers and well-behaved dogs, enticing city parks—all of which allow dogs—and no fewer than three leash-free dog runs. At the Baylands, you and your leashed dog can watch birds and get a good workout at the same time. And many student-oriented restaurants with outdoor seating welcome your dog. If you're lucky enough to have a Palo Alto address, or a friend with one, you may bring your dog to the glorious Foothills Park on weekdays. And the nearby Foothills Open Space Preserve is open to everyone and their dogs—so long as dogs wear a leash.

Parks, Beaches & Recreation Areas

Esther Clark Park 

This is a beautiful piece of undeveloped land with some dirt paths, right on the border of Los Altos Hills. The city leash rule applies—dogs must be leashed everywhere, except in official dog runs. There are no facilities, but plenty of meadow and eucalyptus. A creek bed promises water in wet season, but in the drought-plagued Bay Area, you can never count on it.

7-8a Where Old Adobe Road bends to the left and makes a cul-de-sac, the park is the undeveloped land on your right. Open from sunrise till sunset. (415) 496-6950.

Foothills Park

To use this park, privately owned by the city of Palo Alto, you must prove you're a resident or be the guest of one. And dogs are allowed only on weekdays, on-leash, but they can go on all the trails.

There's a large lake surrounded by unspoiled foothills, and 15 miles of hiking trails of varying difficulty. At sundown, deer are plentiful. The park's sole creek, **Los Trancos Creek**, has been dry for several years, but someday will fill again. This park is heaven on Earth for dogs and people alike. If you don't pass the entry test, though, don't despair—drive one mile down Page Mill Road to **Foothills Open Space Preserve** (see the next listing).

> ***7-8b*** To find Foothills Park from Interstate 280, exit at Page Mill Road and drive about 2.5 miles south. As usual, when you're searching for a really good Santa Clara County park, the road will become impossibly narrow and winding, and you'll think you're lost. But you aren't. Entry fee for Palo Alto residents is $2 per car, $1 for hikers and bicyclists. Open 8 a.m. to 7:30 p.m. (415) 496-6950.

Foothills Open Space Preserve

This is pretty country too, but dry and completely undeveloped—as in all open spaces, there's not even a portable toilet. Be sure to carry plenty of water for both you and your dog. You'll walk through lovely oak and brush with views of wooded hills and the populated valley below. The somewhat rough dirt trail is full of deer tracks, and your dog will be fascinated by mysterious rustlings. Leash is the rule. The place is often full of ticks, but to your dog, it's worth the trouble.

> ***7-8c*** Follow directions to Foothills Park (see listing above) and go one mile farther down Page Mill Road. Watch carefully for the obscure turnout on the left (south) side. The worst feature of this park is that there is barely room for two cars at the turnout that constitutes the entrance, and turning around in the winding road is dangerous. The preserve is open from daybreak to one-half hour after sunset. (415) 949-5500.

Greer Park

This is one of Palo Alto's parks with an off-leash dog run, but it isn't the largest (see Mitchell Park, page 227). The park is green and pleasant, as are all the city's parks, but it's somewhat noisy from nearby Bayshore Road. Dogs have to be leashed outside the dog run.

There are athletic fields, picnic tables and two playground areas, one of which forbids dogs. The dog run, near the Bayshore side, is small and treeless, but it's entirely fenced, if that's what your dog needs. Bring your own scoopers and water.

The rules for all three city dog runs are: No unattended dogs when other dogs are present; no children under eight; aggressive dogs must wear a muzzle; keep the gate closed; let other owners know before you let your dog in; and clean up.

7-8d Open from sunrise to 10:30 p.m. At Amarillo Street and West Bayshore Road. The parking lot is off Bayshore, conveniently near the dog run. (415) 496-6950.

Hoover Park

This small park has two features to recommend it—a stream, wet during non-drought years, and a small dog run. It also has tennis, basketball and handball courts, a softball field, picnic tables and a playground.

7-8e At Cowper Street between Colorado Avenue and Loma Verde Avenue. Open from sunrise to 10:30 p.m. (415) 496-6950.

Mitchell Park

Another generous, green park with many amenities, including some unusual ones—two human-size chess boards and a roller-skating rink. This park is a standout in the canine book, too: Its dog run is the largest and best of the three that Palo Alto offers. It's completely fenced and furnished with loose balls and water dishes, and has a row of pine trees on one side. A soccer field and a creek (in wet season only) are nearby. The dog run is a short walk from the parking lot. Rules for dog comportment in the leash-free area are the same as for the dog run in Greer Park (see listing, page 226).

The park itself has plenty of shade to delight a dog. Remember to leash outside the dog run. For kids, the playground area has sculptured bears for climbing and a wading pool (sorry, no dogs).

7-8f On East Meadow Drive just south of Middlefield Road. Open from sunrise to 10:30 p.m. (415) 496-6950.

Palo Alto Baylands

This is the best-developed wetlands park in the Bay Area for adults, children and dogs, laced with paved bike trails and levee trails. Along the pretty levee paths are benches facing the mudflats. Don't forget your binoculars on a walk here. A cacaphony of mewling gulls, mumbling pigeons and clucking blackbirds fills the air; small planes putt into the nearby airport; and your dog will love the fishy smells coming from the marshes. This seems to be a popular spot for dog exercise. Keep yours leashed and on the trails.

Dogs shouldn't go near the well-marked waterfowl nesting area, but they are welcome to watch children feed the noisy ducks and Canada geese in the duck pond, as long as they don't think about snacks *à l'orange.*

7-8g From Highway 101, exit at Embarcadero Road East and go all the way to the end. At the entrance, turn left for the trails, ranger station and duck pond. A right turn takes you to a recycling center. The Interpretive Center is open weekends from 1 p.m. to 5 p.m., Wednesday through Friday 2 p.m. to 5 p.m. The park itself is open during daylight hours. (415) 496-6997.

Rinconada Park 

Dogs are welcome here on-leash. Like most Palo Alto parks, it's quiet and green and full of mothers with kids. It has a shuffleboard court, a pool and tennis courts, and a kids' gym. The small redwood grove is a welcome relief when it's hot.

7-8h At Embarcadero Road and Newell Road. Open from sunrise to 10:30 p.m. (415) 496-6950.

The Stanford Dish 

"The Stanford Dish" is not a park but Stanford University property, surrounding the satellite dish used by the physics department. Stanford lets dog owners enjoy it, so long as dogs stay on-leash and on the trails, and their owners pick up after them. The hill is quite popular, with its grasslands reclaimed from cattle pasture, dotted with oaks. A reforestation project is under way, so in the future it'll be even nicer. Cattle still graze on the Interstate 280 side, so there's good reason for the leash rule. A ranger patrols to enforce it.

7-8i You can park on campus across the street from the Tressider Student Union and walk up a path to Junipero Serra Boulevard. The dish property borders Junipero Serra. Don't park in the nearby residential areas. It's open during daylight hours. (415) 723-2862.

RESTAURANTS

Downtown Palo Alto is walker-friendly and dog-adoring. It's full of benches and plazas for sitting, and quite a few restaurants will serve both of you out on the sidewalk or patio. Here are several from the Stanford end of University Avenue—like most student-occupied neighborhoods, a good bet for a restaurant that will welcome a dog. Also a good bet for students who'll hug your dog and feed him treats. You may have to dodge bikes whizzing by on the sidewalk.

As we strolled past the corner of Bryant and University, Dabney was irritated by the mural on the wall of Wiedeman's department store, showing—at eye level—a man pushing a cat in a stroller.

Cafe Montmartre: This place is so elegant, with its stone patio and plantings, that we approached the waiter praying he'd let Dabney stay. "Totally cool," he said. Sit outdoors at one of a dozen tables, some shaded, and enjoy delicious soups, salad bar, desserts and coffees. If he's neat about it, your dog is welcome to drink from the patio pool. 150 University Avenue. (415) 324-9536.

Il Fornaio: Fine coffee and pastries. There are about six sidewalk tables subject to heavy foot traffic, but most of the feet will be of students who miss their dogs and want to stop and make a fuss over yours. "Dogs encouraged!" says the manager. 388 University Avenue. (415) 325-9353.

Rodger's Plaza Ramona: Gourmet sandwiches and coffee, in the mug or by the pound. You're welcome at the relatively quiet sidewalk tables with your dog, so long as he's leashed. Corner of University Avenue and Ramona Street. (415) 324-4228.

Lodgings & Campgrounds

Holiday Inn—Palo Alto: From Highway 101, exit at Embarcadero West; go 2 miles to Highway 82, then go one-half mile north. It's opposite Stanford University. 625 El Camino Real, Palo Alto, CA 94301. A double is around $115. A refundable $50 required for dog. (415) 328-2800.

Hyatt Palo Alto: 4290 El Camino Real, Palo Alto, CA 94306. $120 to $150 for a double; $50 refundable deposit for dog. (415) 493-0800.

Hyatt Rickeys: 4219 El Camino Real, Palo Alto, CA 94306. A double is $125 to $150. $50 refundable deposit for dog. (415) 493-8000.

Diversions

Compete in the four-footed race: The city of Palo Alto stages an annual Dog's Best Friend Run at the Baylands (see listing). The five kilometer (3.1 mile) course, which you may run or walk with your leashed dog, begins and finishes at the athletic center. Rules are: You must have your dog on a regular six-foot leash, not a retractable one; you can't carry the dog; and she must cross the finish line before you do. (The idea of this last rule is to restrain hot-dog owners who drag their poor dogs across the finish line.) The record will show your dog's racing time, not yours. Nearly 500 dogs now show up every year, yet the organizer, recreation supervisor Tom Osborne, says he's never seen a dogfight in all the years he's hosted the race.

For your entry fee of $10 or $12, you get a T-shirt and the dog gets a bandanna and plenty of treats. Winners receive plaques and photos. At the Baylands, around the second week of April. Call (415) 329-2380 for this year's date.

Shop with a best friend: It's perfectly legal to bring your dog to the huge, open-air Stanford Shopping Center, so long as he stays outside the stores. Dogs haven't quite mastered the art of shopping without wearing out the merchandise. And "No deposits," the managers plead. This mall has plenty of outdoor snacking places. On El Camino Real and University Avenue, next to Stanford University. (415) 328-0600.

7-9

SAN JOSE

Everyone knows the San Jose jokes, and everyone's heard about San Jose's new "Renaissance city" image. Both are true. Blocks from the marble and glass towers of the new downtown, you can still see chickens scratching in people's front yards. But the city is changing every day.

We visited San Jose's downtown center hoping to find plenty of dog-friendly outdoor eateries and shopping malls, but we were disappointed. Only one mall—The Pavilion, next to the Fairmont Hotel, with an inviting array of shops and outdoor tables—looked as if it might allow dogs, but it didn't. The same went for outdoor restaurants. But a dog can drink from a fountain featuring wrought-iron fish in elegant St. James Square Park, or gaze at 20 terrific pillars of water shooting from the fountain at Park Plaza. Keep your eye on the area if you have a boulevardier-type dog. Any day now, San Jose may change into his kind of place.

Dogs are welcome in most of the city's parks. Leashes are mandatory in all the parks, and there are no leash-free dog runs.

San Jose residents must enjoy most of their city parks—even the best ones—in the shadow of freeways (some literally) and under the buzz of airplanes landing at the central airport. This listing describes several of the larger, clean, green parks; many others are undistinguished or full of litter.

The city parks department has a number of new parks planned for the future, often behind newer housing developments, and many of them are shown on maps but aren't actually there yet at all. Caution! Before setting out for a large green spot on the map, check whether it's labeled "undeveloped." That may mean it isn't there. Call the parks department before going: (408) 277-4661.

PARKS, BEACHES & RECREATION AREAS

Almaden Quicksilver County Park 

This rustic, 3,600-acre park allows dogs on about half of its 30 miles of trails. Some of these trails are popular for horseback riding, so watch out, because although leashes are the law here, they don't always stop dogs who like to chase hooves.

In the spring, the hills explode with wildlife and wildflowers. Any of the trails will take you through a wonderland of colorful flowers, and butterflies, who like to tease safely leashed dogs.

Dogs are allowed on the **Guadalupe Trail**; the **Hacienda Trail**; portions of the **Mine Hill Trail**; the **Mockingbird Picnic Area**; portions of the **New Almaden Hiking Trail**; the **No Name Trail**; and the **Senator Mine Trail.**

7-9a Call the park for more information about the trails and the locations of their trailheads. You can enter the park at several points. We prefer the main park entrance, where New Almaden Road turns into Alamitos Road, near Almaden Way. Open from 8 a.m. to sundown. (408) 268-3883.

Cataldi Park 

Very green and clean, Cataldi Park has no creek but does have a wide variety of trees—eucalyptus, pepper trees, willows and pines. Paths are both paved and smooth dirt, and picnic tables are shaded. There is a parcourse, a soccer field and tennis courts. The children's play area boasts an attractive high-tech design. Dogs on-leash, as usual.

7-9b Morrill Avenue at Cataldi Drive. Open from sunrise to one hour after sunset. (408) 277-4661.

Coyote-Hellyer County Park

Dogs are not officially allowed in this park's best feature—**Coyote Creek**—or in the lake. They can't go on athletic fields, either, and they must be leashed everywhere. But visit the beautiful picnic area beside the creek, lined with big sycamores and other trees.

It's a generous, rustic park, popular with bicyclists. The best deal for dogs is the **El Arroyo del Coyote Nature Trail**, which by some miracle allows dogs. Walk to the left at the entrance kiosk and cross under Hellyer Avenue on the bike trail to find the entrance to the nature trail. Cross the creek on a pedestrian bridge to your right; once across, take the dirt path to your left. Bikes aren't allowed, making it all the nicer for dogs. Willows and cottonwoods are luxuriant here, and in spring, poppies and serpentine bloom. There's occasional shade from eucalyptus groves. Watch out for bees and poison oak; otherwise, this is heavenly territory for your dog. It is ridiculous that he's not allowed to dip his paws in the largest creek in the Santa Clara Valley, but them's the rules.

7-9c From Highway 101, exit at Hellyer Avenue and follow prominent signs to the park. A parking fee of $3 is charged on weekends and holidays. Open from 8 a.m. to sunset. (408) 358-3741.

Coyote Creek Bicycle Trail

When this trail is completely paved—it may be ready by the time you read this book—it will furnish your dog with 13 miles of trail, if she doesn't mind sharing space with bicycles. Some pooper-scooper dispensers are being installed, too. You may take your dog, leashed, on any portion between the **Coyote-Hellyer County Park** end and **Parkway Lakes**, a private fishing concession at the south end close to Morgan Hill. (Your only reason to go there would be to pull in some of the club's stocked trout or enter one of its fishing derbies.)

7-9d See the directions to Coyote-Hellyer County Park above. (408) 358-3741.

Emma Prusch Park

One of San Jose's most attractive working farms is a museum—this park. Like a symbol of the county, it lies in the shadow of the intersection of three freeways. Yet it's a charming place, and surprisingly, it allows dogs to wander on-leash around the farm with you so long as they stay out of the farm animal areas. A smooth paved path, good for strollers and wheelchairs, winds among a Victorian farmhouse (the visitor center), a multicultural arts center, farm machinery, a barn, an orchard and gardens. There are picnic tables on an expanse of lawn with trees.

During the summer and through October, farmers' markets are held here every Sunday from 8:30 a.m. to 1 p.m. Also here, the city's K-9 Corps of trained police dogs occasionally shows off for children. If you think your own dog won't be intimidated by dogs in uniform, call the park to find out when they'll be there.

7-9e Entrance is on South King Road, near the intersection of Highway 101 and Interstate 680/280. The park is open from 8:30 a.m. to 5 p.m., till sundown in summer. The buildings close at 4:30 p.m. (408) 926-5555.

Guadalupe Oak Grove Park 

This park is a pleasant exception to most of the others in San Jose—it's undeveloped, beautiful and doesn't allow bicycles—and sure enough, it may not be open to dogs for long. It may soon be declared an oak woodlands preserve. For now, go there and enjoy it.

Dirt trails wind through hills, alternately semi-open and covered with thick groves of oaks. Birds are plentiful and noisy. Be aware of high fire danger in the dry season, and don't even think of letting your dog off-leash. The park's ranger loves dogs, but she'll ticket you, and she's heard all the excuses—"He just slipped out of his collar for a moment...." or "I couldn't get my dog through the gate with his leash on...."

7-9f Guadalupe Oak Grove Park is at Golden Oak Way and Vargas Drive. Open during daylight hours, closing promptly at sunset (the ranger locks the gate). (408) 277-4661.

Joseph D. Grant County Park 

Here's another huge, gorgeous, wild park that your dog may barely set foot in. Dogs are limited to the campgrounds, picnic areas, the **Edwards Field Hill** and the **Edwards Trail**. But if you don't mind a long, winding drive for one short—albeit satisfying—trail hike, by all means try this park. Stop in at the homey old ranch house that is now the visitor center for directions to the Edwards Trail, which isn't easy to find.

Or try these directions: On Mount Hamilton Road midway between the intersection with Quimby Road and the park border is a white barn on your right as you're heading out of the park. Just past the white barn is an unmarked pedestrian gate on the left. This is the trailhead. This trail is a fine walk through mixed deciduous forest, but there's no creek. Carry water for your dog.

7-9g To get to the park from Interstate 680, exit at the Capitol Expressway and take it south to Quimby Road. Turn left (east) on Quimby and wind tortuously to the park entrance. It's a long six miles, and the road is often a one-lane cliffhanger. Alternatively, you can get to the park from Interstate 680 via Highway 130 (Mount Hamilton Road). It's similar, but at least it's two-lane. The park is open from 8 a.m. till sunset. (408) 358-3741.

Kelley Park 

Kelley is a big, welcoming city park that's heavily used for Japanese birthday parties, company picnics, Mariachi bands, formal Filipino weddings, gospel church picnics and every other stripe of San Jose's cultural rainbow. Dogs, on-leash, are allowed everywhere except on the grounds of the San Jose Historical Museum, in the Japanese Friendship Garden and in the Happy Hollow Park and Zoo (for children).

But there's plenty more for a dog to do. An old orchard behind the museum, bordering **Coyote Creek**, reminds you of what Santa Clara Valley once was. (It's now part of the museum.) The park offers lots of picnic tables, a variety of trees, walking paths and chances to plunge into the creek. (Unfortunately, the section that Dabney chose for his plunge contained half a dozen rusty shopping carts, and when he emerged, his paws were dripping with black goo. Fortunately, the goo turned out to be only silt that dried and fell off. But the park could use some heavier cleaning. Dabney's scrap hunt in the picnic areas was a bit too successful.)

7-9h The park is on Senter Road between Tully Road and Keyes Street. Hours are 8 a.m. to one-half hour after sunset. A $3 parking fee is charged on weekends and holidays. (408) 277-4661.

Los Alamitos—Calero Creek Park Chain 

Six miles of multi-use trail, both dirt and paved, run along **Los Alamitos Creek** and **Arroyo Calero** from the southern end of Almaden Lake Park (which doesn't allow dogs) south to the western entrance of Santa Teresa County Park. San Jose dogs love these trails for their easy creek access. There's plenty of shade. Two small adjacent city parks, Graystone Park and Carrabelle Park, have picnic tables and drinking fountains, for a break if you and your dog are making a trek of it. Keep your dog leashed and watch for bicycles and horses sharing the trail with you. You can park on a neighborhood street, but not along Camden Avenue.

From Camden at Villagewood Way or Queenswood Way, you can pick up a new segment of the Bay Area Ridge Trail that runs all the way to Santa Teresa County Park's western entrance, about 1.3 miles. Where the trail forks, take the westernmost fork—the trail paralleling Camden Avenue—westward across Harry Road and continuing to Santa Teresa County Park.

7-9i The creek park chain runs parallel to the southern end of the Almaden Expressway. The trails run along the north side of Camden Avenue and along the east side of Queenswood Way. The trails along Camden are open 24 hours; the segment of Bay Area Ridge Trail leading to Santa Teresa County Park closes at dusk. (408) 277-4661.

Motorcycle Park 

The only reason you'd want to bring your dog here is if he's your sidecar companion, and you want him to mingle with friends at a picnic. Besides the parking lot, the picnic area is the only place here that allows dogs—leashed, of course. For obvious reasons, dogs are not permitted anywhere near the 13 miles of dirt trails—they're for motorcycles and all-terrain vehicles only. If you do take him for some picnicking with fellow bikers, beware: A biker named Buddy told us a small dog with a big appetite once chewed a hole straight through the arm of his leather jacket. Buddy laughed it off. Others might not.

7-9j Exit Highway 101 at Metcalf Road and follow it to the parking area. Fee is $5 per vehicle. Hours are subject to change, and are usually limited to Thursday through Sunday. Call for details. (408) 226-5223.

Penitencia Creek County Park 

This county park is largely a four-mile paved streamside trail designed for hikers, bicyclists and roller-skaters. Leashed dogs are welcome, and it usually isn't dangerously crowded. From the western end, at North King Road, you can connect with the **Coyote Creek Bicycle Trail** (see listing). The **Penitencia Creek Trail** is paved from end-to-end, but it is not designed to go under roads like the better bicycle trails in Walnut Creek, for example. You will have to scramble your way across highways or around fenced portions. Or you'll be confronted with a locked gate protecting water district equipment.

(Dabney celebrated his arrival here by instantly plunging into the cool, clean creek, which has a stony bottom—praise be! no mud in your car). At the Jackson Avenue end, large walnut trees line the creek and shelter some picnic tables. Restrooms are scattered along the route.

7-9k There are parking lots on Penitencia Creek Road and on Jackson Avenue. This is the best portion of the trail for a dog, because there's a dry lake bed. Hours are sunrise to one hour after sunset. (408) 358-3741.

Santa Teresa County Park

From a distance, the few trees here look like old broccoli, and the hills are nearly barren. But there's a stark beauty here that dogs seem to appreciate. With more than three miles of hiking trails for people with dogs, there's plenty of room to roam. Humans can get a great view of the valley, while their leashed dogs sniff at all kinds of hidden, hill-dwelling critters.

Dogs are allowed only on the **Ohlone Hiking Trail, Mine Trail,** and **Pueblo picnic area** and playing field. We like to start at the base of the Ohlone Trail and walk to the top of the steep hill and then down to the picnic areas via the Mine Trail. There, we refill our water bottles, have a picnic and hike back. Round trip, it's about six miles.

7-9l From Highway 101, take Bernal Road to Santa Teresa Boulevard, and go right on Avenida Espana. You'll skim the northeast rim of the park. Stop when you see a sign for the archery range. Walk into the park here. You'll be far from the archers' arrows, and just at the foot of the Ohlone Hiking Trail. You can also follow Bernal Road into the park and start hiking at the picnic area, but the Mine Trail is a little tricky to find from there. Open from 8 a.m. to dusk. (408) 268-3883.

RESTAURANTS

Aussie's: At several outdoor tables here, you can enjoy fishburgers or teriyaki chicken and steak. 1187 Saratoga-Sunnyvale Road. (408) 446-3170.

LODGINGS & CAMPGROUNDS

Best Western San Jose Lodge: From Interstate 880 or Highway 101, exit at North First Street. 1440 North First Street, San Jose, CA 95112. Around $60 double. (408) 453-7750.

Holiday Inn, Airport: From Highway 101, exit at North First Street; From Interstate 880, exit First Street and drive east on Rosemary Street. 1355 North Fourth Street, San Jose, CA 95112. A double is about $90. (408) 453-5340.

Holiday Inn Park Center Plaza: From Interstate 280, exit at Almaden/Vine. 282 Almaden Boulevard, San Jose, CA 95113. A double is about $75. (408) 998-0400.

Joseph D. Grant County Park Family Campground: There are 20 campsites, $8 a night for up to eight people and two cars; extra car is $4. For seniors and handicapped, sites are $4 weekdays, $8 weekends and holidays. Pay by envelope. Sites are first-come, first-served. No showers. Open daily from April 15 to October 31; open weekends in November and in March; closed from December to February. (408) 274-6121.

Red Lion Hotel: From Interstate 880, exit at North First Street. 2050 Gateway Place, San Jose, CA 95110. A double is about $150. If you aren't using a credit card, the hotel asks for a refundable $50 deposit for the dog. (408) 453-4000.

Fairs & Festivals

Tapestry in Talent: Visual, performing and culinary arts are all on display at this multicultural arts festival. Seven stages feature every kind of live music, and you can watch modern, ethnic, square and folk dancing. There are potential dog treats here from all over the world. Your pup will love this festival, no matter what his ancestry. Just make sure he doesn't mind crowds and the occasional firecracker, and that the weather isn't too warm for him. Held the weekend closest to July 4 in downtown San Jose. (408) 293-9727.

Diversions

Get clean with your dog: Wear old clothes and take her to the Santa Teresa Self-Serve Pet Wash. You'll get help heaving a large dog into the tub; after that you're on your own. Dogs think being washed by their own dear master is a good improvement on a bad idea. They are allowed 30 minutes under the spray gun, and they feel that's quite enough. A shampoo for any size dog costs $10 for regular shampoo, $12 for flea shampoo, and $3 for extra flea dip. 7136 Santa Teresa Boulevard. (408) 281-8209.

7-10

SANTA CLARA

PARKS, BEACHES & RECREATION AREAS

Central Park

This Santa Clara city park, like all the others, has a sign that reveals a certain slant: "No Dogs Allowed Except on Leash." If you can get past that, the park is large and has a wide assortment of trees. Its creek is large and deep, but dry in summer. A beautiful round picnic pavilion has tables fully shaded by wisteria vines, the most we've ever seen in one place. There's an **International Swim Center,** two softball fields, basketball and tennis courts, a parcourse and a lawn-bowling green. This park is the only one in the city whose restrooms are never locked in winter.

7-10a On Kiely Boulevard between Homestead Road and Benton Street. Open 8 a.m. to sunset. (408) 984-3223.

FAIRS & FESTIVALS

Santa Clara Art & Wine Festival: Music, art and wine blend perfectly on a September day. The Santa Clara Art and Wine Festival is a good daytime outing for you and your dog, if the weather isn't too warm. Leash up and make sure your dog's manners are perfect, if she's going to look at artwork. There's a petting zoo here, too, though it's not for dogs. Held the second weekend in September in Central Park (see listing). (408) 984-3257.

LODGINGS & CAMPGROUNDS

Econo Lodge: On Highway 82 (El Camino Real), one-half mile west of San Tomas Expressway. 2930 El Camino Real, Santa Clara, CA 95055. A double is $50 to $90. Dogs are $5 extra. (408) 241-3010.

Santa Clara Travelodge: From Highway 101, exit at Lawrence Expressway, then drive two blocks east on El Camino Real. 3477 El Camino Real, Santa Clara, CA 95051. Small dogs only. (408) 984-3364.

The Vagabond Inn: On Highway 82 (El Camino Real) at the Lawrence Expressway Cloverleaf. 3580 El Camino Real, Santa Clara, CA 95051. Around $65 for a double; $3 extra for dog. (408) 241-0771.

DIVERSIONS

Go on a pilgrimage: Mission Santa Clara, on the Santa Clara University campus, allows leashed dogs on its grounds. You might make it part of your walk if you're exploring the campus. The building, dating from 1929, is a replica of one version of the old mission, which was first built in 1777 but destroyed five times by earthquake, flood and fire. Preserved fragments of the original mission, and the old adobe faculty club, are the oldest college buildings standing in the western United States. On campus, off The Alameda. (408) 554-4023.

7-11 SUNNYVALE

PARKS, BEACHES & RECREATION AREAS

Las Palmas Park 

This park is good for a walk among rolling hills. There are paved paths around the edge, a dozen tennis courts and two kids' playgrounds. Soon, there will be something better: A brand-new dog run! Call the city to find out its status.

7-11a At Danforth Drive and Russet Drive. Open from 8 a.m. to dusk. (408) 730-7350.

Sunnyvale Baylands Park 

This wetland area is partly managed by the county and partly by the city. Only the county section allows dogs. It's a good place to stretch your six legs on the levee trails—there are no other amenities, not even bicycle trails—or bring binoculars to watch water birds. Dogs should be leashed.

7-11b At the end of Lawrence Expressway, at Moffett Park Drive. Street parking only. (408) 358-3741.

LODGINGS & CAMPGROUNDS

The Vagabond Inn: From Highway 101, exit at Mathilda Avenue and drive south. 816 Ahwanee Avenue, Sunnyvale, CA 94086. About $65 for a double, $3 extra for the hound. (408) 734-4607.

MORE INFO

WHERE YOUR DOG CAN'T GO

- Almaden Lake Park, San Jose
- Alum Rock Park, San Jose
- Calero Reservoir County Park (except for picnic areas)

- Campbell Park, Campbell
- Columbia Park, Sunnyvale
- Ed R. Levin County Park (except for picnic areas)
- El Sereno Open Space Preserve
- Field Sports County Park, San Jose
- Foothills Park, Palo Alto (dogs whose owners live in Palo Alto only, and only on weekends)
- Guadalupe Reservoir
- Gilroy Garlic Festival, Gilroy
- Hakone Gardens, Saratoga
- Hellyer County Park
- Heritage Oaks Park, Los Altos
- John D. Morgan Park, Campbell
- Lake Cunningham Park, San Jose
- Lincoln Park, Los Altos
- Los Trancos Open Space Preserve
- Mango Park, Sunnyvale
- Marymeade Park, Los Altos
- McClellan Ranch Park, Cupertino
- McKenzie Park, Los Altos
- Monte Bello Open Space Preserve
- Motorcycle Park (except for picnic areas)
- Overfelt Botanical Gardens, San Jose
- Rancho San Antonio County Park
- Rancho San Antonio Open Space Preserve
- San Jose Flea Market
- Sanborn Skyline County Park (except for picnic areas and RV lot)
- Saratoga Gap Open Space Preserve
- Shoreline Park, Mountain View
- Shoup Park, Los Altos
- Sierra Azul Open Space Preserve
- Stevens Creek Shoreline Nature Study Area
- Sunnyvale Baylands (city-owned section)
- Thornewood Open Space Preserve
- Upper Stevens Creek County Park

7. SANTA CLARA COUNTY (map page 212-213)

- Villa Montalvo Arboretum, Saratoga
- Washington Park, Santa Clara

USEFUL PHONE NUMBERS & ADDRESSES

City of San Jose, Department of Recreation, Parks & Community Services: 333 West Santa Clara Street, Suite 800, San Jose, CA 95113. (408) 277-4661.

For a bike paths map: Santa Clara County Transportation Agency, (408) 287-4210 .

County of Santa Clara Parks & Recreation Department: 298 Garden Hill Drive (Vasona Lake Park), Los Gatos, CA 95030. (408) 358-3741.

Humane Society of Santa Clara Valley: 2530 Lafayette Street, Santa Clara, CA 95050. (408) 727-3383.

Midpeninsula Regional Open Space District: 201 San Antonio Circle C135, Mountain View, CA 94040. (415) 949-5500.

·Solano County·

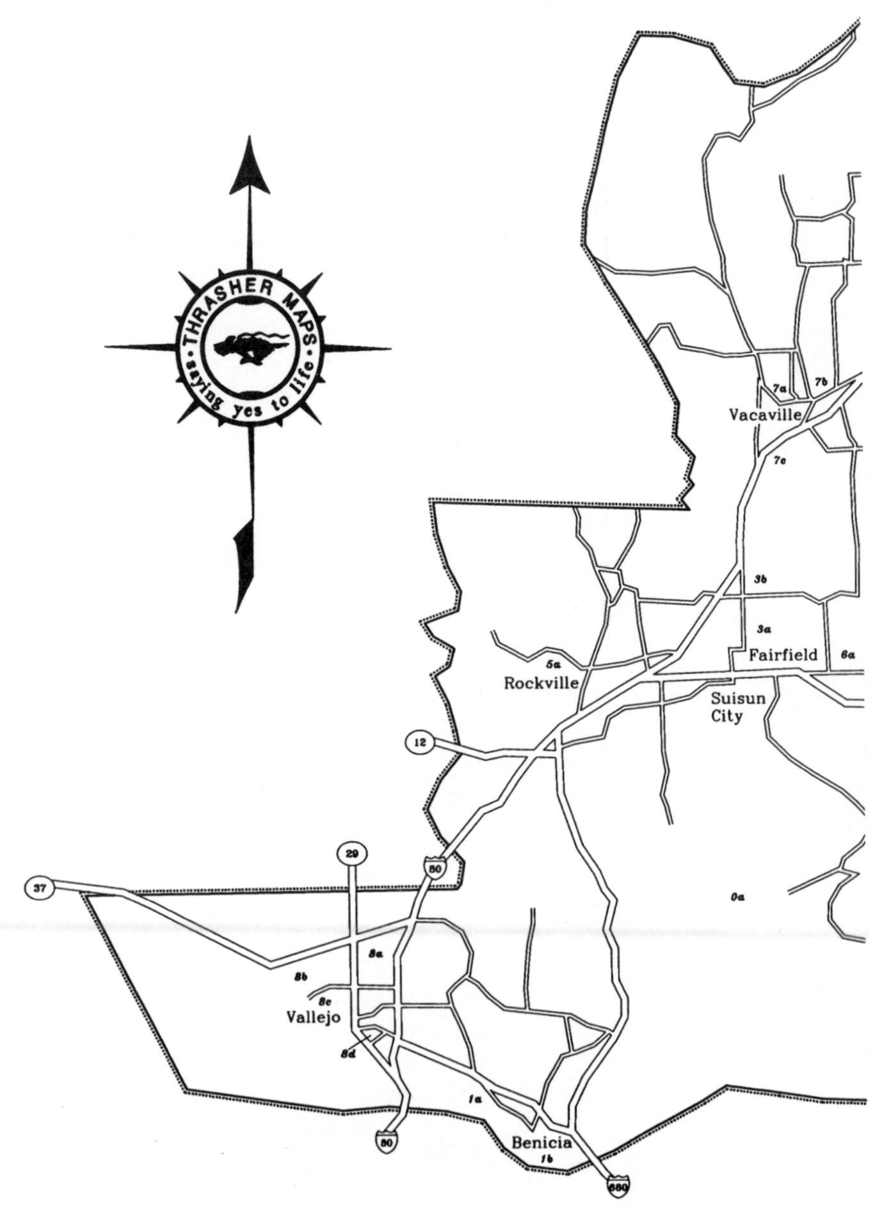
THRASHER MAPS
saying yes to life
7a
7b
Vacaville
7c
3b
3a
Fairfield
6a
5a
Rockville
Suisun
City
12
29
80
37
0a
8a
8b
8c
Vallejo
8d
1a
80
Benicia
1b
680

8. SOLANO COUNTY (map page 244-245)

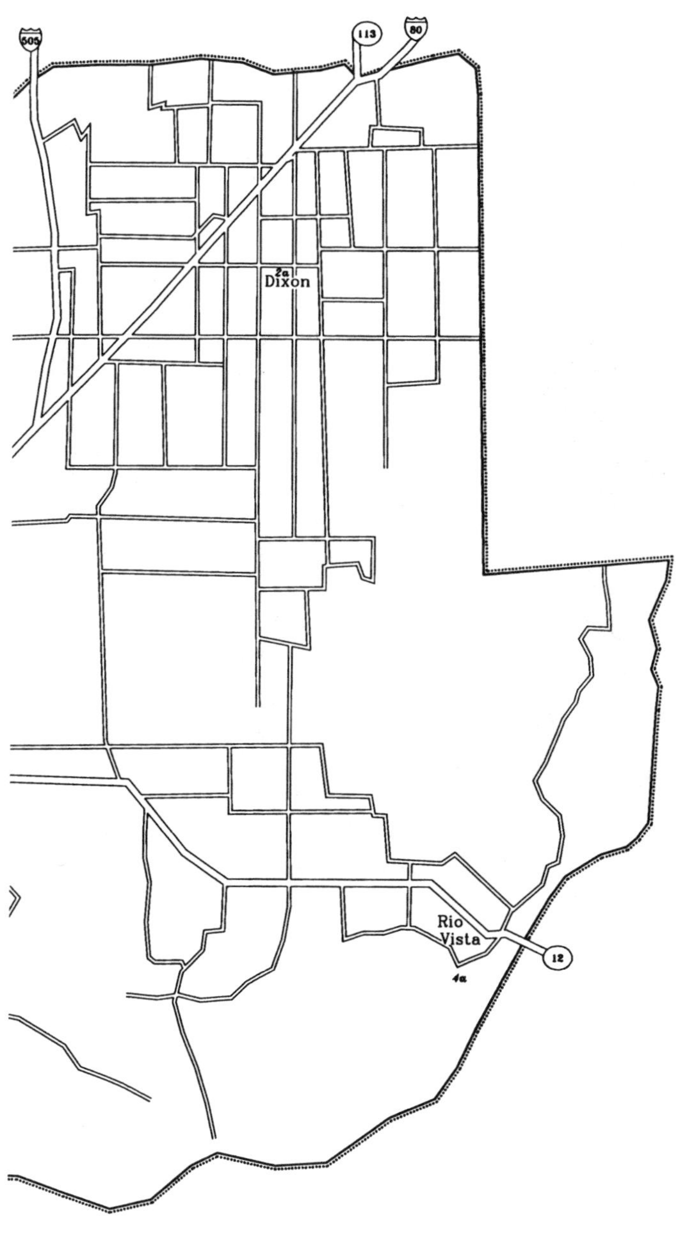

8

One park saves **Solano County** from being devoid of leash-free areas. And what a park it is—8,600 acres of nature as dogs would have created it. The Grizzly Island Wildlife Area, in the thick of the Suisun Marsh, is absolutely worth the trip to Solano County.

The rest of the county offers a mix of small to medium-sized neighborhood parks. Some are enchanting, many are mundane. All demand leashes.

Grizzly Island Wildlife Area 

This is what dogs have been praying for since they started living in cities: 8,600 acres of wide-open land where they can run—leashless—among the sort of wildlife you see only in PBS specials.

This sprawling wetland, in the heart of the Suisun Marsh, is home to an amazing array of fauna: tule elk, river otters, waterfowl of every type, bald eagles, jackrabbits, white pelicans and peregrine falcons.

Of course, walking in marshy areas has its pros and cons. But you don't have to get muddy feet here; the landscapes are as varied as the animal life. Dry upland fields are plentiful. You can also hike along the shores of **Grizzly Bay**, canoe down a slough with your steady dog, or hike on dozens of dirt trails. Many folks bring dogs here to train them for hunting, which brings us to the unfortunate subject of the park's schedule.

Because of hunting and bird nesting seasons, Grizzly Island Wildlife Area is open for you and your dog only between mid-January and March 1, July and early August, and part of September. (Call for exact dates. These are approximate and are subject to change.)

If your dog helps you hunt for elk, ducks or pheasant, she's allowed to join you during some of the hunting seasons. Rangers also occasionally open small sections to people during the off-season, but it's unpredictable from one year to another when and if they'll do it. Even when the park is open, certain sections may be off-limits to dogs. Check with rangers when you come in.

8-0a To get to the Grizzly Island Wildlife Area, exit Interstate 80 at Highway 12 heading toward Rio Vista. Turn onto Grizzly Island Road at the stoplight for the Sunset Shopping Center. Drive 10 miles, past farms and sloughs and marshes, until you get to the ranger station. You'll have to check in here and pay a $2.50 fee. Then continue driving to the parking lot nearest the area that you want to explore (rangers can advise you). Open from dawn to dusk, and only during the months mentioned. Don't forget your binoculars. (707) 425-3828.

8-1

BENICIA

Drive into this quaint town, and you're immediately greeted by the friendly sign: "Welcome to Benicia—A California Main Street City." The sign stands in front of a park straight out of Disneyland's Main Street USA, white gazebo and all.

You'll feel like jumping out of your car and bounding to the nearest green space with your dog to wait for the marching band. But wait! Read the *other* signs—the ones in every single Benicia town park: NO DOGS. The nerve!

But all isn't lost. There's a state recreation area that allows dogs—barely. And there's a fishing area at the end of First Street. It's not dog heaven, but at least it smells good.

The one consolation for being in Benicia with your dog is that the First Street area is full of some of the most dog-friendly restaurants around. Your dog can eat here and use some other city's park to powder his nose.

PARKS, BEACHES & RECREATION AREAS

Benicia State Recreation Area 

While dogs *are* allowed here, the red carpet isn't exactly rolled out for them. Signs everywhere warn against dogs being here or there, and tell owners the many rules of the road. That's partly because for years owners didn't clean up after dogs, and the trail was often a mess. So now we all pay with stricter regulations.

Dogs are allowed only on the virtually shadeless paved trails that are heavily used by bikers and joggers. Dogs aren't supposed to wander into the beckoning fields and hills. And, as in all state parks, they must be leashed.

8-1a The park is off Columbus Parkway at Rose Drive. Park in the area to the left and walk onto the trail there. As of this printing, it's a free parking area, but the state park system may start charging for that area, too. On this trail, it's three-fourths of a mile walk to the Carquinez Strait. Dogs aren't supposed to swim, unfortunately. If you drive to the right on entering the park, you have to pay a $5 fee, and it's a 2.5-mile walk to Dillon Point, overlooking the strait. Open from sunrise to sunset. (707) 745-3385.

Point Benicia Fishing Pier Area 

Park and fish at this big drive-on pier at the end of First Street that juts into the Carquinez Strait. It's a popular spot among local anglers. If you're not up for fishing, bring a lunch from a nearby restaurant and park yourself on one of the benches near the old train station here. You'll be amazed at the numbers of seagulls vying for your crusts.

Dogs enjoy the smells of the strait. While the pier itself isn't conducive to dog exercise, there's an area of undeveloped land nearby where they can cut loose as much as their leashes will allow.

8-1b At the southern end of 1st Street, just past A Street. Open 24 hours. (707) 746-4285.

RESTAURANTS

Morgan's Grill: If your dog slips his leash anywhere in Benicia, check for him here first. They've got great burgers (digna-fried, says owner Lynda Morgan), and they'll cut them in quarters for dogs who dine at their outdoor picnic tables. They even cook them to order. Morgan says most dogs prefer burgers medium rare. 1034 First Street. (707) 745-4466.

Pacifica Pizza: Choose from a large selection of pizzas to eat at tables shaded by umbrellas. 915 First Street. (707) 746-1790.

Waterfront Cafe: The owners will bring your dog a bowl of water while you're awaiting your order at the outdoor tables. They love dogs. They also make a mean bowl of minestrone soup—some of the best we've ever sampled. We also like to take our meal down to the end of First Street, where our dogs can sniff the Carquinez Strait and watch people fishing. 127 First Street. (707) 745-4635.

FESTIVALS

Benicia Peddler's Fair: This August antique sale is held on First Street, starting at the waterfront. Leashed dogs are permitted, but with the valuables they're peddling here, make absolutely, positively certain your dog isn't lifting his leg on anything but a tree. (707) 745-2120.

LODGINGS & CAMPGROUNDS

Best Western Heritage Inn: Dogs are allowed here if you can put up a $50 deposit, returnable on room inspection. Average cost for a double room is $65. 1955 East Second Street, Benicia, CA 94510. (707) 746-0401.

8-2

DIXON

Although it's no more stringent than most, the pooper-scooper law in Dixon has such a formidable name we had to pass it on. It's called the "Canine Defecation Ordinance." Beware.

PARKS, BEACHES & RECREATION AREAS

Hall Memorial Park 

If you have to conduct business with city government, and you want your dog to conduct business too, you couldn't have asked for a better location for a park. It's right behind city hall.

There's not much in the way of shade here, but on cooler days this park proves a decent stroll for dogs, provided they're leashed or at very firm heel. The park also has a playground, a swimming pool, tennis courts and picnic areas with barbecues, so it's even better for people.

8-2a Open from dawn to 10 p.m. At Hall Park Drive and East Mayes Street. (916) 678-7000.

FESTIVALS

Lambtown Festival: Dixon claims the title of having once been the Lamb Capital of the World. The town still celebrates its sheep industry every year with a two-day festival of events that will bring a grin to your dog's face. Young children get to ride sheep rodeo style; people race the clock to dress sheep in boxer shorts. And there are wool shearing, spinning and weaving displays, live music and lots of food (lamb dishes are big here, of course).

Dogs have to be leashed, even on the dance floor. If you've got any kind of herding dog, you may want to leave her at home or risk a dislocated shoulder.

The fair is held the first full weekend in August at the Dixon Fairgrounds, 655 South First Street. Admission is $4 for teens and adults, $2 for children and senior citizens. Toddlers under age five are admitted free. (916) 678-2650.

8-3

FAIRFIELD

PARKS, BEACHES & RECREATION AREAS

Dover Park 

The atmosphere here is right for relaxing. It's a fairly small park, but it has two ponds with lots of ducks, and big, shady willows, oaks and firs. It's the place to go if you want to take a stroll with your leashed dog, then sit against a willow tree to read your favorite book.

On the other hand, if your dog doesn't feel like relaxing, this park can be a little too stimulating: Chaseable ducks abound. And the picnic areas are so popular that the smells just beckon dogs. We saw one unleashed mixed-breed fellow swipe a toddler's bag lunch and run away to eat it in peace. He came to the right place.

8-3a At Travis Boulevard and Flamingo Drive. Open from 6 a.m. to 10 p.m. (707) 428-7428.

Laurel Creek Park 

Remember the kind of park you used to play in as a kid—the big neighborhood park with a great playground where the ice cream truck visits several times a day? This is it. Only it's better, because there's some room for leashed dogs to roam.

The entire west side of this 40-acre park is open fields and undeveloped land. It's the right environment for running around with a dog, but the wrong place for keeping cool on hot days—there's no shade.

8-3b The park is on Cement Hill Road at Peppertree Drive. Open from dawn until 10 p.m. (707) 428-7428.

LODGINGS & CAMPGROUNDS

Best Western Cordelia Inn: Dogs are allowed here at the discretion of the manager. About $54 for a double. 4373 Central Place, Cordelia Village, CA 94585. (707) 864-2029.

Holiday Inn of Fairfield: From Interstate 80, exit at Travis Boulevard West and go one-quarter mile south. About $70 for a double. 1350 Holiday Lane, Fairfield, CA 94533. (707) 422-4111.

8-4

RIO VISTA

Humphrey the humpback whale visited this Delta town, and so should your dog. This is a real, dusty Old West town—not one of those cute villages loaded with boutiques and "shoppes." It's refreshing to find a town with more bait shops than banks.

Rio Vista isn't bursting with dog amenities. In fact, it's really appropriate to visit with your dog only if you're on a fishing holiday. Then you can slip your boat into the water and take off on the Delta for a few hours. Come back with your catch and eat dinner at the county park/campground as the sun goes down on another Delta day.

PARKS, BEACHES & RECREATION AREAS

Sandy Beach County Park

Dogs can't just jump into the Sacramento River here. Although it's part of the day-use area of the park, pooches are not even allowed in that section.

Your dog's best chance of getting wet is to follow you into the showers at the campground. Dogs are allowed at the campground, but it's not a very hospitable place. It's flat and dry, and its trees are more like bushes. With the campsites as close together as they are, and no foliage to give you privacy, it's like sleeping in one big commune.

8-4a Take Highway 12 all the way to Rio Vista; follow Main Street to Second Street and go right. When the street bears left and becomes Beach Drive, the park is within a quarter mile. Bring proof of a rabies vaccination. The campground is open 24 hours, but a ranger isn't always on duty. (707) 374-2097.

RESTAURANTS

Delta Deli: After a long day of fishing, there's nothing like the homemade barbecued beef, ribs and chicken they serve here. 659 Highway 12. (707) 374-6539.

Food Farm: They've got every kind of fast food you could ever want here, and several picnic tables for your feast. Try the southern fried chicken, but watch that your dog doesn't dispose of the bones for you. 650 Highway 12. (707) 374-2020.

LODGINGS & CAMPGROUNDS

Sandy Beach County Park: Camping fees are $10 per vehicle and $1 per dog. (See above for directions.)

DIVERSIONS

Roll on the river: Hire a houseboat. There's nothing like cruising around the Delta in your very own house. Your dog can feel right at home, and nothing makes her happier than having you home all the time! Just remember that, as on land, you have to walk your dog—and you have to dock to do it. Call the Rio Vista Chamber of Commerce for information on houseboat rentals in the Delta. (707) 374-2700.

8-5

ROCKVILLE

PARKS, BEACHES & RECREATION AREAS

Rockville Hills Recreation Center 

Hike, fish and enjoy nature in this 500-acre park filled with trees and trails. The main trail is fairly steep and takes you to the top of the park, where you'll find two small ponds for fishing. After this hike on a summer afternoon, many dogs jump in when they reach the summit. A man told us that a small beagle once disappeared for several seconds and came up with a tiny fish flailing in her mouth.

Once you enter the park, you're safe from traffic. But dogs are supposed to be leashed anyway, since the park is officially run by the city of Fairfield, which has a strict leash law. The city can provide you with a pamphlet on a nature trail that a local Eagle Scouts troop created. It's a great way to learn about the flora of this fragile environment.

But for the most vigorous workout, try the main trail. It's the one that bends slightly to the left and up a steep hill as you enter from the parking lot. The park is often desolate, so use judgment about hiking alone.

8-5a It's on Rockville Road, just west of Suisun Valley Road. Open from 9 a.m. to 9 p.m. (707) 428-7428.

8-6

SUISUN CITY

PARKS, BEACHES & RECREATION AREAS

Montebello Park 

Because of its location at the east end of Suisun City, this is probably the city's least-used park. So if you want to avoid trampling youngsters at play, it's the city's most appropriate park. But it's only a few acres, made up of sports fields with a small playground. A few young trees pop up here and there, but they're nothing dogs will get excited about.

8-6a The park is at Montebello and Capistrano drives. It's open 24 hours a day. (707) 421-7340.

FAIRS & FESTIVALS

Bathtub Races: There's nothing most dogs would enjoy more than watching 20 bathtubs disappear down a slough. That's why they love the Bathtub Races, held in July. Unfortunately for them, the bathtubs usually return at the end of the race. To make up for this disappointment, there's food and live music. The races are held at the end of the Suisun Slough, near the yacht club. (707) 422-0584.

8-7

VACAVILLE

PARKS, BEACHES & RECREATION AREAS

Alamo Creek Park 

The creek here is fenced off from human and canine contact, and in any case, it's bone-dry in summer. With tennis courts, a heart course and a playground, this 10-acre park is more fun for humans than for dogs. But a few young trees and grass provide sufficient pleasures.

8-7a At Alamo Drive and Buck Avenue. Open from dawn to dusk. (707) 449-5390.

Andrews Park 

If you need a shopping cart, try this park first. For some reason, the creek that cuts through the west end of the park contains more shopping carts than most supermarkets.

The chunk of park to the east of the creek is graced with gentle rolling hills, picnic areas, barbecues, deciduous trees, and a lawn as green and smooth as a golf course. But dogs must be leashed.

The west side of the creek is just a shady trail that officially stops at the first overpass and can get pretty seedy if you continue.

8-7b The best parking for the east side is on School Street, near Davis Street. For the west side of the creek, park in a lot at Kendal Street, off Dobbins Street. Open from sunrise to sunset. (707) 449-5390.

Lagoon Valley Regional Park

The hills you see in the background of this sprawling county park are off-limits to your dog. So are the two reservoirs. In fact, most of the park bans dogs. All this for only $3.

Dogs are allowed to walk by the reservoirs on-leash, but that's as close as they can go legally. The section of park that you first enter is the only place dogs are allowed. There are a couple of open grassy areas, and a trail that runs along one reservoir. We've seen people fishing with their dogs, which is the most fun you'll have together at this park.

8-7c Exit Interstate 80 at Cherry Glen Road and follow the signs to the park. It's open from 8 a.m. to dusk. The park currently is closed on Tuesday and Wednesday, but this may change, so call first. (707) 448-7258 or (707) 421-7925.

Lake Solano Park

It's no picnic here for dog owners. In fact, dogs aren't allowed in the picnic/day use area at all. The only way to visit this isolated county park with a dog is to use the camping area across the street. It costs $12 per vehicle, and $1 per dog—a fair slightly higher than the day-use section.

But for dogs who love to swim, it's worth the price of admission. The big freshwater lake here is an ideal respite on a hot summer day. Dogs are allowed off-leash for swimming—and only for swimming. There are a couple of skinny trails along the shore, but they're very short.

The camping here is typical "pack 'em in" camping. Sites are so close together you can hear your neighbors unzip their sleeping bags. But if you scout it out, you may be able to nab a site that has a little more privacy. There are even a few sites on the lake.

Don't forget to bring proof of rabies vaccination for your dog. This can be his certificate or just his up-to-date tag.

8-7d The park is at Highway 128 and Pleasant Valley Road, about five miles west of Interstate 505. Rangers are generally on duty from 8 a.m. to 6 p.m. to check in campers. (707) 421-7925.

Fairs & Festivals

Onion Festival: You're allowed to bring your dog to this onion lover's extravaganza (as if she didn't have bad enough breath already!), but she must be left with SPCA dogsitters volunteering at the gate. They'll keep your dog comfortably shaded from the September sun, and provide lots of water and companionship. Call (707) 448-6424 for this year's dates.

DIVERSIONS

Eat, drink and look in strange mirrors: Most people who visit the **Nut Tree** go there for the shopping or the western-style cuisine. But dogs and their people visit exclusively to enjoy the strange array of activities in front of this gigantic restaurant.

Vain dogs get offended, but most dogs seem highly amused by the funhouse mirrors perched on the restaurant's outer wall. From one moment to the next, your dog becomes fat and thin and distorted beyond belief. (Joe was initially taken aback. Cautiously, he sniffed behind the mirror to see what horrible creature lurked on the other side of the glass. Then he got brave and started barking at his image. A dalmation-basset hound mix joined him with howls and pranced back and forth, never taking his eyes off his reflection.)

There's also an instant photo booth. Pop in a few quarters, pick up your dog somehow, and bango—four wallet-size photos. Just the right size to pull out and show the folks at the office your date for the weekend.

Some dogs pass the time watching the mini-train steam its passengers around the grounds of the Nut Tree. Others like to romp in the shaded, grassy portion that runs parallel to the parking lot. But all dogs love at least one of the many outdoor food concessions in front of the restaurant.

The Sandwich Garden offers dozens of shaded tables and live entertainment. There are also ice cream shacks, places to buy popcorn, cookies and drinks, and plentiful benches.

If your dog doesn't like crowds, you may want to avoid the Nut Tree on weekends and during school breaks. But even in the busiest times, there's always an empty spot of grass, or at least an unused photo booth.

Exit Interstate 80 at Monte Vista Avenue. You can't miss it. (707) 448-1818.

LODGINGS & CAMPGROUNDS

Best Western Heritage Inn: Only very small dogs are allowed here. Don't try to pass your Saint Bernard off as a lapdog, even if he *is* your lapdog. A double room is about $50. Exit Interstate 80 at Monte Vista Avenue. 1420 East Monte Vista Avenue, Vacaville, CA 95688. (707) 448-8453.

Brigadoon Lodge: Small pets only, for $5 extra a day. A double room costs about $45. Exit Interstate 80 at Monte Vista Avenue. 1571 East Monte Vista Avenue, Vacaville, CA 95688. (707) 448-6482.

Gandydancer RV Park: The office here is made up of old cabooses. You camp among groves of eucalyptus trees. Tent sites are $10, RV sites $16. Dogs must be leashed. Take Interstate 80 to the Midway exit. 4933 Midway Road, Vacaville, CA 95688. (707) 446-7679.

Vacaville Super 8: Average double-room rate is $43. Exit Interstate 80 at Monte Vista Avenue. 101 Allison Court, Vacaville, CA 95688. (707) 449-8884.

8-8

VALLEJO

PARKS, BEACHES & RECREATION AREAS

Dan Foley Park 

You won't see *this* at Marine World Africa USA: Professional waterskiers practicing their acts over sloping jumps, and landing head first in the water when everything doesn't work out perfectly.

You and your dog will be treated to this unpolished spectacle if you visit this park on the right day. It's directly across **Lake Chabot** from Marine World, so you get to witness a good chunk of the goings-on there. Since dogs aren't allowed at Marine World, this is an ideal place to walk them, if your kids are spending a few hours with more exotic animals. You still get to hear the sound of jazz bands and the roar of amazed crowds.

Dan Foley Park is so well-maintained we initially were afraid it was a golf course. Willows and pines on rolling hills provide cooling shade, and there's usually a breeze from the lake. Leashed dogs are invited everywhere but the water. Even humans aren't supposed to swim in it. Picnic tables are located right across from the waterski practice area, so if your dog wants entertainment with his sandwich, this is the place.

8-8a The park is on Camino Alto North just east of Tuolumne Street. Open from dawn to dusk. (707) 648-4600.

River Park

With goldenrod as high as an elephant's eye, and a preponderance of low brush, this waterfront park looks more like a huge abandoned lot. That's actually one of its charms—you don't have to worry about your dog mowing over children in a playground, or digging up a plug of green grass. The only park-like features here are a couple of benches along the **Mare Island Strait**.

A wide dirt path leads you toward the water and far from traffic danger. Unfortunately, the leash law is in effect here. And unless your dog is inclined to wade through several yards of mucky marsh to get to the water, he's not going to go swimming. It's still fun to walk along the water and watch the ships at the Mare Island Naval Shipyard across the strait. One ship looks straight out of central casting for McHale's Navy.

8-8b There are two entry points. If you're driving, use the south entrance on Wilson Avenue, just north of Hichborn Street, which has a small parking lot. Otherwise, you can enter at Wilson Avenue just across the street from Sims Avenue. Open from dawn to dusk. (707) 648-4600.

The Wharf 

This is *the* place for hip Vallejo dogs, and it's not even an official park. The paved path along the **Mare Island Strait** looks toward the Mare Island Naval Shipyard on the other side of the strait. There's a real nautical atmosphere here.

It's also the perfect place to take your dog while you're waiting for your ship to come in: This is where the Vallejo-San Francisco ferry stops.

There's a substantial strip of grass beside the path where dogs like to take frequent breaks. Here, they can socialize without getting under joggers' sneakers. Leashes are a must.

8-8c The wharf area covers almost the entire length of Mare Island Way, starting around the Vallejo Yacht Club. Your best bet is to park at the public parking area of the ferry terminal. The wharf is open 24 hours a day. (707) 648-4600.

Wilson/Lake Dalwigk Park 

What you've got here is a big neighborhood park that's mostly undeveloped, leaving lots of land for trotting around. A cement walkway takes you by fields, big palm trees and **Lake Dalwigk**, a small, fairly dirty body of water that can smell slightly of Port-A-Potty.

Cross over the lake on a small footbridge, and your dog will be in a grassy section surrounded by bushes that shelter her from traffic, in case she happens to slip the leash. Be careful, though—it's so secluded that you may not want to go there alone.

8-8d At Fifth and Lemon streets. Open from dawn to dusk. (707) 648-4600.

RESTAURANTS

Gumbah's Beef Sandwiches: Here's the beef. If your dog is your lunch partner, this meaty place is where he'll ask to go. Dine at the tables out front. 138 Tennessee Street. (707) 648-1100.

Sardine Can: Get a view of the strait, while you eat some of the freshest seafood available. Dogs get great treatment here, including a big bowl of water. 0 Harbor Way. (707) 553-9492.

LODGINGS & CAMPGROUNDS

Best Western Royal Bay Inn: There's a non-refundable $5 cleaning fee for dogs. A double room costs around $55. 44 Admiral Callaghan Lane, Vallejo, CA 94590. (707) 643-1061.

Holiday Inn Marine World Africa USA: Dogs allowed in first-floor rooms. There's a $25 non-refundable deposit. A double room costs around $65. Exit Interstate 80 at State Road 37 and go a quarter-mile north. 1000 Fairgrounds Drive, Vallejo, CA 94590. (707) 644-1200.

FAIRS & FESTIVALS

Whaleboat Regatta: Enjoy live entertainment, food and crafts at the fair celebrating the annual race of these big, old, eight-person rowboats. It's sponsored by the California Maritime Academy, and is usually held along the waterfront during the first weekend in October. (707) 648-4216.

MORE INFO

WHERE YOUR DOG CAN'T GO

- Any Benicia city park
- Blue Rock Springs Park, Vallejo
- Pena Adobe Park, Vacaville
- Vallejo's fishing pier at the Sears Point Bridge

8. SOLANO COUNTY (map page 244-245)

USEFUL PHONE NUMBERS & ADDRESSES

Solano County Department of Parks & Recreation: 301 County Airport Road, Vacaville, CA 95688. (707) 421-7925.

State Department of Fish and Game, Grizzly Island Wildlife Complex: 2548 Grizzly Island Road, Suisun City, CA 94585. (707) 425-3828.

Sonoma County

101
Cloverdale
1
Gualala
5a
2a
Geyserville
Sea
Ranch
Healdsburg
8a
17a
Windsor
7b
17b
7a
Timber
Cove
Guerneville
7c
Jenner
9a
9b
15a
Occidental
Sebastopol
Freestone
Bodega
Bay
1b
1a
1

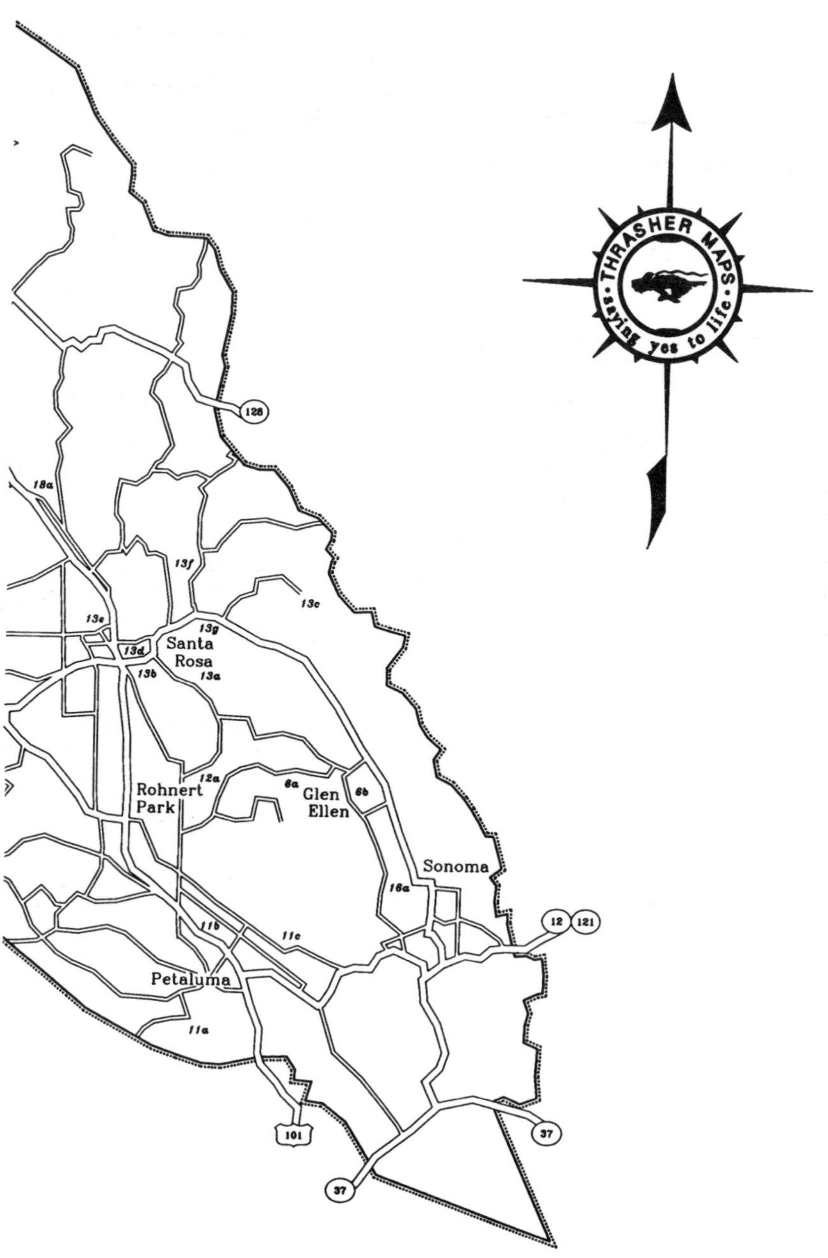
THRASHER MAPS
saying yes to life
128
18a
13f
13c
13e
13g
13d
Santa
Rosa
13b
13a
12a
6a
Rohnert
Park
Glen
Ellen
6b
Sonoma
18a
12
121
11b
11c
Petaluma
11a
101
37
37

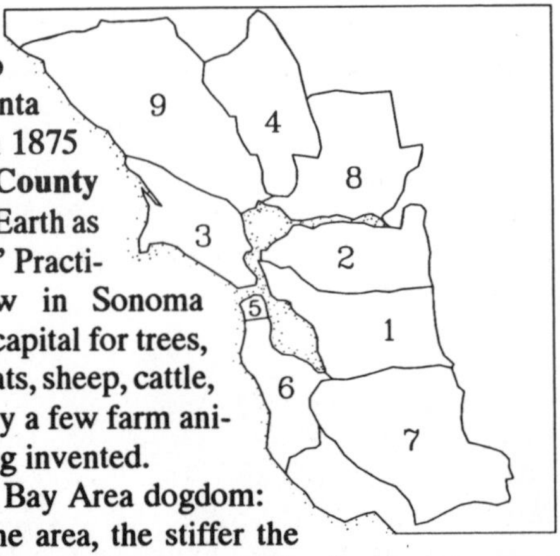

9 The horticulturalist Luther Burbank, who made his home in Santa Rosa and Sebastopol from 1875 to 1926, called **Sonoma County** "the chosen spot of all the Earth as far as nature is concerned." Practically anything will grow in Sonoma County. It's the Bay Area capital for trees, flowers and vegetables, goats, sheep, cattle, chickens, pigs and probably a few farm animals that are just now being invented.

But there's an irony in Bay Area dogdom: Often, the more bucolic the area, the stiffer the penalties for an unleashed dog. On every inch of unincorporated Sonoma County land, and in every single public park, your dog must be on a six-foot leash. As far as we know, there's not a single off-leash beach or public dog run in the county.

If you think about it, though, it makes sense—dogs and farm animals don't mix. Some Sonoma sheep ranchers have been known to impose the ultimate penalty on loose dogs that they see near their livestock: They shoot them.

They're not acting under the law of the Wild West, either; it's a county ordinance that dogs harassing livestock in unincorporated areas or on private property may be shot by the property owner.

The first idea you might have, thinking about Sonoma or Napa counties with your dog, a car and a beautiful day, is: Could I bring my dog wine-tasting?

We asked around, and the general answer is: The wineries want your business, but not your dog's. In other words, if you call ahead and ask if you may bring your dog along, they often find it difficult to say no—but they are very unhappy when owners let their dogs behave badly, or don't pick up after them. So no winery wanted to be listed as welcoming dogs. Still, if you call ahead the winery may say it's all right. Just remember your part of the bargain.

A better idea for a dog is exploring Sonoma's magnificent beaches. You can drive from Bodega Bay (just over the line from Marin County) to Gualala (just over the line in Mendocino County) in about one hour and 15 minutes, if traffic is light. Then work your way down, stopping at one or more of the beaches listed below that allow dogs. You'll have to leash, but you and your dog will sniff incomparable salt air and get sand between your toes.

STATE PARKS

The leash law in the state parks is as strict in Sonoma County as elsewhere. Areas off-limits to dogs—such as nature preserves and historic restoration areas—are clearly marked, and listed at the end of this chapter.

SONOMA COUNTY REGIONAL PARKS

All of Sonoma's county parks require that dogs be on a six-foot leash, and rangers began stepping up enforcement in 1990. (A first citation can cost you up to $62.) The parks are **Crane Creek, Doran Beach, Foothill, Gualala Point, Helen Putnam, Maxwell Farms, Ragle Ranch, Sonoma Valley, Southwest Community, Westside** and **Shiloh Ranch parks, Stillwater Cove, Hudeman Slough** and the **Pinnacle Gulch Trail.** At Shiloh Ranch Park, dogs are allowed only in the parking lot and picnic area. Also under county jurisdiction are several coastal access trails across Sea Ranch, a private development.

You can get a year's pass to the regional parks for $30, free for those age 60 and older. Write to: Sonoma County Regional Parks, 2403 Professional Drive, Number 100, Santa Rosa, CA 95403. (707) 524-7175.

9-1 BODEGA BAY

PARKS, BEACHES & RECREATION AREAS

Doran Beach Regional Park

This Sonoma County Regional Park offers marshland full of egrets, herons and deer—if your dog is very polite with them—and access to the **Pinnacle Gulch Trail,** where your dog is also allowed on-leash. There's a campground (see Lodgings) and a boat ramp. The plain but serviceable beach has almost no surf, great for dog swims, and there are picnic tables near the beach.

9-1a Fee for day use is $3 and $1 for dog. The park is open sunrise to sunset. On Highway 1 just south of Bodega Bay. (707) 875-3540.

Westside Regional Park 

This is an undistinguished but handy park and campground built on landfill right on the water, with picnic tables and barbecues. The non-campground areas close at sunset. **Spud Point Marina**, just to the north, also allows dogs, on-leash.

9-1b The fee for day use is $3, $1 for a dog. On Westshore Road, a westward turn off Highway 1 in town. (707) 524-7175.

LODGINGS & CAMPGROUNDS

Bodega Coast Inn: 521 Coast Highway/Highway 1, Bodega Bay, CA 94923. This inn welcomes dogs with owners who'll promise to be responsible for the dog's behavior. Double rooms around $80, $165 on Saturdays; $10 extra for dog. (707) 875-2217.

Doran Beach Regional Park Campground: 138 tent or RV sites with tables, barbecues, showers and dump station. No trailer hook-ups. Sites are $12 ($10 for Sonoma County residents) plus $3 for each extra vehicle and $1 for each dog, first-come, first-served. On Highway 1 one mile south of Bodega Bay. (707) 875-3540.

Westside Regional Park Campground: 47 tent or RV sites with tables, barbecues, showers and dump station. No trailer hook-ups. Sites are $12 ($10 for Sonoma County residents) plus $3 for each extra vehicle and $1 for each dog, first-come, first-served. On Westshore Road, Bodega Bay. (707) 875-3540

FAIRS & FESTIVALS

Bodega Bay Fisherman's Festival: Annually on the third or fourth weekend in April, the fishing fleet is blessed at the beginning of the salmon season. Surrounding the traditional blessing is a parade of more than 100 decorated boats. You can also join in a 6K run, a bathtub race, pony rides—all the usual silliness—and dogs love silliness, as we all know. Music is provided by a Navy band, an oompahpah band and Scottish bagpipes; lamb and oysters are barbecued.

The festival is held at Westside Park, off Highway 1 at Bodega Bay. Turn west on Westshore Road to the park. (707) 875-3422.

9-2

CLOVERDALE

PARKS, BEACHES & RECREATION AREAS

Lake Sonoma Recreation Area

This is the only recreation site in the nine counties of the Bay Area run by the Army Corps of Engineers, and it's too bad. The Corps has a liberal attitude toward dogs, and this park is beautifully developed and managed, clean and free. You must keep your dog on a six-foot leash, and he's not allowed on the swimming beach at the north end, but rangers told us there's no rule against dogs swimming anywhere else.

At the visitor center is a large lawn with picnic tables, some in shade. You can rent a boat from the private concession on the lake, which allows dogs—leashed—on all boats. Follow signs from the visitor center. To reserve a boat, call (707) 433-2200. Water skiing and camping are also popular here.

For a good dog hike, pick up a map at the visitor center and drive west on Dry Creek Road to the trailheads, which have their own parking lots. There are 40 miles of trails. Here are two of our favorites: There's a bit of shade at the **Digger Pine Flat Trailhead.** This smooth foot trail goes down to the lake through an unusual forest of digger pines, madrone, manzanita and blooming desert brush. The buzz of motorboats on the lake blends with the hammering of woodpeckers. You get a good view of the lake fairly quickly. If you'd prefer less of a climb back to the trailhead, take the **Little Flat Trail**, which starts lower down.

Horses are allowed on these trails, but bikes aren't—a plus for your dog's safety. It's bone-dry here in summer; carry water. And watch for clumps of poison oak.

9-2a For the main entrance at the south end, turn south off Highway 101 on Dutcher Creek Road and drive four miles to the entrance. Take a right at the only fork. The park is open from 8 a.m. to 8 p.m., and it's free. (707) 433-9483.

LODGINGS & CAMPGROUNDS

Lake Sonoma Recreation Area Campgrounds: Developed, primitive and boat-in sites are available. **Liberty Glen Campground** has 113 individual campsites with hot showers and two group camp areas for recreational vehicles. To use the primitive sites (no water), you must get a free permit from the visitor center. There are seven secluded sites reachable only by boat. All these sites are first-come, first-served; reservations are taken for the group sites and handicapped access sites. Dogs must be leashed or "restrained" in the campgrounds, which in this case means you can put him on a generous rope tether. The idea is to keep him from invading other campsites.

Sites are $8 per night during spring and summer, free in the "off season." Call for exact dates, which vary. (707) 433-9483.

9-3 FREESTONE

Lodgings & Campgrounds

Green Apple Inn: This is a homey bed and breakfast sited in meadows and redwoods. Breakfast includes plenty of apple-based dishes. "Of course we accept dogs here," says owner Rosemary Hoffman. "I think dogs are even nicer than people." Rosemary and her husband, Rogers Hoffman, offer a relaxed welcome and good conversation. You can also pet their goats, Emily and Charlotte. All the rooms have separate entrances, and there's one stand-alone cabin with a yard. Prices are around $80 double including breakfast. 520 Bohemian Highway, Freestone, CA 95472. (707) 874-2526.

9-4 GEYSERVILLE

If you just want a pretty drive with your dog—scenery for you, head out the window for him—Highway 128 between Geyserville and Calistoga, in Napa County, is one of the best in Northern California. Be sure to leash at pit stops.

9-5 GUALALA

Parks, Beaches & Recreation Areas

Gualala Point Regional Park

This is the pristine, driftwood-strewn beach you can see from the town of Gualala, just over the Mendocino County border from Sonoma. The small, friendly visitor center offers displays of shore life, Pomo Indian artifacts and old machinery. Outside is a sandstone bull sea lion. From there, it's a half-mile walk to the beach on a smoothly paved trail negotiable by strollers or wheelchairs, through mixed grasses, ferns, berries, dunes and rows of pines and cypresses.

(Leash is required.) At the beach, you can take a trail through marsh or along a coastal bluff. On the beach are driftwood and piles of kelp bulbs, good for jumping on for their satisfying pop.

9-5a From Highway 101, turn just south of Gualala at the sign announcing the park and the Sea Ranch Golf Links. Day-use fee is $2; dog is free. Open 6 a.m. to sunset. (707) 524-7175.

LODGINGS & CAMPGROUNDS

Gualala Point Regional Park Campgrounds: There are 26 sites, about half big enough for trailers; seven are walk-in sites. $12 fee per night; Sonoma County residents, $10. No showers, no trailer hookups. Two vehicles allowed per site; extra vehicles $3. Dogs allowed on-leash for a $1 fee. First-come, first-served only. From Highway 101, turn west just south of Gualala. (707) 785-2377.

9-6 GLEN ELLEN

PARKS, BEACHES & RECREATION AREAS

Jack London State Historic Park 

The extensive backcountry trails here are off-limits to dogs, but the parts of historic interest are not: You're free to take your dog (leashed) the half-mile to the **Wolf House**, visiting Jack London's grave en route, and around the stone house containing the museum of Londoniana (open 10 a.m. to 5 p.m., no pets inside). The trail is paved and smooth enough for strollers and wheelchairs as far as the museum, but then becomes dirt and too narrow. Oaks, pines, laurels and madrones cast dappled light, and the ups and downs are gentle. Signs warn against poison oak and rattlesnakes. Note the antique wagons alongside the trail. The ruins of the huge stone lodge that was London's dream Wolf House are impressive and sad. Fire of unknown origin destroyed it in 1913. London planned to rebuild, but died three years later.

Dogs are also allowed in the picnic areas by the parking lot and by the museum.

9-6a From Highway 12, follow signs to the park: Turn west on Arnold Drive, then west again on London Ranch Road. Fee is $5 for day use, $1 for dog; it's open from 8 a.m. to sundown. (707) 938-5216.

Sonoma Valley Regional Park 

This park is large and welcoming. Just remember that all Sonoma County parks are enforcing their leash rules. A paved, level trail winds alongside a branch of **Sonoma Creek,** and dirt trails head off into the oak woodlands above. Varied grasses and wildflowers, madrones and moss-hung oaks make this a pretty walk, but unfortunately the stream will be dry in warm weather. If you start at the park entrance off Highway 12 and walk westward across the park to Glen Ellen, about a mile, you'll end up at Sonoma Creek and the old mill, with its huge working wheel. You can visit the Jack London Bookstore or just walk around the lovely old town.

9-6b The park lies just south of Glen Ellen between Arnold Drive and Highway 12. The entrance is off Highway 12. It's open sunrise to sunset. Parking fee $1. (707) 539-8092.

9-7

GUERNEVILLE

Parks, Beaches & Recreation Areas

Armstrong Redwoods State Reserve 

As usual, in this state park, you can take a dog only on paved roads and into picnic areas, but here you can give your dog and yourself an exceptional treat. The picnic grounds are a cool, hushed redwood cathedral, and you can walk on the **Armstrong Woods Road**, which winds along **Fife Creek** (usually lush, but dry in the heart of summer) all the way to the top of McCray Mountain, about three miles. The drive is fairly terrifying, so you might rather walk anyway. Hikers, bicycles and autos all share the road, so be very careful. Your dog must be leashed everywhere in the park.

9-7a From Guerneville, go about 2.5 miles north on Armstrong Woods Road. Hours are 8 a.m. to one hour after sunset. Day-use fee is $5, $1 for dog. (707) 869-2015 or (707) 865-2391.

Austin Creek Recreation Area 

Austin Creek's open grassy hills nestle just to the north of Armstrong Woods. Rules there are even stricter, since dogs aren't allowed on dirt trails, and only one paved road goes partway in. But you may picnic or camp with a pooch at the Bullfrog Pond Campground (see Lodgings).

9-7b To get there, follow directions to Armstrong Woods and drive all the way through. There's no extra charge after you pay

$5 and $1 dog fee to enter Armstrong Woods. (707) 869-2015 or (707) 865-2391.

Vacation Beach

Vacation Beach, not really a beach but an access point where the **Russian River** is dammed by two roads across it, is one of several public spots where you and your dog can legally jump into the drink. Here, people picnic, swim, put in canoes and let their dogs cool their paws. It's free, and there are no posted leash rules, but watch cars going over the dam roads. No overnight camping is allowed.

9-7c From Highway 116 between Guerneville and Monte Rio, turn south at the unmarked road where you see Old Cazadero Road going off northward. You can park at the approaches to the dams, but not on the crossing itself.

Lodgings & Campgrounds

Austin Creek Recreation Area, Bullfrog Pond Campground: This campground has 24 primitive tent sites, available on a first-come, first-served basis year round. Tables and flush toilets, fire rings and drinking water are provided, but no showers. Follow directions to Armstrong Woods State Reserve and drive about three miles from the entrance on Armstrong Woods Road to the campground. Sites are $12 plus $1 dog fee. (707) 869-2015.

9-8

HEALDSBURG

Parks, Beaches & Recreation Areas

Healdsburg Veterans Memorial Beach 

The bad news, predictably, is that you can't take a dog to this prime summertime county swimming beach on the **Russian River**, open from Memorial Day to Labor Day. The good news is that you may have her with you, on-leash, in the shady picnic area. And there are some shady spots in the parking lot for your car if you arrive early enough to nab one. Don't plan on leaving your dog in your car while you swim, though, even in the shade. It's much more dangerous than you think (see page 300).

9-8a Exit Highway 101 at Healdsburg Avenue/Old Redwood Highway and drive north; the beach is south of Old Redwood Highway where it crosses the Russian River. Parking fee is $2 or

$3 when the water level drops after Labor Day. Open 8 a.m. to sunset. (707) 524-7175.

RESTAURANTS

Costeaux French Bakery: Stroll around Healdsburg's good-looking town square, with its old buildings and benches for shady rest stops, and then drop in here for dinner or a wonderful pastry snack at an outdoor table. 417 Healdsburg Avenue. (707) 433-1913.

LODGINGS & CAMPGROUNDS

Best Western Dry Creek Inn: Exit Highway 101 at Dry Creek Road. 198 Dry Creek Road, Healdsburg, CA 95448. $60 to $70 for a double. Small dogs only. (707) 433-0300.

9-9

JENNER

PARKS, BEACHES & RECREATION AREAS

Russian Gulch State Park

Your dog will enjoy this small, wild park whose streams drain Russian Gulch. You must leash up, though. A rough dirt trail leads in through deciduous forest. Huge groves of willows line the gulch. In wet season, you'll have to wade across the gulch to reach the beach, a small one with cliffs at each end. The surf is ferocious; don't let your dog near it! Swimming in the fresh creeks is much more fun for her, anyway.

9-9a About three miles north of Jenner, watch for a small brown sign marking the turnoff. There's a dirt parking lot at the entrance. Open sunrise to sunset. (916) 653-6995.

Sonoma Coast State Beaches

A string of beautiful, clean beaches runs from Jenner south to Bodega Bay. From **Goat Rock Beach** south to **Salmon Creek Beach**, you can't go wrong: Gorgeous bluff views, stretches of brown sand, gnarled rocks and grassy dunes welcome you. Always keep your eye on the surf.

The beaches are all open 24 hours and allow dogs on-leash. Dogs are not allowed on any of the trails that run on the bluffs above the beaches, on **Bodega Head**, in the **Willow Creek** area east of Bridgehaven, or in the seal rookery upriver from Goat Rock Beach. (Watch for the warning sign.) No unofficial camping is permitted on any of the beaches. All are free of charge except **Bodega Dunes** and

Wright's Beach, which have campgrounds. These two charge a $5 day-use fee. (707) 875-3483.

LODGINGS & CAMPGROUNDS

Bridgehaven Campground: This friendly place welcomes dogs, leashed or not, so long as they are under control—and charges no extra fee. It's in the hamlet of Bridgehaven, where Highway 1 crosses the Russian River south of Jenner. For a day-use fee of $3, you and your dog can swim together — "and if he doesn't make a mess, I'll forget the $3," says the campground owner. Camp tent sites are $10. There are 23 sites with barbecues and two shower bathrooms, one with hot water. Open year round. PO Box 59, Jenner, CA 95450. (707) 865-2473.

Sonoma Coast State Beach Campgrounds: Bodega Dunes Campground has 98 developed tent/trailer sites with restrooms, a campfire center, hot showers and a trailer sanitation station. Wright's Beach Campground has 30 developed sites with no showers. Sites are $14, a night plus $1 for each dog. They're open year round; advance reservations are highly recommended in summer and early fall (you may reserve up to eight weeks in advance): (800) 444-PARK, or write to MISTIX, PO Box 85705, San Diego, CA 92138.

9-10

OCCIDENTAL

LODGINGS & CAMPGROUNDS

Negri's Occidental Lodge: Right in Occidental—you can't miss it. PO Box 84, Occidental, CA 95465. Around $50 for a double. Pets are an extra $3.25. (707) 874-3623.

9-11

PETALUMA

Petaluma is a captivating Sunday afternoon stroll, with its leafy streets and pocket parks for your dog's pleasure, Victorian buildings, old feed mills and a riverfront that remains mostly original, but not dilapidated. An informal survey told us that you can go almost everywhere with your dog in town, which has a tolerant character. Several eating places will gladly serve you and your dog along the riverfront at outdoor benches and tables (see Restaurants).

Parks, Beaches & Recreation Areas

Helen Putnam Regional Park 

This county regional park is, and will remain, a minimally developed stretch of converted cow pasture with oak trees. A wide paved trail shared by hikers and bicyclists runs between the main entrance and the Victoria housing development (to enter from that end, go to the end of Oxford Court). Dogs must be leashed. Carry water if you plan to stay long. There's no shade from the scrub oaks, and it can be windy. The paved trail takes gentle ups and downs; some other dirt trails give you steeper hill climbs. About one-quarter mile in from the main entrance is an old cattle pond good for a dog swim.

At the main entrance, you put $1 in a machine for parking, and restrooms and water are provided. Next to the lot is a kids' play area and a picnic gazebo, by a creek that's only a gully in summer. At the development end, there's a water fountain but no restroom, no parking lot and no fee. You have to park along the road.

9-11a Drive south on Western Avenue, which becomes Chileno Valley Road. Watch for the turnoff to the park. Open sunrise to sunset. (707) 524-7175.

Lucchesi Park 

A well-kept, popular city park with an impressive postmodern community center, playing fields, horseshoe pits, kids' playground, picnic tables, a huge pond with fountain and ducks, and paved paths. Sadly, no dog swimming is allowed in the pond. And of course, leash is mandatory. Nevertheless, we saw crowds of happy dogs being trained to heel or catch frisbees.

9-11b At North McDowell Boulevard and Madison Street. Curfew is 10 p.m. to 6 a.m. (707) 778-4386.

Petaluma Adobe State Historic Park 

Leashed dogs are welcome here, if they behave well around goats and such, and if you avoid the gardens and the farm animals' courtyard. From the parking lot, walk across a wooden bridge over a wide, willow-lined creek (dry in summer) to the house, built in 1836 as headquarters for General Mariano Vallejo's 66,600-acre Rancho Petaluma. Clustered around the house are tempting displays of animal skins, saddles and tallow makings, and loose sheep, a donkey and chickens. Dogs must use their best manners. You may tour the building and visit the museum, but without your dog. There are some shady spots in the parking lot in which to leave him, and bicycle racks and picnic tables nearby.

9-11c The park is northeast of Petaluma at Adobe Road and Casa Grande Road. From Highway 101, you'll see an exit sign for the Petaluma Adobe. The park and museum are open 10 a.m. to 5 p.m. Admission is $2 for adults, $1 for children. (707) 762-4871.

RESTAURANTS

Apple Box: A store of antiques and housewares that also serves good desserts, teas and coffee. There's a bookshop next door and five or six tables outside, right by the river. Dabney loves the smell of sun on river water, mixed with baking cookies. 224 B Street. (707) 762-5222.

Que Pasa: At this Mexican place on the river, you can tie your dog up outside the patio fence and munch tacos close by. 54 East Washington Street. (707) 769-8396.

Perry's Charburgers: Order a burger and eat it in the tiny, pretty Putnam Plaza Park right next door. Then order onion rings, mozzarella sticks and a milk shake to wash it down. (Healthier fare is also available.) The eatery furnishes around 10 tables, or pick a park bench. 139B Petaluma Boulevard North. (707) 762-9559.

Rocket Cafe: Light meals, desserts, beer and wine. On weekends, the owners offer barbecue and live music. And they love dogs. 100 Petaluma Boulevard, Number 104. (707) 763-2314.

The Old River Inn: This elegant spot in a restored Victorian serves Italian and French brunch, lunch and dinner on a sunny riverfront patio. The owner, very fond of dogs, regrets that the board of health frowns on dogs on the patio, but she'll let you tie yours on the nearby shaded lawn while you eat. By the walk-across floating bridge, at 222 Weller Street. (707) 765-0111.

DIVERSIONS

Go ahead—you won't hurt your dog's feelings: Petaluma's annual Ugly Dog Contest is a good time for you and your dog, ugly or not. (Beautiful dogs are welcome, so long as they don't mind losing.) It's held on the last day of the Sonoma-Marin Fair, and open to any dog owner for a $3 entry fee. For your $3, you get free admission to the fair for that day, but your dog is allowed only in the contest area. Water and shade are provided; bring your own pooper scooper.

A winner is chosen in the Mutt and Pedigreed categories; these winners square-off for the Ugly Dog of the Year award. Then there's the Ring of Champions division, in which past winners compete for the title of World's Ugliest Dog. Don't miss it! Held at 12:30 at the Grandstand Park Stage on a Sunday in late June, at the Sonoma-Marin Fair grounds. Call for this year's date: (707) 763-0931.

9-12 ROHNERT PARK

PARKS, BEACHES & RECREATION AREAS

Crane Creek Regional Park

This patch of grazing land in the middle of nowhere is undeveloped open space for your dog's pleasure. Unfortunately, the leash law is enforced here, and a sign tells you why: "Dogs Caught in Livestock May Be Shot." Carry water; you may get thirsty just trying to find the place in your car.

9-12a From Rohnert Park, drive east on the Rohnert Park Expressway to Petaluma Hill Road; turn south on Petaluma Hill Road to Roberts Road; go east on Roberts Road. Shortly after Roberts turns into Pressley Road, there's the park. A machine hopes to collect a $1 parking fee from you. Future improvement plans include only an upgraded parking lot. (707) 524-7175.

9-13 SANTA ROSA

Santa Rosa no longer looks quite as it did in Hitchcock's *Shadow of a Doubt*, but it's still a nice town with neat, green city parks that get good use. All require dogs to be leashed.

PARKS, BEACHES & RECREATION AREAS

Dan Galvin Community Park 

Volleyball, tennis courts, soccer field, picnic tables with barbecues under trees, parcourse and kids' gym—all nice, but nothing special for a dog to do. Keep him leashed.

9-13a At Bennett Valley Road and Yulupa Avenue, next to the Bennett Valley Golf Course. Open 6 a.m. to 6 p.m., to 9 p.m. during Daylight Savings Time. (707) 524-5116.

Doyle Park 

This is a perfect small-town park, much appreciated on summer evenings, when kids play softball under huge oaks and mariachi music fills the air. Even in summer, there's water in Spring Creek for your leashed dog to enjoy. Besides the big softball diamond, there are volleyball courts, a parcourse and a kids' gym.

9-13b From Sonoma Avenue, turn south on Doyle Park Drive to the parking lot. Open 6 a.m. to 6 p.m., to 9 p.m. during Daylight Savings Time. (707) 524-5116.

Hood Mountain Regional Park 

Dogs and people love the trails in this park, but it's open only on weekends and holidays and closes every summer when fire danger gets high—and usually reopens only in late September. Make sure your dog wears a leash. If a sign appears at the Los Alamos Road turnoff saying that the park is closed, believe it. Be sure to carry water for you and your dog; the few vernal creeks are low to nonexistent in warm weather.

To get to the only entrance, from Highway 12, turn east on Los Alamos Road (not Adobe Canyon Road, which leads only to Sugarloaf Ridge State Park—where dogs aren't allowed on trails). The road is long, winding, steep and narrow for the last two miles, not for nervous drivers. It's a beautiful four-mile drive, with a good close-up of Hood Mountain's bare rock outcropping "hood," if you're in the mood for such a road.

9-13c Open from 8 a.m. to sunset, weekends and holidays only; closed in summer after start of fire season. Call to make sure it's open before driving there! (707) 524-7175.

Juilliard Park 

A pleasant city park near the Luther Burbank home and gardens and the Ripley's Believe It or Not Museum. It has picnic tables under redwoods, a softball diamond, volleyball courts, a parcourse and a kids' gym. Leash up.

9-13d Juilliard Park Drive is a westward turn off Santa Rosa Avenue. There's no parking lot, but the street parking is shaded on South A Street, the western edge. Open 6 a.m. to 6 p.m., to 9 p.m. during Daylight Savings Time. (707) 524-5116.

Northwest Community Park 

Green lawns are available here, plus a parcourse, a softball diamond, a playground, other athletic fields and picnic tables by a creek, which is small but wet even in August, and lined with willows.

9-13e It's a bit hard to find; the entrance is off West Steele Lane, east of Marlow Road. Open 6 a.m. to 6 p.m., to 9 p.m. during Daylight Savings Time. (707) 524-5116.

Rincon Valley Community Park 

This city park has a softball field, picnic tables, parcourse and kids' gym, and ponds in which three happy dogs were swimming (with leashes on, like good dogs) the day we visited. There's an attractive picnic area with shade trees by one pond.

9-13f On Montecito Boulevard, west of Calistoga Road. (707) 524-5116.

Spring Lake Regional Park 

In winter, this county park isn't much more than a pleasantly dutiful trot on-leash around the lake. But in summer, it's leafy and full of the summer sounds of kids yelling and thumping oars. This is a good spot for a picnic, roller skating, a parcourse workout, a boat ride or human swimming (no dogs in swim area). The path around the lake is paved for skaters, strollers and bicycles, and there are short dirt paths off into the open oak and brush woods. You can fish from the banks, where they're cleared of tules and willows.

Dogs must be leashed. It's more fun here for people than for dogs; in summer, there are a lot of bicycles.

9-13g From Highway 12—the Farmer's Lane portion in Santa Rosa—turn east on Hoen Avenue, then left (north) on Summerfield Road, then immediately right (east) on Newanga Avenue to the entrance. Parking fee is $2; the large lot has some shady spots. Open from 7 a.m. to sunset daily from May 15 to September 15; weekends only from September 16 to May 14. (707) 539-8082.

Lodgings & Campgrounds

Best Western—Garden Inn: From Highway 101, exit at Baker Avenue (northbound) or Corby Avenue (southbound). 1500 Santa Rosa Avenue, Santa Rosa, CA 95404. About $60 for a double. (707) 546-4031.

Best Western Hillside Inn: Two and one-half miles east off Highway 101, on Highway 12, at Farmers Lane and Fourth Street. 2901 Fourth Street, Santa Rosa, CA 95409. About $50 for a double.

Los Robles Lodge: From Highway 101, exit at Steele Lane. 925 Edwards Avenue, Santa Rosa, CA 95401. About $80 for a double. (707) 545-6330.

Santa Rosa Travelodge: From Highway 101 northbound, take the second Santa Rosa Avenue exit; southbound, exit at Santa Rosa Avenue/Corby. 1815 Santa Rosa Avenue, Santa Rosa, CA 95407. About $50 for a double. (707) 542-3472.

Spring Lake Park Campground: 31 sites with tables, barbecues and hot showers, $11 plus $3 for each extra vehicle and $1 for a dog. Ten sites are reservable; 20 are first-come, first-served. Dogs must have proof of rabies vaccination. The campground is open daily between May 15 and September 15, weekends and holidays only after September 15. To reserve, call (707) 539-8082.

Sugarloaf Ridge State Park Campgrounds: The Family Campground, which accepts dogs, has 50 campsites with tables and fire rings, but no showers. The sites accommodate trailers and campers up to 24-feet long. Sites are $12 per night, plus $1 for each dog. (707) 833-5712, or reserve through MISTIX, (800) 444-PARK.

9-14

SEA RANCH

Sea Ranch is a private development, but seven public foot trails cross the property leading to the beach, which is also public property as everywhere in the state. The smooth, wide dirt trails are managed by the Sonoma County Regional Parks. They offer incomparable solitary walks through unspoiled grassy hills.

All the trails are clearly marked on Highway 1. At each trailhead are restrooms, and you're asked to deposit $2 in a box for parking. The trailhead gates are locked at sunset. No motorcycles, bicycles or horses are allowed. Keep your dog on-leash, and if you step off the trail, you're trespassing. Here are the distances to the beach, listing trails from north to south: **Salal Trail**, .6 mile; **Bluff-Top Trail**, 3.5 mile; **Walk-On Beach Trail**, .4 mile; **Shell Beach Trail**, .6 mile; **Stengel Beach Trail**, .2 mile; **Pebble Beach Trail**, .3 mile; **Black Point Trail**, .3 mile.

9-15 SEBASTOPOL

PARKS, BEACHES & RECREATION AREAS

Ragle Ranch Park

This Sonoma County regional park, right in the town of Sebastopol, is surprisingly large and wild, once you pass the fields and picnic areas. Unlike most urban parks, it's not very crowded, except when sports are going on on weekends. Level hiking and equestrian trails wind alongside vineyards and apple orchards, in bloom beginning in early April. Waterfowl breed in marshy spots around the creek, so in that area, at least, you shouldn't yield to the temptation to let your dog off the leash. (Leashing is the rule.) The landscape is gently rolling, with reeds and willows lining the creek and oaks with mistletoe on the higher rises.

9-15a At Healdsburg Avenue and Ragle Road. Admission is $1 per car. Opening and closing hours vary with season, but are usually 7 a.m. to sunset. (707) 524-7175.

RESTAURANTS

So-N-So's: Don't miss the truly delicious burgers, fries and shakes at this roadside drive-in, a favorite of ours. 915 Gravenstein Highway/Highway 116. (707) 823-3398.

FAIRS & FESTIVALS

Apple Blossom Festival: As with all the farm festivals held in the county, this one is not particularly fun for dogs, since they must be leashed everywhere and mind their manners impeccably. But if your dog likes jumping in and out of the car, and behaves well in crowds on-leash, by all means bring her along. Stroll through town and browse the arts and crafts and food displays. This two-day festival is usually held in April. Call the Chamber of Commerce: (707) 823-3032.

Gravenstein Apple Fair: Even on the hottest, dustiest, most crowded day, this fair is sure-fire fun. Dogs are allowed on-leash, and you'll see plenty there. The begging is excellent. Listen to country-western or bagpipes, shake hands with someone in a cow costume, watch cooking demonstrations, and pet farm animals (only you—not your dog). Admission is $3.50, $1 for kids. Held all weekend in August, 10 a.m. to 6 p.m., in Ragle Ranch Park. For exact dates: (707) 829-GRAV.

Diversions

Sniff out the farm trail: If you're serious about buying home-grown produce and dairy products, or just like farms—and your dog wears a leash at all times and won't do leg-lifts on the vegetables—pick up a Farm Trails map from Sonoma County Farmtrails, (707) 544-4728, or from the Chamber of Commerce, PO Box 178, Sebastopol, CA 95473. (707) 823-3032.

9-16

SONOMA

Sonoma's historic buildings and Town Plaza are a fine stroll with a canine on a summer day. But even on-leash dogs aren't permitted in the square park, which on a good day is full of picnickers wolfing down fine wine and Sonoma jack.

Parks, Beaches & Recreation Areas

Maxwell Farms Regional Park 

This Sonoma County Regional Park offers playing fields, picnic tables, a generous kids' playground, smooth paths for strollers, and a large undeveloped area where paths follow Sonoma Creek under huge laurels wound with wild grapevines. The creek is dry in summer, though. Dogs must be leashed.

9-16a The entrance is off Verano Avenue, west of Highway 12. Day-use fee is $1. The park is open from 7 a.m. to sunset. (707) 524-7175.

Restaurants

The Feed Store Cafe & Bakery: Delicious lunch, dinner and snacks, coffee and desserts, beer and wine can be enjoyed by both of you at cafe tables in front or in the roomy and beautifully landscaped back patio, with almost 20 umbrella tables. A fountain provides the soothing sound of flowing water and also serves as an elegant water dish. (It should be elegant, but Dabney fell in and ruined the effect.) The owners welcome well-behaved dogs at any hour. 529 First Street West. (707) 938-2122.

Lodgings & Campgrounds

Best Western Sonoma Valley Inn: One block west of Town Plaza, at 550 Second Street West, Sonoma, CA 95476. Around $120 for a double. Small dogs only; a refundable $10 deposit is charged. (707) 938-9200.

9-17 TIMBER COVE

PARKS, BEACHES & RECREATION AREAS

Salt Point State Park

Dogs are allowed only on **South Gerstle Cove Beach**—south of the rocky tidepool area, which is an underwater reserve—and in the **Gerstle Cove, Woodside and Fisk Mill Cove** picnic areas and campsites. On-leash, as always. Gerstle Cove picnic area is right above the allowed portion of the beach, though, so that's your best bet. The surf is usually gentle here, but if in doubt, you can call an ocean-conditions recording: (707) 847-3222.

9-17a The park is about five miles north of Timber Cove and six miles south of Stewarts Point, off Highway 1. Parking fee is $5, $1 for dogs. Open sunrise to sunset. (707) 847-3221.

Stillwater Cove Regional Park 

This is a tiny but delightful beach at the foot of spectacular pine-covered cliffs. Park in the small lot beside Highway 1, leash your dog and walk down. There is a larger picnic area above the highway, where a $2 day use fee is charged. From here, you have to cross the highway to get to the cove. Look both ways!

9-17b The turnout is about 1 mile north of Fort Ross State Park, where dogs are excluded. Open sunrise to sunset. (707) 847-3245.

LODGINGS & CAMPGROUNDS

Salt Point State Park Campgrounds: Dogs are allowed on-leash in all campsites here except the walk-in, group and environmental sites. The park has about 30 units in the upland portion of the park, each with table and fire pit, water and nearby bathrooms. East of Highway 1 are 80 family sites, with all those same facilities, but no showers. Sites are $14 per night, dog fee $1. Between March 2 and November 30, reserve through MISTIX: (800) 444-PARK. The rest of the year, it's first-come, first-served. (707) 847-3221.

Stillwater Cove Regional Park Campgrounds: There are 23 tent or RV sites with showers. No trailer hook-ups. First-come, first-served only. Sites are $12 per night for two vehicles, $10 for Sonoma County residents; extra vehicles $3 each. Dogs allowed on-leash for $1. (707) 847-3245.

9-18

WINDSOR

PARKS, BEACHES & RECREATION AREAS

Foothill Regional Park 

This unimproved patch of land near Windsor will be developed in the future by the county for "passive use"—low-tech amusements such as hiking, bicycling and dog-walking. It's legal now to walk your dog there, on-leash.

9-18a From the Old Redwood Highway, take the Windsor exit and follow Vinecrest Road all the way to the end. No toilets or water are available. (707) 524-7175.

9-19

MORE INFO

WHERE YOUR DOG CAN'T GO

- Armstrong Redwoods State Preserve, Guerneville (except for paved roads and picnic areas)
- Austin Creek State Recreation Area, Guerneville (except for paved roads, picnic areas and one campground)
- Bodega Head State Park trails
- Fisk Mill Cove beach
- Fort Ross State Historic Park, between Jenner and Timber Cove
- Jack London State Historic Park, Glen Ellen—backcountry trails
- Kruse Rhododendron State Reserve
- Olompali State Historic Park, Novato
- Russian River beaches from Goat Rock inland on state park lands (a seal rookery)
- Salt Point State Park (except for paved roads, campgrounds and picnic areas)
- Shiloh Ranch Regional Park, Windsor (except for picnic areas)
- Sugarloaf Ridge State Park (except for paved roads, campgrounds and picnic areas)

Useful Phone Numbers & Addresses

California State Parks: Department of Parks and Recreation, Office of Public Relations, PO Box 942896, Sacramento, CA 94296. (916) 653-6995. To call within California for MISTIX campsite reservations (you may reserve up to eight weeks in advance): (800) 444-PARK, or write to MISTIX, PO Box 85705, San Diego, CA 92138.

Corps of Engineers, Lake Sonoma Recreation Area: 3333 Skaggs Springs Road, Geyserville, CA 95441. (707) 433-9483. Boat rentals: (707) 433-2200.

Sonoma Coast State Beaches: Bodega Bay, CA 94923. (707) 875-3483.

Sonoma County Regional Parks: 2403 Professional Drive Number 100, Santa Rosa, CA 95403. (707) 524-7175.

Appendix

BEYOND THE BAY

There comes a time when a dog owner must venture beyond the Bay Area. Whether traveling for business or pleasure, we're faced with the difficult choice of bringing our dog along or leaving him with a kennel or dog sitter. People often opt to travel solo and not risk that seemingly dog-unfriendly world out there. It's a shame, because if you're willing to do a little research, you and your dog can find happiness almost anywhere in California—even in Los Angeles.

Bear in mind, though, if you've been in the San Francisco area long enough to forget, that temperatures in other parts of the state can be scorching. Check weather reports before you decide to take your dog into oven-like regions. And if you're flying, and will be gone only a few days, your dog will probably prefer to stay behind: Air travel can be grueling for dogs.

For more information on West Coast lodgings for you and your dog, we recommend the book *On the Road Again With Man's Best Friend* by Dawn and Robert Habgood (Dawbert Press).

And there's a nationwide directory listing more than 3,000 hotels and motels that allow pets. To order the PETS-R-PERMITTED Travel Directory, send $8.95 plus $1.05 postage to the Annenberg Communications Institute, PO Box 66006, West Des Moines, Iowa, 50265-9410. Or call (515) 224-4872.

GOLD COUNTRY

The folks at Gold Prospecting Expeditions, in Jamestown, say they've never met a dog who didn't like helping his owner pan for gold in the cool rivers and creeks here. You and your dog can take a walking tour guided by a prospector, then get down to the business of panning for yourselves. You keep what you find, and the folks here say you'll always get something in their section of the Mother Lode.

If your dog can pan like Twinkles, the poodle on the premises, you'll be rich. Twinkles sticks her head under water in a panning trough and comes up with a gold nugget every time. Of course, she's been trained, and the nugget is always there, so don't be too disappointed if your dog doesn't scoop up a retirement fund for you.

For a real outback prospecting experience, you and your dog (so long as he's of calm disposition) can fly in a helicopter to some of the most remote swatches of gold country in California. You can stay for just a day or camp for two weeks, panning and digging into gold veins the whole time. The adventure isn't cheap, but it won't matter if you find that big vein of gold.

Prices range from $25 for an hour to hundreds of dollars per week for a camping excursion via helicopter. Write or call Gold Prospecting Expeditions, 18170 Main Street, Jamestown, CA 95327. (209) 984-GOLD.

LAKE TAHOE

This isn't an adventure for people or dogs who get panicky looking out a second-story window: Your excursion—should you choose to take it—will find you and your leashed dog dangling hundreds of feet above the mountainside at the Squaw Valley ski resort.

During summer and autumn months, cable cars normally reserved for skiers will lift you to new heights (8,200 feet above sea level, to be precise) and set you down in the midst of miles of hiking trails. You can either hike to the bottom or explore the mountaintop and take the cable car back down.

In early summer, when wildflowers are blooming on the bare mountain, this experience is especially spectacular. If you have a swimming dog, take her to Shirley Lake for a refreshing splash. But avoid the lake after midsummer—without snow runoff, it turns stagnant and unappealing.

Round-trip tickets cost $10 for adults. Dogs ride free. The cable cars operate from approximately 9:30 a.m. to 4:40 p.m. during summer and fall. (Don't forget that dogs aren't allowed at all during ski season.) Call (916) 583-6985.

LOS ANGELES

Los Angeles isn't all freeways and suburbs, as Northern Californians like to imagine. There really *are* unpaved pieces of land where dogs can run and have fun.

PARKS BEACHES & RECREATION AREAS

Griffith Park

There's something for every dog in this sprawling 4,100-acre park. For canines who are into locomotives, there's a small-scale version of an 1880s steam train that chugs past big steamer trains, pony rides and patches of trees. People pay $1.75 each for this 1.5 mile ride; dogs ride free. Call (213) 662-9678 for more information.

Nature dogs who want to learn more about the environment enjoy occasional interpretive hikes sponsored by the Sierra Club. For further details and a hike schedule, call the Sierra Club at (213) 387-4287.

For dogs who just want to hike and do their business without an audience, the park offers many miles of trails. Dogs must be leashed, but it seems a small price to pay as you wander through towering redwoods, thick ferns and huge eucalyptus and oak groves. (You should be extremely cautious in the park's remote areas.)

- The park is open from 6 a.m. to 10 p.m. Park ranger headquarters are at 4730 Crystal Springs Drive. Call (213) 665-5188 for information and directions from nearby freeways.

Laurel Canyon Park

Do you and your dog long to throw his leash to the wind? City parks officials tell us that in all of Los Angeles, this is the only park that allows dogs off-leash. The dog run area is actually just a small portion of this 20-acre park. It's fenced and supplied with drinking water and pooper scoopers. If you hope to catch your favorite movie star walking his dog, you've got a good chance here. This is a favorite relief area for dogs of the rich and famous.

- The dog run area has very restricted hours. It's open from 7 a.m. to 10 a.m. and from 3 p.m. to dusk. The park is at 8260 Mullholland Drive, in Studio City. (213) 485-5555.

MENDOCINO AREA

This charming region, with its miles of beaches, should be rife with running room for dogs. Alas, the best beaches demand leashes. But it's still a magical place to visit with your best friend. There's something about the New England atmosphere here that deeply relaxes both canines and people. Inland, the Mendocino National Forest permits dogs off-leash (see National Forests, page 292).

Parks Beaches & Recreation Areas

MacKerricher State Park

You can camp here with your dog, but even better, you can spend hours hiking along a breathtaking, fairly desolate Northern California beach. The place is so full of scents dogs love that they don't even seem to mind their mandatory leashes.

■ The park is two miles north of Fort Bragg, along Highway 1. Open dawn to dusk. (707) 937-5804.

Lodgings & Campgrounds

Sears House Inn

This Victorian inn in the heart of Mendocino is surrounded by several small cottages where dogs are welcome. All have Franklin fireplaces. One cottage is atop an old watertower, with great views of the area. Average cottage cost is $95. Pets are $5 extra per night. On Main Street near Evergreen Street. The mailing address is PO Box 844, Main Street, Mendocino, CA 95460. (707) 937-4076.

Sheep Dung Estates

Staying at this secluded Boonville-area cottage is a blissful experience for dogs and their people. The statistics speak for themselves: 90 percent of the guests bring dogs.

And if you stay here you don't need to traipse around looking for a place to romp with her, either. Just walk out your door: This studio cottage, with wood-burning stove, sits on 40 acres of land that dogs love to explore. If you're up for a long hike, there are eight miles of very remote country roads. The cottage is especially inviting in the winter. It snows two or three times in the coldest months—the kind of snow that doesn't stick around, but that invigorates dogs and people alike.

The cottage costs about $75 a night. It's two miles off Highway 128, and about 40 miles south of Mendocino. PO Box 49, Yorkville, CA 95494. (707) 462-8745, ask for unit 5285.

The Stanford Inn By The Sea

This cozy redwood inn is the perfect spot for people and dogs who want to get away, but not get away from it all. On one side of the property is the ocean, on the other, the Big River. But you're only a quarter-mile from town.

You can rent a canoe here, but your dog might prefer to take a leashed romp on the inn's 11 acres. The rooms all have fireplaces and French doors leading to private decks—most with an ocean view. But if you decide to use the swimming pool or dine out, the rule here is that you mustn't leave your dog alone in the room, no matter how tempting.

Dogs do get the red carpet treatment here. They stay for free; dog sheets are provided "so your dog can be his hairy self and sit on the couch," says reservations manager Norris Crawford; and they always get the canine equivalent of a pillow chocolate: dog biscuits wrapped with ribbons.

The average room rate is $170. It's located at Highway 1 and Comptsche-Ukiah Road. The mailing address is PO Box 487, Mendocino, 95460. (707) 937-5615.

MONTEREY BAY AREA

This is one of the most picturesque areas in which a dog could ever hope to cavort. The coastal towns are home to dozens of public beaches and many restaurants where dogs are welcome to join you at outdoor tables. Since it's only a very scenic two and one-half hour drive south from San Francisco, via Highway 1, you can make this jaunt a habit. Just make sure your dog isn't prone to motion sickness, because the road is very curvy in places.

Parks Beaches & Recreation Areas

Carmel City Beach

Dogs are allowed off-leash on this pristine mile-long beach. It's not often very crowded, so it's an ideal spot for stretching all six of your legs after a long drive.

■ Take Highway 1 to the Ocean Avenue turnoff, drive through town toward the ocean, and you'll soon be at the beach. Open dawn to dusk. (408) 624-2781.

Manresa State Beach

Just south of Santa Cruz, this is the only state beach in the region that allows dogs both on the beach and in the campground. And since the beach isn't heavily used, it's a decent place to take a leashed dog.

■ To make camping reservations, call (800) 444-7275. Campsites are approximately $15 a day. Day use of the beach is $6 per vehicle. Dogs are $1 extra. Take Highway 1 to Larkin Valley Road in Watsonville, and go west to the beach. (408) 688-3241.

Monterey State Beach

Leashed dogs can explore this large, fairly calm beach that's within smell of Monterey's Fisherman's Wharf. Dogs are magnetically drawn to the fishy, fried-food odors wafting from the wharf area.

If you venture onto Monterey's sidewalks, be sure to always carry along some kind of evidence that you'll clean up after your dog. Otherwise you can get a stiff fine.

■ The beach is off Highway 1, at Dunes Drive, in the northeast section of the city. (408) 384-7695.

Lodgings & Campgrounds

Cypress Inn: The owner of this elegant Mediterranean-style hotel in Carmel doesn't just *allow* pets—she adores them. That's because the owner is none other than Doris Day, actress turned animal-rights activist.

Considering this vintage 1929 hotel's fine oak floors, delicate upholsteries and valuable antiques, you'd think she'd allow only the tiniest of teacup poodles as guests. But all well-behaved dogs are welcome. In fact, by decree of Doris Day, the inn supplies pet beds and pet food to its four-legged customers.

Doris Day devotes most of her time to helping pets through the Doris Day Pet Foundation and the Doris Day Animal League.

"Sometimes I think I will take a role in a movie just to be able to get some rest," she says.

She's had pets all her life, but the childhood pet that may have most influenced her pursuit of animal welfare was Tiny, a little black and tan mutt. When Doris Day was 15, she broke her leg and had to stay in bed for months. "Tiny," she says, "was my constant friend. He seemed to understand my moods, and never left my side. Those long days of companionship gave me a beginning insight into what it is that sets a dog apart from all other animals....Tiny taught me how much love and affection and undemanding companionship a dog can give—he was such an antidote for loneliness."

It was only logical that when she bought the Cypress Inn, the first thing she did was change the 59-year-old "No Pets Allowed" policy. She even welcomes—be sure to warn your dog—cats.

She says if she had her way, most businesses would have an open-door policy for pets.

"With all the animal guests we have had, there has not been one problem. It is important for people to be able to choose to have their pets with them if they would like. I would actually like to encourage apartment building owners to adopt a 'pets welcome' policy as well. There are so many loving people who would make wonderful pet owners, but they are restricted by where they live," she says.

The average double room rate is $100. Dogs are $15 extra per night. At Lincoln and 7th Streets. The mailing address is PO Box Y, Carmel, CA 93921. (408) 624-3871.

Manresa State Beach Campground: (See page 290 for details.)

NATIONAL FORESTS

If you want to hike hard with your unleashed dog beside you, the national forests in California provide you with hundreds of thousands of acres of dog heaven. National forests generally allow dogs off-leash—*au naturel*—in most areas except camping spots and designated wilderness. That means days and weeks of sheer pleasure bounding through nature's finest unfettered land.

Watch out, though, because all those wild scents can trigger a dog's chromosomal memory to shift back to his wolf days. If it looks as if your dog is chasing something other than his shadow, leash him immediately, for his sake as well as his prey's. And don't be fooled if your dog is a dignified city slicker. Once he feels that hunting impulse, there's no stopping even the most sophisticated cafe society dog.

A few more safety tips for your dog: Some streams or lakes can harbor the giardia parasite (the same reason humans shouldn't drink from *any* untreated California water source). Dogs can end up with giardiasis, which can be a real problem when you're in the middle of nowhere. One of its symptoms is debilitating diarrhea.

If you see your dog poking around rodent holes, stop her. Fleas from rodents may carry bubonic plague; the animals themselves can carry rabies. In country areas with a heavy rattlesnake population, it's best to leash your dog. Fortunately, rattlers will almost always hear you or a dog coming and disappear before a confrontation occurs—but a surprised snake can be deadly. (See Emergencies, page 300, for help if your dog needs first aid in the wilderness.)

National forests are all over California, but they're all more than three hours from San Francisco. For information and advice on terrain and dog hazards, call the U.S. Forest Service at (415) 705-2874. Or write: Office of Information, USDA Forest Service, 630 Sansome Street, San Francisco, CA 94111.

By day, Joe is a brave wanderer in the national forests, but at night he insists on sleeping inside a tent, generally on top of its occupants. When morning breaks, he turns into his fearless self again. Twice he has walked through the no-see-um bug screen in an effort to escape before anyone noticed he really spent the night inside. He walks to the end of the campsite and strikes a Sphynx pose, as if he'd been on guard duty through the wee hours. When we eventually crawl out of our tents, we try to go along with his story. You've never seen a prouder looking dog.—M.G.

YOSEMITE

We recommend against taking dogs to this magnificent park. The rules are so restrictive—and understandably so because of wildlife—that dogs are barely allowed to venture out of the car. But while dogs can be a menace to many wild animals, some can really do a job on dogs. Bears, especially, are a real danger to dogs.

You'd probably enjoy the freedom offered by a national forest more. But if you must bring your dog to Yosemite, be aware she can't go on any hiking trails, in either the backcountry or the valley. Meadows are off limits, too. If you plan to hike, Yosemite operates an outdoor kennel during the milder months where you can keep your dog for $6 a day. Call (209) 372-1248 for kennel information.

Dogs are allowed in certain campgrounds. And since dogs aren't permitted in any lodging facility at Yosemite, these campgrounds are your only hope for staying overnight together. Some campgrounds are seasonal, and some require reservations. Campground costs range from $4 to $12 per night. Call (209) 372-0200 for more information, or write the National Park Service, PO Box 577, Yosemite National Park, CA 95389. For reservations, call (800) 551-7328.

Lodgings & Campgrounds

Yosemite campgrounds where pets are allowed:

- **In Yosemite Valley:** Upper Pines Campground
- **Along Highway 120:** Hodgdon Meadow Campground; Crane Flat Campground, section A; White Wolf Campground, section C; Yosemite Creek Campground, front section; and Tuolumne Meadows Campground, west end.
- **Along Glacier Point Road and Highway 41:** Bridalveil Creek Campground, section A; and Wawona Campground.

MISCELLANEOUS DOG ADVENTURES

The Red & White Fleet

A great secret to know is that the Red & White ferry system lets you bring your dog with you on all its lines, free. You must leash her or carry her in a traveling box, and if there's an "accident" on board, you're responsible for cleanup. Two destinations are forbidden—Angel Island and Alcatraz, both state parks that don't allow dogs. That leaves you a choice of voyages between Fisherman's Wharf in San Francisco (Piers 41 and 43) and Tiburon, Belvedere, Sausalito or Vallejo, and a bay cruise. Phoning (415) 546-2896 will give you fares, daily schedules and departure locations.

Unfortunately, the Blue & Gold Fleet (running between San Francisco and Alameda and Oakland) and the Golden Gate Transit Ferry Service (between San Francisco and Sausalito and Larkspur) don't allow dogs on board.

I'd been told twice over the phone that yes, you can bring a dog on the Red & White Fleet ferries—no muzzle necessary, just leash—but I stood in line for a ticket wondering if we'd really get away with it. At the window I mentioned that a dog was coming with me, was that all right? The agent looked dubious. But he turned to another, who said sure, go ahead, and we were off and running to the gangplank just in time to catch the 11:20 to Sausalito. The deck hand was all smiles. "All r-i-i-i-ght, a dog!"

I still didn't believe it. Dabney hadn't even had to buy a ticket. And now he was on the boat, nose aloft in appreciation of the harbor smells and the rising breeze. The deckhand said about three or four dogs a week get on the ferry, "but most people don't have trained dogs like yours," he added. Smothering a snort I glanced at Dabney, who at that moment was holding his leash in his mouth. (This is his cutest trick, but I never taught it to him. It's his own idea.)

Nothing but smiles and free pettings came to us on the ride. Out on the top deck, Dabney thought he was in open-car-window heaven as the wind and fog ruffled his fur and stood his ears straight up. Later we curled up in a booth on one of the snug inside decks, ate potato chips and watched the Sausalito harbor, Tiburon, the headlands, Angel Island and Alcatraz slip by. We could have explored Sausalito or Tiburon, and made a half-day or a whole day of it, but we just stayed on board and got back to San Francisco in exactly an hour.—L.Y.

BOATING

If you're lucky enough to own your own boat, you'll have no dog regulations to worry about except common sense. Probably only a dog who's part monkey should accompany you sailing; motoring is much safer. A Delta houseboat is ideal (see the Solano County Chapter, page 243). You can buy special dog life vests in marine stores and dog specialty stores, and by all means vest her up when boating. Remember, however, that neither a dog nor a person can survive more than about 15 minutes in the cold water of San Francisco Bay.

BUSES & TRAINS

Don't think you have to own a car to own a dog. San Francisco's Muni system—including the cable cars—allows dogs on board if they're wearing an official, effective muzzle (don't improvise). (See the San Francisco Chapter, page 143.)

BART allows dogs only "completely enclosed within acceptable carrying cases." On Golden Gate Transit, AC Transit and SamTrans buses, and on CalTrain, the carrying case must fit on your lap. This regulation means that if you have a large dog, it's Muni or nothing. But if you have a dachshund or teacup poodle, and a carrying case, you can get to the beach or most anywhere on public transportation.

BIKE RIDES

Pick out a relaxed, rural bicycle trail for a ride with your dog. Of course you should check out the route ahead of time to avoid crowds of other bikers, auto traffic or too many hot stretches. And whatever you do, don't overdo. Your dog has physical limits that he may ignore in his desire to keep up with you. Watch for the same danger signals you should know when running with your dog: heavy panting or ropy saliva. Always carry plenty of water and offer it frequently.

Sierra Club Canine Hikes

Dogs aren't allowed on most Sierra Club outings, but the organization holds several canine hikes and camping trips each year. Hikes explore such nearby parks as Redwood Regional Park, Oakland; Tilden Regional Park, Berkeley; and Point Pinole, Richmond. Camping expeditions go to the Sierra and Tahoe National Forest.

You can pick up a four-month activities schedule at Oakland's Sierra Club Bookstore, 6014 College Avenue, for $3, or, to order by mail, send the bookstore a check made out to the Sierra Club for $3.75. Mail your order to Chapter Schedule, 6014 College Avenue, Oakland, CA 94618. (510) 658-7470.

400 Miles Of Future Fun— The San Francisco Bay Trail Project

In 1989, the Association of Bay Area Governments, the Coastal Conservancy, the Metropolitan Transportation Commission and a number of corporations adopted a 10-year plan to close the gaps between the trails that already exist encircling San Francisco and San Pablo bays. As this book goes to press, one-third of the Bay Trail—160 miles—has been completed. Write to ABAG for maps and information: Association of Bay Area Governments, San Francisco Bay Trail, County Maps, PO Box 2050, Oakland, CA 94604.

By 1999, if all goes according to plan, a dog and walker should be able to traipse 400 uninterrupted miles together. Think of bragging about *that* to your grandchildren.

Shopping Malls

The kind of mall that has outdoor corridors is legally a public space and just fine for a well-behaved dog, so long as he's leashed. (Some outdoor malls have rules against dogs; check before you go.) Of course, she can't go shopping with you inside any stores.

One good example of a dog-welcoming mall is in Corte Madera, Marin County. The Town Center features brick outdoor corridors with plenty of seating and cafes with corridor tables. It also has fountains and plenty of friendly cafe workers eager to give your dog treats and water. To get there from Highway 101, exit at Paradise Drive/Tamalpais Drive. Town Center is on the west side of the freeway. The Village, on the east side of the freeway, doesn't allow dogs.

And think of the shopping opportunities for you and your dog in the malls of Santa Clara County. One outstanding example is Stanford Shopping Center in Palo Alto, next to the university on El Camino Real at the border of Menlo Park.

Wineries, U-Pick Farms & Other Private Businesses Open To The Public

Wineries, orchards, produce farms and Christmas tree farms want your business, so they may well give you permission to bring your dog. It's only courteous (and healthy for the dog) to call ahead before bringing her, though. Leaving your dog in the car in warm or even mild weather can be extremely dangerous, and you don't want to face the choice of leaving her in the car or giving up and going home. If your dog is allowed to come with you, *clean up after her! Scoop!* Don't be that one customer in 10 who ruins the business owner's good attitude toward dogs.

Urban Steps

If you like aerobic exercise but would rather not pay someone in Lycra to yell at you in a gym, take your dog on a steps walk. Yes, folks, the York/Goodavage patented Steps Walk is yours for the price of this book, and here it is: Leash your dog and run up steps in urban residential neighborhoods. San Francisco has steps on Lyon Street, Lombard Street, Filbert Street; Sausalito, Berkeley and Oakland all have them. Look at a map and take a steps walk for fresh air, cardiovascular health, a sense of accomplishment and a free architectural tour of interesting neighborhoods all rolled into one.

Blessings On Your Pet

Every year in early October, around Saint Francis' day, many churches hold a Blessing of the Animals. Good dogs and bad alike are welcome—that's what blessings are for! Probably the best known are Father Floyd Lotito's blessing in San Francisco, held at different Roman Catholic churches in the city, and Dean Alan Jones' Episcopal ceremony at Grace Cathedral. But blessings are offered by many churches—even in Marin shopping malls. (See Larkspur listing, page 100.) Call a church near you to find out about one your dog might like.

Outdoor Games

Wherever there's a Little League or amateur softball game, your dog wants to be there. He likes hot dogs and sunshine just as much as you do. Check first that pets are allowed in the ballpark; they usually are, but some city parks exclude them. And of course he should be leashed—you don't want to hear those dread words, "Dog on the field!"

Drive-In Movies

There aren't too many of these left in the Bay Area—we found them hanging on in southern Alameda County, San Francisco, San Mateo County and Santa Clara County—but remember how much fun it can be to snuggle up to a furry date and watch ...well, not *Old Yeller*. Not *Cujo*. But the dog is the hero in *Honey, I Shrunk the Kids*!

EMERGENCIES

Chances are your adventuring will go without a hitch, but you should always be prepared to deal with trouble. In this chapter we'll deal first with common hazards—ticks, foxtails, poison oak and skunk attacks—and then with more serious accidents such as heat stroke, broken bones and snakebites.

Ordinary Trouble

Ticks are hard to avoid in Northern California. They can carry Lyme disease, so you should always check yourself and your dog all over when you get home from tick country. Don't forget to check ears and between the toes. If you see one, just pull it straight out with tweezers, not your bare hands.

The tiny ticks that carry Lyme disease are difficult to find. Consult your veterinarian if your dog is lethargic for a few days, has a fever, loses her appetite, or becomes lame. These symptoms could indicate Lyme disease. Some vets recommend a new vaccine that is supposed to prevent onset of the disease, but others say it's too early to tell if the vaccine is safe and effective, and advise against it.

Foxtails—those arrow-shaped pieces of dry grass—are the seed cases of wild barley. They're an everyday annoyance, but in certain cases can be lethal—they can stick in your dog's eyes, nose, ears or mouth and work their way in. Check every nook and cranny of your dog after a walk if you've been near dry grass. Poor Joe once had to have an embedded foxtail removed from his paw by a vet, to the tune of $200.

Poison oak is also a common California menace. Dogs don't generally have reactions to it, but they can easily pass it to people. Advises Charise McHugh, hospital manager at Belmont Pet Hospital: "If you think your dog has trotted through some poison oak, try not to pet him until you get him home and wash him, wearing rubber gloves. If you do pet him, avoid touching your eyes. I've had poison oak in my eye three times, and it's miserable."

If your dog loses a contest with a skunk (and he always will), rinse his eyes first with plain warm water, then bathe him with dog shampoo. Towel him off, then apply tomato juice (canned tomatoes or sauce works just as well) or a mixture of one pint vinegar to one gallon water, or five or six ounces of Massengill douche powder or liquid mixed with one gallon of water.

Prevention of veterinary emergencies is the best cure. When you're in the wilderness with your dog, you should be aware of certain hazards before your dog encounters them. Some vets advise finding out from a ranger if there's a danger of poisonous snakes, and keeping your dog leashed where the ranger suggests. If your dog is sticking her snout down rodent burrows, stop her, because fleas from rodents can carry bubonic plague. The animals themselves may carry rabies.

And if you're a thoroughly cautious dog owner, you may want to follow the advice of some veterinarians and not let your dog drink out of California rivers and streams, often host to the Giardia parasite.

Serious Trouble

The rest of this chapter describes serious emergency situations that can arise while you're out with your dog. In all these emergencies, *get to a veterinarian as soon as possible.* Don't rely on the treatments listed here as permanent solutions. These are only stopgap measures so your dog can survive until he gets professional medical attention.

If your dog injures an eye, or starts squinting or blinking, don't wait to take her to the vet. Eye injuries are usually easily treated, but even minor ones should be looked at immediately; eye infections can progress very fast.

Always speak to a wounded dog in a calm, reassuring voice. Approach an injured animal with caution. It may be necessary to muzzle her if she's snapping in panic, but a word of warning: If a dog is in shock (see Shock), use a muzzle only as a last resort. You may have to open the dog's breathing passage, and you don't have time to waste with a muzzle. To improvise a muzzle, wrap a wide piece of adhesive tape around the dog's snout. Don't bind it too tightly. You can also use a strip of cloth, a belt or a necktie, wrapped snugly around the animal's muzzle and tied off behind the ears.

Unfortunately, courses in first aid for animals are almost exclusively for animal care workers. Dr. Karl Peter, a veterinarian with Los Altos' Adobe Animal Hospital, suggests an alternative: "Any first aid course for humans is going to give you greater confidence when it comes to dealing with dog emergencies," he says. "While everything may not translate, many techniques do. Those could be the ones that save your dog's life."

Be sure to have a well-stocked first-aid kit close at hand whenever you travel with your dog. It should contain the following:

- Phone numbers of your veterinarian and of a nighttime/weekend vet (probably the single most important item.)
- A veterinary first aid book
- Adhesive tape, one to two inches wide
- Cotton batting
- Large gauze pads
- Gauze roll, three inches wide
- Hydrogen peroxide (3%)
- Petroleum jelly
- Several short, sturdy sticks, such as tongue depressors
- Sterilized knife or razor blade
- Thermometer
- Tweezers or thumbforceps

Bleeding From External Wounds

Almost any bleeding (even spurting arterial wounds) can be controlled by the direct pressure method. Tourniquets should be used only as a last resort.

"It can be difficult to be calm when your dog seems to be bleeding profusely," says Dr. Cara Paasch, a veterinarian at San Francisco's Arguello Pet Hospital. "But the key is not to panic. Sometimes a little blood can look like a lot. Don't rush to make a tourniquet right away."

Get any bleeding dog to a veterinarian immediately. Always check for shock, and treat if necessary (see SHOCK). If the dog is unconscious, elevate his hind end so blood can get to the brain.

If necessary, muzzle the dog. Press gauze, lint-free cloth or even your hand over the wound and maintain firm pressure. If the bleeding doesn't stop, increase pressure. Check bleeding in five or 10 minutes by releasing pressure. Do not remove the cloth, since this could open the wound. If the wound is still dripping, continue direct pressure. Gravity can also help. If the wound is in the front leg, try to stand the dog on his hind legs while you treat him. This raises the wound above the heart, and should slow the bleeding. If you're transporting a dog by yourself and can't maintain pressure by hand, bandage the cloth firmly in place. Get to a veterinarian immediately.

For bleeding from fractures that protrude through the skin, apply pressure between the break and the dog's heart, slightly above the injury. For a compound fracture of the lower leg, for instance, tightly encircle the dog's upper leg with your hands.

Veterinarians advise against tourniquets except in the most dire circumstances. Many say there's rarely a situation when you'll have to use one. If a tourniquet is done improperly, lack of circulation can cause the dog to lose a limb. But if you've tried direct pressure and the arterial bleeding is still profuse, and it looks like a matter of life over limb, you may need to make a tourniquet.

To do so, place a two-inch-wide clean strip of cloth or gauze slightly above the wound, over the bleeding artery. Tightly wrap it twice around the limb, and tie a stick into the wrap. Twist the stick until bleeding is controlled. Secure the stick in place with tape. Cover the dog loosely with a blanket and get to a veterinarian immediately.

Broken Bones

If you're within a short drive of a veterinarian, it may be best to carefully transport your dog (see Transporting A Dog) and let the vet take care of the injury. Some veterinarians say they've seen more harm than good done by improperly applied splints.

But if you're on a long hike, or far from immediate medical care, you may need to make a temporary support for the fracture. Consider muzzling the dog if the injury is painful. Treat only fractures of the lower leg. If you suspect fractures or dislocations elsewhere, carry the dog to a veterinarian as gently as possible (see Transporting A Dog).

If bones protrude, control the bleeding with direct or encircling pressure (see Bleeding From External Wounds).

Wrap the leg with cloth or cotton batting. Place rigid sticks, such as tongue depressors, on opposite sides of the break so that they extend past joints at both ends of the break. Wrap with adhesive tape. Be sure not to wrap too tightly, because a lack of circulation might result in loss of the dog's limb. See a veterinarian as soon as possible.

Heat Stroke

Heat stroke is life threatening, but its prevention is simple. You can avoid most heat stroke by keeping your dog in a cool, shady, well-ventilated area, not exhausting her in hot weather, and providing lots of fresh water.

Never, ever leave your dog in a car on a warm day. Heat stroke generally occurs at temperatures greater than 100 degrees, but it can often happen at much lower temperatures. Although the temperature outside may be tolerable, your car can become an oven, even with the windows partly open—and even in the shade. "The most common problem usually happens when someone parks his car on a hot day to run into a shop for five minutes, and it takes a little longer than he expected," says Dr. Rob Erteman, veterinarian at the Animal Hospital in San Anselmo. "He comes back, and the animal is in big trouble, even if the window is cracked."

Symptoms of heat stroke are rapid panting, bright red gums, high body temperature and hot limbs. Symptoms can progress to uncontrollable diarrhea, collapse and coma. Death can occur in severe cases.

Treatment: Normal rectal temperature for a dog is 100 to 102 degrees. If your dog's temperature is above 103 degrees, and she has heat stroke symptoms, treat her immediately and rush to a veterinarian (see TRANSPORTING A DOG). Rapid treatment is essential, because the dog's condition can deteriorate quickly.

Use any method possible to cool the dog. In mild cases, it is often effective to move the dog to a cool, well-ventilated place and wrap her in a cold, wet towel. But treatment generally calls for bathing the dog in cold water, or even ice. Ice is especially effective when packed around the head. Monitor her temperature every 10 minutes and stop cooling when her body temperature gets down to 103 degrees. Get to a veterinarian as soon as possible.

SHOCK

Shock is insufficient blood flow caused by problems with the heart, or loss of blood volume. It can result from injury or overwhelming infection. If prolonged, it can lead to death.

Symptoms of shock are pale gums; weak, faint pulse; general weakness; shallow, rapid breathing; listlessness or confusion; low body temperature or shivering; semi-consciousness or unconsciousness.

Treatment: Don't muzzle the dog unless snapping becomes a danger to you. Control any bleeding (see BLEEDING FROM EXTERNAL WOUNDS). If the dog is unconscious, keep his airway open by opening his mouth and carefully pulling out his tongue. If the dog is conscious, let him relax and assume the position most comfortable to him. An ideal position is on his side with head extended, but don't force him into it. Cover him lightly with a blanket and transport him immediately to a veterinarian (see TRANSPORTING A DOG).

SNAKE BITES

Although most snakes are not poisonous, California is home to a few types of deadly snakes. Many veterinarians caution that if you know you're in poisonous snake country, you should keep your dog leashed. If your dog is bitten, try to identify the snake, or check the bite marks. Fang marks (two puncture wounds) indicate a poisonous snake. Get your dog to a veterinarian immediately. Depending on where the dog was bitten, and how much venom was injected, serious symptoms can develop rapidly.

Symptoms: At the site of the wound, there may be swelling and severe pain. At first the dog may be restless, panting and perhaps drooling. These signs can be followed quickly by weakness, difficulty in breathing, diarrhea, collapse, convulsions and shock. In severe cases, the dog can die.

Many veterinarians advise against treating snakebites yourself before getting your dog proper medical attention. They say people sometimes tie tourniquets too tightly, or cut too deeply and sever an artery. Their advice is to keep the dog as still and calm as possible, since exercise and struggle increase the rate of absorption of the poison. If possible, slide the dog onto a blanket or board and carry him to a veterinarian immediately (see TRANSPORTING A DOG).

But even most veterinarians who counsel against emergency treatment in the field say that if you're hiking and you're miles from any transportation to a vet, you should probably consider treating the wound yourself.

Of two methods for treating snake bites before you get to an animal hospital, vets generally prefer the tourniquet method only slightly to cutting the wound and sucking the venom. Again, keep the dog calm and quiet, muzzling if necessary. Keep the wound below heart level. If the bite is on a leg or the tail, tie a constricting band tightly between the bite and the heart, a few inches above the bite. It should be just tight enough to prevent venomous blood from returning to the heart. Get to a vet as quickly as possible.

If there's no way you feel you can reach a veterinarian in time, you may opt for the cut-and-suction treatment. Tie a constricting band between the bite and the heart, but not too tightly. Sterilize a knife or razor blade over a flame. Carefully make parallel cuts through each fang mark, about one-half-inch long and no deeper than one-quarter inch. The smaller the dog, and the closer the bone, the shallower the cut. Blood should ooze from the wound. If it doesn't, loosen the band.

Draw the venom from the wound with your mouth, if it's free of cuts and open sores, and spit out the blood. You can also use a suction cup. Continue at five to ten minute intervals for 30 minutes, if possible, while in transit to the veterinarian (see TRANSPORTING A DOG). Watch the dog's symptoms and continue if necessary until you get professional veterinary care.

After your dog has been seen by a veterinarian, remember to keep the wound clean. Snake bites are prone to infection.

TRANSPORTING A DOG

Always use a stretcher to move a dog who can't walk, or greater bodily injury could result. A good makeshift stretcher is a large, sturdy board, but a blanket or even a rug will do.

Carefully slide the dog onto the stretcher, making sure not to bend any part of his body. On a board stretcher, tie the dog gently, but firmly, in place. Speak reassuringly to the dog en route to the veterinarian.

ALL-NIGHT VETERINARY CLINICS

Your dog may need medical attention in the middle of the night, when your own veterinarian is unavailable. Many vets offer on-call emergency service, and there are several all-night clinics in the Bay Area. Be sure to phone first, to be certain hours and location have not changed.

ALAMEDA COUNTY CLINICS

- Berkeley
  Pet Emergency Treatment Service: Open 6 p.m. to 8 a.m. on weekdays, and from noon Saturday to 8 a.m. Monday. Open 24 hours on holidays. 1048 University Avenue. (510) 548-6684.

- Dublin
  Tri-Valley Veterinary Emergency Clinic: Open 5:30 p.m. to 8 a.m. weekdays, and from 5:30 p.m. Friday to 8 a.m. Monday. Open 24 hours on holidays. 6743 Dublin Boulevard. (510) 828-0654.

- Fremont
  Central Veterinarian Hospital and Emergency Services: Open 24 hours for emergencies. 5245 Central Avenue. (510) 797-7387.

- Oakland
  Bay Area Pet Hospital: Open 24 hours for emergencies. 4820 Broadway. (510) 654-8375.

- San Leandro
  Alameda County Emergency Pet Clinic: Open 6 p.m. to 8 a.m. weekdays, and from noon Saturday to 8 a.m. Monday. Open 24 hours on holidays. 14790 Washington Avenue. (510) 352-6080.

Contra Costa County Clinics

- Concord
  Contra Costa Veterinary Emergency Clinic: Open 6 p.m. to 8 a.m. weekdays, and 6 p.m. Friday to 8 a.m. Monday. Open 24 hours on holidays. 1410 Monument Boulevard. (510) 798-2900.

Marin County Clinics

- San Rafael
  Marin County Veterinary Emergency Clinic: Open 5:30 p.m. to 8 a.m. weekdays, and 5:30 p.m. Friday to 8 a.m. Monday. Open 24 hours on holidays. 4240 Redwood Highway. (415) 472-2266.

Napa County Clinics

- As of our publication date, there are no all-night clinics in Napa County.

San Francisco County Clinics

- San Francisco
  All Animals Emergency Hospital: Open 6 p.m. to 8 a.m. weekdays, and 6 p.m. Friday to 8 a.m. Monday. 1333 9th Avenue. (415) 566-0531.

  Pets Unlimited Veterinary Hospital: Open 24 hours for emergencies. 2343 Fillmore Street. (415) 563-6700.

San Mateo County Clinics

- San Mateo
  North Peninsula Veterinary Emergency Clinic: Open 6 p.m. to 8 a.m. weekdays, and 6 p.m. Friday to 8 a.m. Monday. Open 24 hours on holidays. 227 North Amphlett Boulevard. (415) 348-2575.

Santa Clara County Clinics

- Campbell
  United Emergency Animal Clinic: Open 6 p.m. to 8 a.m. weekdays, and 6 p.m. Friday to 8 a.m. Monday. Open 24 hours on holidays. 1657 South Bascom Street. (408) 371-6252.

- Palo Alto
  All Peninsula Veterinary Emergency Clinic: Open 6 p.m. to 8 a.m. weekdays, and 5 p.m. Friday to 8 a.m. Monday. Open 24 hours on holidays. 3045 Middlefield Road. (415) 494-1461.

- San Jose
  Emergency Animal Clinic of South San Jose: Open 6 p.m. to 8 a.m. weekdays, and 6 p.m. Friday to 8 a.m. Monday. Open 24 hours on holidays. 5440 Thornwood Drive (behind the Oakridge Mall). (408) 578-5622.

Solano County Clinics

- Cordelia
  Solano Pet Emergency Clinic: Open 6 p.m. to 8 a.m. Monday through Friday, and from 6 p.m. Saturday to 8 a.m. Monday. Open 24 hours on holidays. 4437 Central Place. (707) 864-1444.

Sonoma County Clinics

- Santa Rosa
  Emergency Animal Hospital of Santa Rosa: Open 6 p.m. to 8 a.m. weekdays, and from 6 p.m. Friday to 8 a.m. Monday. Open 24 hours on holidays. 4019 Sebastopol Road. (707) 544-1647.

  Petcare Emergency Hospital: Open 7 p.m. to 8 a.m. weekdays, 4 p.m. to 8 a.m. Saturday and Sunday, and 24 hours on holidays. 1370 Fulton Road. (707) 573-9503.

ANIMAL SHELTERS

Don't have a dog? Need another one? The Bay Area has more than two dozen shelters full of dogs who are longing to be someone's best friend.

ALAMEDA COUNTY
Alameda City Animal Control—(510) 522-4100
Alameda City Animal Shelter—(510) 828-0824, 551-6860
Alameda County Animal Shelter—(510) 667-7707
Berkeley Animal Shelter—(510) 644-6755
Berkeley Humane Society—(510) 845-7735, 845-3633
Hayward Animal Shelter—(510) 537-7560
Oakland Animal Shelter—(510) 273-3565, 273-3564
Oakland SPCA—(510) 569-0702, 569-1606
Tri-City Animal Shelter—(510) 792-1261
Union City Animal Shelter—(510) 471-1365

CONTRA COSTA COUNTY
Martinez Animal Shelter (East)—(510) 646-2995
Pinole Animal Shelter (West)—(510) 374-3966
Antioch City Shelter—(510) 757-2278

MARIN COUNTY
Marin Humane Society—(415) 883-4621

NAPA COUNTY
Napa County Animal Control—(707) 253-4381

SAN FRANCISCO COUNTY
Animal Care and Control—(415) 554-6364
San Francisco SPCA—(415) 554-3000, 554-3030
Presidio Vet Clinic—(415) 561-3744

SAN MATEO COUNTY
Peninsula Humane Society—(415) 340-8200

SANTA CLARA COUNTY

Palo Alto Animal Shelter—(415) 329-2671, 329-2433
Santa Clara Animal Shelter—(408) 683-4186
Santa Clara Humane Society—(408) 727-8640, 727-3383

SOLANO COUNTY

Solano County Animal Control—(707) 429-6964
Solano County SPCA—(707) 448-7722

SONOMA COUNTY

Sonoma County Humane Society—(707) 542-0882
Petaluma City Animal Shelter—(707) 778-4396
Rohnert Park Animal Shelter—(707) 795-3656
Healdsburg City Shelter—(707) 431-3386
Pets Lifeline of Sonoma—(707) 996-4577

One of the most active shelters in Northern California is the San Francisco SPCA. The SF/SPCA offers all of the following programs:

- **Pets & Older People,** which provides senior pet owners with the extra financial support they may need.
- **Animal Assisted Therapy,** a program that brings the therapeutic presence of animals to people who need it most: those in hospitals, psychiatric clinics and nursing homes.
- **The Hearing Dog Program,** which trains once-homeless dogs to become the ears of deaf people.
- **The Humane Education Program,** which makes speakers, animal visitors and curriculum materials available to San Francisco schoolchildren.
- **A Low-Cost Spay/Neuter Clinic,** which provides cheap "alterations."
- **The Volunteer Program,** which always has openings for dog walkers, dog socializers, adoption counselors and animal behaviorists.
- **Sido Service,** which places pets of deceased SF/SPCA members in new loving homes and provides them with lifetime veterinary care.

INDEX

INDEX

Q

R

S

ABOUT THE AUTHORS

Lyle York and Dabney

Maria Goodavage and Joe

Dabney, mostly collie with a dash of golden retriever, is a Berkeley dog with a refined social conscience. He believes all creatures are created equal and should be treated with respect, with the possible exception of mailmen. To him all foods are created equal as well, whether they appear in his dish, or in the gutter, or on someone else's plate. He loves long walks and shallow water—mud best of all. Dabney moved in with **Lyle York** eight years ago from temporary quarters at the San Francisco SPCA. Lyle, his caretaker and chauffeur, is an editor at the San Francisco Chronicle.

Although **Joe** flunked out of school and never received a formal education, he is a distinguished, debonair airdale-about-town. Born into a lineage of champions in an upscale Palo Alto home three years ago, he was brought to San Francisco and named Joe—a name that still makes him wince. He leads a dilettante's life, lying in his bed and silently contemplating the city streets for hours on end. His dream is to move to the country, near the ocean, close to the seagulls. He shares a flat with **Maria Goodavage,** a writer and news correspondent for USA Today.